STAGING GROUND

LESLIE STAINTON

STAGING GROUND

AN AMERICAN THEATER
AND ITS GHOSTS

THE PENNSYLVANIA STATE UNIVERSITY PRESS
UNIVERSITY PARK, PENNSYLVANIA

A KEYSTONE BOOK®

Keystone Books are intended to serve the citizens of Pennsylvania. They are accessible, well-researched explorations into the history, culture, society, and environment of the Keystone State as part of the Middle Atlantic region.

Portions of this book have been previously published
in somewhat different form:

The Prologue incorporates material from "Stage-Struck," in "The Documentary Imagination (Part Two)," ed. Tom Fricke and Keith Taylor, special issue, *Michigan Quarterly Review* 45, no. 1 (2006).

Chapter 3 incorporates material from "Conestoga," in "Due North," special issue, *Crab Orchard Review* 17, no. 2 (2012).

Chapter 15 incorporates material from "Players," *Common-place* 8, no. 4 (2008). Courtesy of *Common-place*, http://common-place.org.

The excerpt from *Indians*, by Arthur Kopit, is copyright © 1969 by Arthur Kopit. Reprinted by permission of Hill & Wang, a division of Farrar, Straus and Giroux, LLC.

Library of Congress Cataloging-in-Publication Data

Stainton, Leslie, 1955– , author.
Staging ground : an American theater and its ghosts / Leslie Stainton.
p.   cm
"Keystone books."
Summary: "Through both history and personal memoir, examines the role of the Fulton Theatre in Lancaster, Pennsylvania, in the shaping of American identity from colonial times to the present"—Provided by publisher.
Includes bibliographical references and index.
ISBN 978-0-271-06365-2 (pbk. : alk. paper)
1. Fulton Opera House—History.
2. Theater—Pennsylvania—Lancaster—History.
3. Theater and society—United States—History.
4. Stainton, Leslie, 1955– .
5. Yecker, Blasius, 1834–1903.
I. Title.

PN2277.L362F857   2014
792.09748′15—dc23
2013049311

Frontispiece: Yecker's Fulton Opera House, ca. 1897 (fig. 21).
Courtesy of Barbara Dorwart Lehman.

For STEVE

For, indeed, the greatest glory of a building is not in its stones, not in its gold. Its glory is in its age, and in that deep sense of voicefulness, of stern watching, of mysterious sympathy, nay, even of approval or condemnation, which we feel in walls that have long been washed by the passing waves of humanity.

—JOHN RUSKIN

Not to know what happened before we were born is to remain perpetually a child. For what is the worth of a human life unless it is woven into the life of our ancestors by the records of history?

—CICERO

Where memory is, theater is.

—HERBERT BLAU

CONTENTS

Illustrations follow page 88.

ILLUSTRATIONS

ACKNOWLEDGMENTS

Were it not for the men and women who fought to preserve the Fulton Theatre from demolition in the 1960s—among them my dear friends the late Helen and Nat Hager—this storied site might well be a parking garage today. The late Joe Kingston deserves credit for the series of articles he wrote in the *Intelligencer Journal* in the mid-1950s, which did much to persuade Lancastrians of the treasure in their midst. Despite his tendency to embellish the facts, Kingston was the first to attempt a comprehensive history of the Fulton Theatre. Ty Greiner followed in 1977 with a two-volume master's thesis listing every touring show to play the Fulton from 1852 to 1930. His monumental labor has made this book possible in countless ways, and I am deeply grateful.

My friend Barry Kornhauser, former Fulton playwright-in-residence, and his wife, Carol, have been unstintingly generous to me and my family for decades. May this account of a building we all revere serve as partial repayment of the debt I owe them. My thanks to Deidre Simmons, Aaron Young, and the late Michael Mitchell for allowing me to explore the Fulton's multiple nooks and crannies and to sit in on rehearsals, and to Fulton archivist Mary Underhill for her many efforts on my behalf. Paul E. Yecker Sr. has been a godsend throughout this project, and I am grateful to him and his family for their many kindnesses.

On numerous occasions, director Tom Ryan and the excellent staff of the Lancaster County Historical Society (now LancasterHistory.org)—in particular Kevin Shue, Marianne Heckles, and the late John Loose—opened my eyes to the nuances of Lancaster's past, as did archivist Joan Kahler of Trinity Lutheran Church; historian Leroy Hopkins; Christopher Raab of Franklin and Marshall College Library; and Peter Siebert, former director of the Heritage Center of Lancaster County. For their knowledge, suggestions, and indispensable reading lists I am indebted to Lynn Brooks, Christopher Densmore, Gregory Dowd, Raymond Grew, Randy Harris, Alison Kibler, Hank Meijer, Martin Walsh, Gwen Waltz, and the late Gerry Lestz. My thanks to Kate Dernacoeur and Ron Grant for their thoughtful comments on the book. Paul Nevin was good enough to take me (and my inveterately curious mother) out to the Susquehanna petroglyphs one gusty October evening, a trip that continues to inspire my dream life. My friend Chris Hager and my brother, Bill Stainton, offered welcome assistance at critical junctures. I am grateful for the help and encouragement of theater design specialists Ann Sachs and Roger Morgan and theater architect Ed Francis, who collectively oversaw the 1995 renovation to the Fulton. Lee Bollinger, Mark Lamos, and Don Wilmeth all lent their support to this project, and I thank them. Lorraine Boncella-Wiley, Don Hammond, and Genny Gumbrecht have provided indispensable technical assistance. Thanks also to my agent, Carol Mann, and her assistant Eliza Dreier for their vision and perseverance.

Jack Brubaker, Gordon Wickstrom, and Julia Kasdorf shared their expertise and read early drafts of the manuscript, and my gratitude to them is boundless. I am indebted to Kathryn Yahner and the fine staff at Penn State Press for their faith in books in general and this one in particular. Helen Sheehy believed in *Staging Ground* from the start and buoyed my spirits throughout the research and writing process. To my parents, Scarlett and Bill Stainton, who made this book possible in so many ways, my endless gratitude. To Jeremy and Julia Whiting, loyal companions throughout this journey, my thanks and love. And to their father, who keeps me going in all ways and to whom this book is dedicated—everything.

No building is static, least of all a theater, whose primary aim is the telling of stories and whose occupants are, for the most part, transients. The Fulton Theatre in Lancaster, Pennsylvania, is particularly mutable. One of the oldest continuously operating theaters in the United States, its history spans at least two centuries, arguably more. For decades I wanted to tell its story—but I wrestled with the problem of how to do so without resorting to numbing detail. A mere account of the more than ten thousand performances that took place in the Fulton from 1852 to the present—never mind its hundred-year existence as a jail prior to 1852—would not begin to convey the complexity of the place, or the Fulton's significance in the larger story of a young nation struggling to forge an identity. Nor would it capture the bewildering array of personalities who in ways big and small etched their tales into the fabric of this space—from dour James Buchanan and steamy Victoria Woodhull to Richard Jackson, a fugitive slave who in 1825 awaited his fate in what is now the Fulton basement, and the late Michael Mitchell, artistic director of the Fulton from 1999 to 2008, who in his last months of life said he was "at peace," despite a grave illness, because he had lived his life "in places like this. Grand spiritual enterprises."

In my search for a way to structure the unruly story of this great American theater, I eventually settled on a framework of two distinct but complementary narratives: the story of Blasius Yecker, who ran the Fulton during its heyday as an American roadhouse, from 1866 until his death in 1903, and whose experience as an immigrant-turned-entrepreneur-and-civic-leader struck me as quintessentially American; and the story of my own coming of age in the 1970s and '80s, a period when the Fulton reclaimed its status as a venue for live plays, and I worked in the theater as an actress, stagehand, seamstress, office assistant, and member of a children's theater company. "All history is biography," said Emerson. That truism underpins much of this book.

Staging Ground is thus both a history and a memoir. I am far from alone in feeling a personal attachment to this building, and my hope is that by filtering the Fulton's larger story through the smaller lens of my own, I can shed light on both the public and private meanings of this extraordinary space—and convey some sense of the intricate ways that the past and present overlap inside its walls. I could have written about any of the nearly four thousand theaters that existed in towns across America in the late nineteenth century and that shaped the way Americans saw and thought about themselves. Fewer than three hundred of these buildings survive, and most occupy a special place in their communities, as they should. Whether they've been lavishly restored or merely spared from the wrecking ball, these are all haunted houses. But the Fulton Theatre has long seemed to me uniquely ghosted—not just because it's in my hometown or because I worked here in my teens and twenties, but because it is built on sacred ground. Its foundations occupy the site where in 1763 a band of vigilantes murdered the last indigenous people to inhabit Lancaster County when the land was still a wilderness. Those same foundations later served to incarcerate African Americans fleeing slavery. Thus is the Fulton implicated in the two great crimes on which this nation was built. That a working theater should function for nearly two centuries in such a place strikes me as both absurd and acutely poignant. It's as if someone had deliberately tried to create a metaphor for the complicated realities of American culture.

The nineteenth-century Shakespearean actor E. L. Davenport called the Fulton "the most beautiful temple of art in the United States," and it remains one of the most irresistible of American theaters—a crimson and gold wedding cake of a place inside, outside a stately monument to Lancaster-born Robert Fulton, who tinkered with submarines in the Seine and built America's first commercially viable steamship. Here is a building where America invented itself—where actors shed their European roots to create a genuinely American style of performance, where audiences confronted an image of themselves and who they might become, where a nation wrote and rewrote its history. This singular space resonates in ways no other American theater does. Hence this book, a small gesture of gratitude to a place that has given so much to so many.

One Christmas morning I came downstairs in my pajamas and found a pink plastic showboat waiting for me under the tree. The boat was small but ornate, with a waterwheel at one end and shallow bas-relief railings at the other. Along the length of one side, the exterior wall had been cut away, like an anatomical model, except that instead of intestines and lungs this opening revealed a drawing room with a cardboard stage set.

I was six and knew already that I loved the theater. With my finger I traced the outline of the proscenium and touched the stage floor. Somewhere behind me, my father switched on the floodlights and began filming me and my brother and sister, as he did every Christmas morning. Stacked neatly inside the box that had come with the showboat were tiny cardboard flats, props, pieces of furniture, lights, figures on plastic stands. There was a complete cast of *Heidi*, including the Alm-Uncle and Clara in her wheelchair. There were mountain goats and a miniature tea service.

My father, still filming, drifted into view on my right and gestured for me to play. I picked up a character from the box and lowered her onto the stage through an open slot in the top of the showboat. I found another character. Soon I had them bobbing back and forth on their circular stands and jabbering. "Good," my father mouthed, and gave me a thumbs-up. The camera clattered as the reel of film unspooled. I'd tried to understand how the machine caught and preserved our movements in a long sequence of frames, but I couldn't grasp it. In the artificial glow of that Christmas morning, my cardboard actors were more real. They cast long shadows onto the stage. Back and forth they went, talking and arguing, making exits and entrances. I added a footstool and a chaise. A maid sailed down into the room in my hands to ask if anyone wanted supper. Long after my father had shut down his camera and turned off the floodlights, I went on playing.

The word itself was thrilling. Play. I'd seen a real one a year earlier in Philadelphia when my Aunt Betty had taken me to *The Sound of Music* for my birthday. The show had just opened, and we had front-row seats.

Everything inside the theater glowed: the walls, the gold trim along the edges of the balconies, the lights at the base of the aisle seats, the playbill itself, which I've kept to this day. The curtain lifted, and I saw dozens of nuns at prayer in a chapel that stretched to the top of the proscenium and beyond. Someone, I couldn't imagine who, had built a glittering rood screen behind which the women in their dark habits seemed to float. I was besotted. At intermission the curtain dropped and to my disappointment veiled whatever was taking place onstage. I leaned across the railing of the orchestra pit to get a closer look. From somewhere below me, a cellist reached up and tapped my elbow with his bow. I looked down; he smiled. Perhaps he said something, I don't remember. What I wanted him to say was, "Follow me. I'll take you to the other side."

1

HAUNTED

Late at night you feel them. Underneath the stage, in the long tunnel that stretches the length of the theater, the stone walls of the old prison ooze a cold sweat, and in the shadows you think you see shapes huddled under blankets, shivering. You tell yourself they're only curtains piled in the corners, but even so they make you start, and you hurry upstairs.

Onstage, a single lightbulb on a metal stand sheds enough glow for you to make out the ropes and pipes hanging overhead, the canvas flats meant to be someone's front porch, a one-sided automobile. Props from the night's performance lie in a chalked grid on a table in the wings. On a lectern in the corner, the stage manager has left her prompt book open, each page annotated like a medical chart. Out in front in the dark are rows of empty red seats and the curving white edges of two balconies, and on the ceiling, peering down, a pair of plaster angels who've been holding their comic and tragic masks, respectively, for more than a century. Here too you sense you're not alone.

Somewhere in the curlicues of the proscenium is the smudge of a bullet fired by Buffalo Bill. He's standing beside you now, dressed in leather chaps and a fringed coat, smelling of prairie. Over there is Ethel Barrymore, running lines, and George M. Cohan, warbling a patriot song, cane in hand, feet thrumming, and here's Bert Williams in blackface, cradling a tuba. Behind you Thaddeus Stevens slams his fist down on the podium and cries, "Abolition! Yes: abolish everything on the face of the earth but this Union; free every slave—slay every traitor—burn every rebel mansion." Soldiers are upstairs drilling, and President James Buchanan is sitting downstage, lost in thought, and the voices of the slain and their survivors mingle in the high reaches of this space, beyond the pin rail, and suddenly you catch a whiff of scent as Sarah Bernhardt makes her way through the house, skirts sighing, on her way to the dressing room. She refuses to come in by the backstage door, unseen.

Hold still for a moment and feel the stream of time, feel your place in it. Outdoors the city is quiet. The market is locked tight, the nail salon next door is closed, the banks and restaurants empty. Over on Chestnut Street, at the spot where Abraham Lincoln addressed the citizens of this town on his way to his first inaugural, nothing stirs, and it's equally silent at the site of the old railroad depot where his funeral train edged its way through weeping crowds four years later. The bars have issued their last calls, the mayor is asleep, and only the police station and the hospital where I was born in the middle of the twentieth century bristle with life. Gone are the taverns whose painted signs once lined the sidewalks, the White Swan and Cross Keys and Cat, gone is the brick courthouse in the center of town where Indians exchanged shells for the promise of peace and land. A tree shivers in the night air, a taxi idles.

The pale white exterior of this theater is its own phantom. The marquee is dark; you can barely make out the word "Fulton" or the sculpted figure two stories up to whom it refers, a short man with a lantern jaw and a tumble of thick hair who's doing his best to look Napoleonic in a cutaway coat and flowing cape, hand on his breast. He stands in a vaulted niche that looks as though it belongs above the entrance to a cathedral, and he gazes out on the streets where he played as a boy, more than once with British prisoners of war in a game he and his friends called Rebels and Tories. Eleven-year-old Robert Fulton, eventual inventor of submarines and steamboats, sketched these scenes, he and the other boys leaping across a rope to pummel the enemy.

I was eleven myself when I first set foot inside the Fulton Theatre in downtown Lancaster, Pennsylvania. Johnson was president; the headlines were full of body counts in Southeast Asia. At home, I watched *The Monkees* every week on TV and listened compulsively to Julie Andrews on my record player. I came to the Fulton for movies and the occasional concert. When a film bored me, I scooched down in one of the theater's seats and shot my legs up in the air and bicycled. The place was dilapidated, paint peeling and carpets worn. There was talk of tearing it down to build a parking garage. Outside, a neon sign proclaimed, "A Landmark in Motion Picture Making!"

Inside, the spectral faces of Alan Bates and Julie Christie glimmered on the screen. As I watched their love blossom and then burn, I slipped from my own skin into theirs, glad to exchange the tedium of my junior high existence for their pain. I was just waking to the world. The cone of light trembling in the ether above me contained every future I might possibly want: the Austrian hills, a Dorset field, the pomp and circumstance of the Royal Ascot. If I could only reach up and nab a speck of it.

The room was dark, the furnishings shabby, the stage (for I knew there was one behind Bathsheba and Gabriel) a gray, impenetrable cave I longed to investigate. Soon afterward, watching my first plays on that stage, I was struck by how distant things became when they were real. Absent the giant screen we were genuinely little, I saw, but that was OK, because we belonged to a larger and quite beautiful cosmos. Moons flew in unannounced from the flies, summers burst into kaleidoscopic falls. You could see dust mites dancing in the tall black air and the shadows of strangers in the wings; clearly we were surrounded by all kinds of things visible and invisible.

By the time I turned thirteen I'd resolved to make a life for myself in the theater. I took acting lessons and memorized monologues about young women striving to understand themselves (Joan of Arc, Emily Webb). At a moment when I despaired of ever having a boyfriend for more than three consecutive days, I donned a crinoline to play Elizabeth Barrett Browning in a two-person show about love. One day I auditioned for a musical at the Fulton. I must have been sixteen. I wore a pink corduroy Betsey Johnson pantsuit I'd sewn expressly for the occasion. Shortly after I began to sing I realized that I was also, at the same time, standing to my own left and back a little ways, watching myself sing. It's the only out-of-body experience I've ever had. I remember nothing else about the event, except that I didn't get the part.

Two years after that audition I went back to the Fulton to work as an apprentice in a summer equity company at $15 a week. We opened four shows in a month and ran them in rep for another month. I sang in the chorus of an Amish musical, ran lights for *The Crucible*, scrounged props for *Tobacco Road*, and spent weeks building eighteenth-century hoopskirts and vests for a revival of Royall Tyler's *The Contrast*, a comedy about pure-hearted Americans and foppish Brits. Tyler's play made its debut in 1787—nearly fifty years after real-life colonists put mortar to stone to build what would eventually become the foundations of the Fulton Theatre, and more than twenty years after a group of Indians died inside the confines of those stone walls.

I spent whole days and nights threading plastic stays into muslin corsets and jamming yards of taffeta into bodices no bigger than my neck. Ronni, the costume designer, smoked long, filter-tipped cigarettes and used a ripper to stir powdered cream into the tall cups of coffee she sipped all day long. Several months pregnant, she'd come down from New York for the summer to run the shop with her sister Joanie and a woman named Poof, who cut patterns. We all had what we called theater-gray complexions.

The costume shop stood down the street from the Fulton, in an old warehouse with the words "Mack, the Coffee Man" painted in black letters on its side wall. A pair of picture windows opened at street level onto our chaotic interior, and I often wondered what passersby thought went on inside. We were in a slightly seedy part of town. A private bar stood halfway between the costume shop and the theater, and at night you could see glimmers of fluorescent light behind the bar's shuttered windows. To this day, when I hear the word "speakeasy" I think of that building. One morning a few years after our summer rep season, a costume designer spotted a shoe sticking out of the garbage skip next to the Mack building and tried to grab it for her shop but found it was attached to a foot. A homeless man had climbed into the dumpster the night before and died.

Things like this might explain why my mother once told me there were two careers she preferred I not pursue: funeral direction and the theater.

Theater was all I wanted to do, even if it meant subsisting on coffee and Tab from the neighborhood diner for days on end in order to get the show up on time, a feat we barely achieved with *The Contrast*. By 7:30 P.M. on opening night, I was still trying to finish a waistcoat for an actor who was due to go onstage at approximately 8:15. The coat was a deep blue ribbed silk, verging on plum, with huge cuffs and fluttering tails, and the actor was Michael Lewis, the misanthropic son of Sinclair. All summer long, Lewis *fils* had sat in his tiny dressing room sulking when he wasn't smoking Tiparillos and complaining about something—the building, the pay, his fellow actors, the rehearsal schedule, *us*. He bristled if you so much as mentioned his dad, so we'd all learned not to say a word, but we knew who he was. It was right there in his playbill bio: "Mr. Lewis is the son of the late Nobel Prize–winning novelist Sinclair Lewis and the journalist and commentator Dorothy Thompson." Just what those parents had done to make Michael the ogre he was, we couldn't imagine. He was in his early forties, tall and stooped, with a long, curving nose that made me think of Captain Hook. He kept mostly to himself. Everyone knew he drank; in rehearsals you could sometimes detect the hazy aftermath of a round with the bottle.

That he was somehow wounded may have occasionally crossed my eighteen-year-old mind, but not that night as I stitched buttons into place and rushed over to the ironing board. Lewis, I knew, had been grumbling all day about our incompetence. He didn't want to go onstage in a blouse, he wanted the waistcoat, and what in God's name had we been doing all summer for it to come to this. I remember my frenzy, the uncomfortably pregnant Ronni urging me on, Joanie cheering as I pumped the last shot of steam into the coat and bounded out the door. The two sisters physically pushed me off on a hundred-yard sprint from our shop to the theater, shouting go, go, *go*. I tore down the street, past the speakeasy and the bums, the silver diner glistening in the dusk, onto the sidewalk and through the back door of the Fulton into the greenroom where Lewis was pacing. The red of his fury bled through his makeup. I threw the coat over his shoulders, yanked his arms through the sleeves, adjusted the front while he fiddled with the lace jabot at his neck, and then he was gone, upstairs and onstage, not a second to spare. I could hear applause through the ceiling, the creaking of the old floorboards as the son of the author of *Main Street* and *Babbitt* made his entrance that evening in one of the first American plays ever produced.

Within a year Michael Lewis was dead. Forty-four years old, he left a daughter and two sons, a wife and an ex-wife. The obituaries didn't give the cause of death, but we could all guess, right or wrong, and anyway it didn't seem right that someone so mean could survive for long. By then my own life had spun off in untoward directions. I'd quit the Christian theater group I'd joined in high school and taken up with a married set designer who seduced me in my college theater. I thought it a fitting location, given my passions. I look back now and see that I craved drama so desperately I didn't mind wrecking lives in order to get it.

When I go back to the Fulton today, among the ghosts I find is the specter of my adolescent self. She and Michael Lewis have more in common than I would have imagined back then. Having now outstripped him in years, I recognize some of the devil that gnawed at him: the compromises of middle age, the burdens of family, the urge to secure your place in a country that disappoints as often as it inspires. Sinclair Lewis called America "the most contradictory, the most depressing, the most stirring, of any land in the world today." Perhaps Michael Lewis shared that view. Perhaps as he stormed onto the Fulton stage in his silk waistcoat that long-ago August night he was invoking his father's spirit.

We called our season the American Heritage Festival; exactly what that meant I couldn't have said. It made me squirm whenever I heard John Proctor defend his integrity that summer. Week after week I sat offstage listening to him, my fingers on the light board, waiting for the cue to illuminate his desperate face. "My name!" he'd cry. "My name!" I pushed the levers up. What had provoked the madness of Salem, I wondered, never mind the madness that prompted Arthur Miller to write those lines? One night toward the end of our season, Richard Nixon resigned. The audience that evening was small, and I hurried home after the show to catch the real theater on my parents' TV. The Vietnam War was raging; that year in college I'd read Arthur Kopit's *Indians* and for the first time been urged to consider the connections between what we were doing in Asia and what we'd done on our own frontier.

I was too fixed on the future to realize a portion of that frontier lay under my feet every time I walked onto the Fulton stage. Scrambling up onto the pin rail to hang lights, I was a sailor charting the swells of my own possibility. Occasionally I went downstairs into the storage tunnel below the auditorium to retrieve a lamp or gel. Inside the subterranean gloom I could see the log piers the first Fulton architect had installed to help hold up the place. They'd since been reinforced with concrete, but beyond them lay soft earth you could touch. I had no idea how long that soil had been there, probably centuries. Further off in the dark were the limestone walls that ran like a maze through the underbelly of the opera house. They were the old jail walls, I knew, and without them the theater would collapse. But I seldom thought more about their presence, about the American saga they'd helped beget. I hadn't yet learned the pull of the backward gaze.

The notion of the theater as a memory machine dates back at least to the sixteenth century, when an Italian scholar named Giulio Camillo suggested using components of a stage and auditorium as mnemonic prompts. The metaphorical implications of his choice have beguiled theater people ever since. "We all know these buildings are haunted," a director friend said to me when I told him about my obsession with the Fulton. Camillo was after personal as well as collective memory, and for me, of course, the Fulton holds both. The lamps I hauled up from the basement and helped string over the Salem courtroom where John Proctor repeatedly went on trial in the summer of 1974 belong to more than one narrative.

I've been told that cells from Julius Caesar still circulate in the world, that with each breath I draw I'm inhaling molecules from ancient Rome. If I keep going back to the Fulton, it's to suck in the past, of which my own is just a fraction. A child sees little but herself until one day she wakes and discovers she occupies a sliver of chronology in a ticking universe. I'd spent most of my life dreaming of what was to come, but that summer I shifted my gaze by a degree, and I've been turning counterclockwise ever since. I see now that we belong equally to the dead and the living, that if you put your hand out and touch the cold stone walls of history you can feel the thrum of your predecessors, those dim beings who've faded into the earth. I know now that if you race down a street at dusk, carrying a silk waistcoat in your arms, you just might make it in time for their story to begin.

2

MR. YECKER OPENS A THEATER: 1866

Six months had passed since the end of the War between the States, and Lancaster was thriving. The funerals of boys too young to die had stopped; the papers no longer published accounts of battles so ghastly they defied belief. Instead of troops, trains carried ordinary men and women back and forth to places like Philadelphia and Baltimore. Ships on the Susquehanna heaved under the weight of new merchandise: plows and threshing machines, carriages, firearms, wagons, umbrellas, cigars, hats, distilled liquors. Soon the cotton mills would be back in business and gaslights would flicker in every home in the city. Soon work would begin on a granite monument in the center of town to commemorate those who had given their lives in the terrible fight to preserve the Union. Already those brave men had begun to lapse into memory, their vibrant selves reduced to quicksilver images inside little cases their mothers and widows kept on the parlor table or carried in their pockets.

The circus came to town, and families went in throngs to see the clowns and acrobats. From time to time someone lit a gas valve under a giant balloon and rose from downtown into the blue sky over south-central Pennsylvania, while hundreds below watched in wonder. People craved amusement.

They wanted to laugh at minstrel shows and see cowboys shoot Indians and hear famous actors declaim Shakespeare.

Blasius Yecker thought it might be a good time to open a theater. A small man with a round face and dark hair who spoke English with a German accent, he said little publicly about why he wanted to go into show business. He was in his early thirties. He'd come to America from Europe at thirteen, leaving his widowed mother and traveling by diligence to Paris from his Alsatian birthplace, then by train to Le Havre, then by boat across the Atlantic in the dead of winter to New York and finally to Lancaster, where he'd worked first as a farmer and miller, then apprenticed as a saddler and opened a harness shop. Now he wanted to be Barnum.

He had a petite, German-born wife and four children, soon to be seven, and they belonged to a large German community whose members attended German-language churches and sang in German choirs and drank lager at picnics in the woods on the edge of town. Yecker had fled hunger and revolution in Europe and survived a war in his adopted land, and he was an optimist. The saddlery business had prospered during the war—the demand for trunks and bridles and knapsacks ever mounting—and he now had the means to buy property. Accordingly, on November 23, 1865, he and a business partner, Hilaire Zaepfel, a former saddler turned hotel-keeper, paid $16,200 for a "three-story brick tenement" with a creamy white façade near the corner of Prince and King Streets, in downtown Lancaster. The building, Fulton Hall, was thirteen years old, although its stone foundations went back more than a century.

Behind its pale veneer, Fulton Hall was little more than an assortment of meeting rooms and a large auditorium with rows of wooden benches and a small platform at one end. Since 1852, this building had served the citizens of Lancaster as a courthouse, stage, chapel, armory, auditorium, boot camp, warehouse, meeting place, concert hall, lecture room, exhibition space, ball-room, campaign rally ground, and occasional funeral parlor. Yecker wanted to turn it into a theater, a place to see and be seen. He envisioned a wide stage and a drop curtain with scenes of Europe, tiered seats, a domed ceiling, low footlights. It's doubtful he knew anything about Thespis or the Teatro Olimpico or London's Globe, about the myriad ways theater had entered people's imaginations through history and shaped civilizations and occasionally threatened governments. He simply saw a chance to make money and perhaps his mark.

Competition was scarce. One block up the street, a stereoscope belonging to the Messrs. Hambright offered fifty different views of battlefields and landscapes. There were occasional concerts by German men's choirs and traveling singers. The Fulton had its own bookings. Two days after Yecker bought the place, a local fire company held a fair inside the hall, with flags and prizes and music by a cornet band. From an arch suspended over the stage, gas jets spelled out the company's motto: "When Duty Calls 'Tis Ours to Obey." Below it stood a pedestal with a statue of the goddess of Liberty cradling an American flag in the hollow of one arm. In her other arm she held a scroll inscribed with the names Grant, Sherman, Sheridan, Meade, Reynolds, and Hooker.

Within the month, the famous Siamese twins Chang and Eng would play Fulton Hall on their farewell tour, together with a pair of "wild" Australian children who had reportedly been captured by gold hunters and who, according to the ads, had "long, sharp teeth" and curiously small heads.

On New Year's Day 1866, two months after Yecker's purchase, Fulton Hall presented a series of sixty-three tableaux based on Milton's *Paradise Lost*. The spectacle had enjoyed a long run in London, including a performance at Buckingham Palace before Queen Victoria, and was said to be an ideal vehicle for teaching children "the solemn and sublime truths of man's disobedience and fall, and God's omnipotence." Perhaps young Americans needed such instruction, although it's likely the recent war had taught them plenty about man's disobedience.

Still, it was a new era. For the first time in four years, Americans could wake on the first of January free from the cloud of battle. There were problems, of course: what to do with the nation's newly emancipated black population, how to reunite North and South. Lancaster's representative to Congress, Thaddeus Stevens, a Radical Republican who had often used the stage of Fulton Hall to trumpet abolition, wanted to remake the South entirely, to take land from plantation owners and distribute it to former slaves and to give every African American the right to vote. He decried the bigotry that had oppressed black men and women for two centuries and was now depriving them "of every right in the Southern states. We have joined in inflicting these wrongs," he said.

But Stevens hadn't long to live, and his vision of a beneficent South would die with him. Meanwhile, people north of the Mason-Dixon Line were interested in a new kind of America. The nation was pushing west. Photographs and prints brought radiant mountain vistas home to citizens in the eastern United States, and dime novels and frontier dramas captured the exploits of scouts and buffalo hunters. The Union Pacific had already reached Nebraska. In another year, General William Tecumseh Sherman would be sent west to help clear the way for trains, much as he'd cleared Georgia for federal troops. "Eastern people must not allow their sympathy with the Indians to make them forget what is due to those who are pushing the 'frontier' farther and farther west," Sherman declared. In three years, rail lines would span the continent.

If some Americans believed in progress more than God, it was understandable. There were new deities to exalt: the self-made man, entrepreneurs like Yecker, exemplars of a budding plutocracy. If some Americans found greater solace in entertainment than prayer, that too was understandable. God's hand "is amputated now / And God cannot be found," Emily Dickinson would write. People worshipped capital and technology, sought redemption not just at church but in nature and on the stage. Why not put your faith in the giant redwoods of northern California or in a $60,000 theatrical extravaganza whose sixty-three scenes included depictions of the Creation, the Garden of Eden, Adam's fall, and a massive spectacle in which heaven's hosts put down a rebellion by Satan's followers?

Hundreds of Lancastrians turned out to see the *Miltonian Tableaux* at Fulton Hall on the first of January 1866. Hundreds more were turned away. Inside the auditorium, which could hold a thousand, it was standing room only. The show's popularity, wrote the *Lancaster Evening Examiner*, "proves the good taste and moral worth of the community in which we live." But Blasius Yecker had a hunch his tasteful community wanted even more.

He had avoided military service himself. When Abraham Lincoln imposed a draft in 1863—the first in the country's history—Yecker and twenty other Lancaster men had each put $50 into a common fund with the understanding that should any of them be called up, $300 would be withdrawn to buy the draftee's way out of the army. Thus did the burden of preserving the nation pass from its older immigrants to its newest and poorest, notably the Irish, who were often dragooned into service the moment they stepped off the boat. Yecker (whose name never did appear on the long lists of the conscripted) stayed home and watched his fortunes and family grow.

He was a savvy businessman. He would eventually buy out his partner's share of the Fulton and take over management of the theater himself, but for now, in the first months of 1866, he focused on turning their musty hall into a posh attraction. Inside the Fulton's main auditorium, the sight lines were bad, and you couldn't reach the stage except by walking from the back of the room to the front. Ventilation was poor, and, thanks partly to a shooting gallery upstairs and a basement full of beer and tobacco, the hall stank.

Shortly after the *Miltonian Tableaux* closed, Yecker hired a crew of workmen to overhaul the Fulton. They cut a new door into the rear of the building, replaced its two dingy dressing rooms with four clean compartments, tore out the dilapidated sets and rolling stage machinery, and installed modern fixtures, including footlights low enough to see over. They introduced a new ventilation system, widened the makeshift stage to fifteen feet, and exchanged the uncomfortable wooden benches in the auditorium for orchestra chairs that rose in tiers toward the lobby, so that people at the back of the room no longer had to stand or "roost" on the backs of the seats in front of them in order to see what was happening onstage.

A pair of artists from Philadelphia created twenty new pieces of scenery for the stage—ten flats and ten wings—showing landscapes, cities, parlors, and streets. But the pièce de résistance was the Fulton's new drop curtain, for which Yecker reportedly paid $200. It featured a panorama of Venice: the Rialto and Grand Canal, Saint Mark's Basilica, sundry palaces, gondolas and barges. Beneath it Yecker hung a quote from Byron: "Those days are gone—but Beauty still is here." The poet was referring to Venice, but Lancastrians would have understood it to mean them. Here in this small town sixty-five miles west of Philadelphia, once the nation's largest inland city, inside this newly refurbished hall—this *theater*—here too was beauty and myth, a longing for the past and a conviction that the best was still to come.

Yecker engaged a Philadelphia company under the management of actor George W. Harrison to provide nightly shows in Fulton Hall. Harrison's was a permanent troupe of "artistes from the first-class Eastern Theaters," not a "strolling company," the *Lancaster Intelligencer* informed readers. The *Evening Express* assured those who might fear the idea of a theater in their midst—might fear, especially, the drunken brawls theater so often provoked, the sordid personalities it attracted—that Harrison would impose "the strictest decorum in the hall" and present "the best and most unexceptionable plays." Months earlier, the same paper had called for an end to the "disorderly conduct of boys and young men at public exhibitions at Fulton Hall."

Despite above-average ticket prices, Harrison drew a healthy crowd on February 10 with the first of his offerings, a comedy and two farces, preceded by an orchestral overture. Over the next week audiences grew, and reporters gushed. The *Examiner and Herald*: "Lancaster has never been famed for its support of the Stage, but this was owing more to the character of the actors who visited us, than to any want of inclination upon the part of the public to patronize a well ordered and respectable theater." The *Evening Express*: "We are pleased to see a class of persons visiting Fulton Hall who heretofore rarely patronized similar exhibitions. These performances have thus far been entirely free from those objectionable features which are urged—and with good reason—against most of the entertainments of this character."

In his second week at the Fulton, Harrison presented *Our American Cousin*, the comedy Lincoln had been watching ten months earlier when the actor John Wilkes Booth stole into his flag-trimmed box at Ford's Theatre and shot the president below his left ear. Walt Whitman would note the paradox—that in the middle of the farce occurred "the main thing, the actual murder" of "the leading actor in the stormiest drama known to real history's stage."

Lancaster audiences understood the play's significance, and perhaps for that reason a sizable crowd came out to see the show. Among them, almost certainly, were men and women who had gone to the city's rail depot ten months earlier to glimpse Lincoln's funeral train on its way from Washington to Illinois. All told, more than seven million Americans witnessed the train's sixteen-hundred-mile odyssey. Lancastrians spent six hours that day draping their depot in black, and when the somber train finally pulled in, they removed their hats and bonnets and stood bareheaded, many in tears, and stared at the funeral car. Through its windows they could see Lincoln's casket and two soldiers standing guard. The whole spectacle lasted a matter of minutes, but forty years later those who were there could describe it in detail.

"Why, if the old Greeks had had this man," Whitman would write of the slain president, "what trilogies of plays—what epics—would have been made out of him!" But Americans didn't need epics: they had the artifact itself, the guilty play.

In the aftermath of Lincoln's assassination, people across America had lashed out against the theater, against actors in particular, reviving prejudices that went back to Plato, who believed mimesis provoked foul thoughts and dreams. Within minutes of Booth's lurid plunge to the stage and Shakespearean cry—*Sic semper tyrannis!*—audience members in Ford's Theatre were calling for the building to be burnt and its actors killed. A Washington shopkeeper who dared to suggest that the cast of *Our American Cousin* was not responsible for the president's death had his neck put in a noose. In Detroit a minister barked, "Would that Mr. Lincoln had fallen elsewhere than at the very gates of Hell—in the theater." An Illinois clergyman announced that by going to see a play, Lincoln had forfeited God's "divine protection."

Actors everywhere were suspect. Booth's brother Edwin, one of the most celebrated of American players, declared his career ended. Papers in Lancaster carried this statement: "While mourning in common with all other loyal hearts, the death of the president, I am oppressed by a private woe not to be expressed in words. But whatever calamity may befall me or mine, my country one and indivisible, has been my warmest devotion. Edwin Booth." His assurances fell on mostly deaf ears; in the next weeks death threats poured into Booth's New York apartment, where he remained under house arrest.

Fulton Hall stayed open after Lincoln's assassination, even as local businesses hung black bunting from their windows and rumors circulated that John Wilkes Booth was on the run in Pennsylvania, not far from Lancaster. Within twenty-four hours of the president's death, the Fulton presented an evening of comedy and burlesque that included both a "laughable farce" and a panorama of the recent war. Wittingly or not, those who attended the show were rendering homage to Lincoln, who had loved the theater. Even in the bleakest months of his presidency, as the number of Union dead and wounded climbed, Lincoln found time to go to plays—farces, melodramas, Irish comedies, Shakespeare. He had seen John Wilkes Booth in *Richard III* and other works, and he had liked the actor. Whitman marveled that so powerful a leader drew such pleasure from "those human jack-straws, moving about with their silly little gestures, foreign spirit, and flatulent text." But Whitman too loved playgoing; he admired especially John Wilkes Booth's late father, Junius Brutus Booth, an alcoholic rogue who had thrilled American audiences in the first half of the nineteenth century with his volcanic performances.

In a sense, Lincoln's murder both cursed and sanctified the American theater. All faiths establish holy sites in places where significant events occurred or are presumed to have occurred, in places haunted by memory, and the secular faith of the American stage in 1865 was no different. Walk into a theater after April 14 of that year, and you beheld the setting for a crime: here were the audience, the actors, the melodrama. On the night of the actual assassination, some in the crowd thought Booth's histrionics were part of the play. "Down in front!" people shouted when others stood to see what was happening. "Sit down!" What was real that evening? Certainly not the actress Laura Keene, who emerged from Ford's Theatre in a yellow costume spattered with blood. Witnesses gasped: she looked like a ghost.

Harrison's reenactment of the play that killed Lincoln drew a large crowd to Fulton Hall on February 22, 1866. Yecker must have been pleased; soon he would start filling a book with records of Fulton engagements. That same month in New York City, Edwin Booth returned to the stage in his signature role, Hamlet—a part he would later reprise at the Fulton. Passions had cooled since his brother's capture and death the previous spring, and Edwin needed money. Despite threats from the public and attacks by the press ("Is the Assassination of Caesar to Be Performed?" the *New York Herald* asked), his return was a triumph, and the audience that evening showered Booth with flowers and applause. Watching him step into the light, they may have felt as Marcellus does when he sees the specter of Hamlet's father: "What, has this thing appeared again tonight?"

Likewise at the Fulton, patrons of *Our American Cousin* must have felt a frisson when George W. Harrison, as Asa Trenchard, the play's hapless Yankee hero, spoke the very words actor Henry Hawk had uttered at Ford's just before Lincoln was shot: "Wal, I guess I know enough to turn you inside out, you sockdologizing old man-trap." Lest Lancastrians forget the horror of that moment, the *Evening Express* had published an account of it the day before the performance, noting how Hawk's hilarious delivery had given way to the crack of a pistol and then chaos.

Now they were reliving the instant here in Lancaster, imagining the president in his box, the audience shouting, "Who was he?" and "Hang him!," as the villain Booth, clad in black, leapt to the stage, and Hawk fled, afraid Booth would stab him. Later that February evening, as they made their way home along Lancaster's gaslit streets or stopped for a glass of beer at Henry Struble's Fulton Hall Restaurant, members of the Fulton crowd may have pondered the irony that it was an actor, of all people, who had conjured the shocking finale to the long war. As Thaddeus Stevens would observe, "In the midst of the most exquisite enjoyment of his favorite relaxation, [Lincoln] was instantaneously taken away." That too was part of the theater's spell.

Two weeks after *Our American Cousin*, the Harrison company presented Dion Boucicault's *The Octoroon*, the story of a mixed-blood Louisiana free woman who is sold back into slavery to save her family from debt. Harrison followed this with the antebellum hit *Uncle Tom's Cabin*, well on its way to becoming the single most produced play in the history of the American theater. Slavery may have ended elsewhere in America, but it flourished onstage, and Yecker hoped to profit from it.

The novelty of his new theater soon faded, though, and by the end of Harrison's inaugural season, in April 1866, ticket sales had plunged. One of Harrison's actors returned for a six-day run in May, but audiences were so sparse he closed three days early. As it happened, Yecker's fifth child was born the next day. He couldn't afford to keep his theater dark, not even in the sticky heat of a mid-Atlantic summer, and so he improvised. In June he brought in a pair of pianists; in July, a minstrel show; in August, another acting company. For the next year Yecker kept up the pattern: theater troupes alternated with comedians, singers with magicians, lecturers, trained dogs, acrobats, and dioramas, among them the *Great Lincoln Memorial Tableaux*, a series of sixty "lifelike and thrilling" panoramas devoted to the late president's memory and the pursuit, capture, trial, and execution of his killer. But audiences continued to dwindle, and the Fulton increasingly fell to local use: church fairs, commencement ceremonies, fundraisers for a monument to honor the city's fallen soldiers and sailors.

Yecker was thirty-two and handsome, with brooding, almost melancholy eyes and dark hair, which he combed back from his face in immaculate waves. In the few photographs of him that survive, he is a model of bourgeois respectability in a tailored suit, crisp white shirt and bow tie, glistening black shoes. It's hard to know what drove this immigrant saddler to create a theater in the middle of his adopted city. Civic pride? A thirst for adventure? The conviction that he could make money as a showman? If so, he was reckoning against the odds. A fellow nineteenth-century theater manager said he could recall "scarcely a single instance . . . of a persevering manager dying in comfortable circumstances."

In his 1855 *Autobiography*, Phineas Taylor Barnum had set forth ten rules for entrepreneurial success, among them "select the *kind* of business that suits your natural inclinations." Yecker, like Barnum, chose entertainment, the presentation of "varieties." "Work at it if necessary early and late," Barnum advised, "in season and out of season, not leaving a stone unturned, and never deferring for a single hour that which can be done just as well now." P. T. Barnum had made a fortune in show business, largely by peddling humbug—a black woman whom he advertised as the 161-year-old former nanny of George Washington, the desiccated remains of a supposed mermaid, an African American man who dressed in a suit of black hair, grunted on cue, and shambled across the stage like a monkey. Barnum labeled him "What Is It?"

Yecker had little interest in hawking tricks, but he shared Barnum's eye for spectacle and grasp of middlebrow taste, and both men understood the need for propriety, personal as well as professional. Yecker attended Mass on Sundays and during his first years at Fulton Hall continued to operate his harness shop, turning out bridles and martingales for his neighbors even as he tried to lure them into his theater with the promise of escape.

Fulton Hall did not tower as high as Saint Mary's Roman Catholic Church, where Yecker worshipped. It had no steeple whose chimes pealed repeatedly through the day, as did Trinity Lutheran Church a few blocks up the street. It lacked the stained-glass windows and stately pews of the city's Episcopal and Presbyterian sanctuaries, but Yecker's hall did have an unmistakable grandeur. The beveled stones at the base of its façade evoked the mansions of Florence, its arched windows the lagoons of Venice, its Gothic lines the cathedrals of northern Europe. Everything conspired to lift your eyes up to the top of the building, where a gabled roof erupted in tiny crenellations pointing heavenward. "Whenever men have become skillful architects at all, there has been a tendency in them to build high," John Ruskin had written a decade before Yecker bought his hall, "not in any religious feeling, but in mere exuberance of spirit and power—as they dance or sing—with a certain mingling of vanity—like the feeling in which a child builds a tower of cards."

A white building in a red-brick city, a pleasure palace in a workaday world—Fulton Hall was indeed exuberant. Cross our threshold, its doors seemed to proclaim, and you will find harmony and goodwill, laughter, the strangeness of other worlds. Above all you will encounter actors, men and women possessed of a curious energy, whose resonant voices and powerful bodies recount the myths on which our lives rely. "Those days are gone," the curtain inside Yecker's spacious auditorium read, "but Beauty still is here." Beauty, yes, and hope, an image of the epic future.

Here too was the ghosted past. If you were to tunnel down through Yecker's hall, from its pitched roof through its wood floors and timber joists to the stone foundations of the building and beyond, into the earth, you would find arrowheads and clay pipes, the precolonial beginnings of the country, and if you were to dig further, into the soft, erosion-prone bedrock of this place, you would touch the skeletons of fish swimming in stone. Long before Blasius Yecker bought Fulton Hall, before the magistrates of colonial Lancaster picked this site for their jail, before Charles II granted this land—with all its "fields, woods, underwoods, mountains, hills, fenns, isles, lakes, rivers, waters, rivulets, bays and inlets"—to William Penn, long before Susquehannocks walked here in search of berries and deer, water covered the surface of this particular earth, and pale creatures glided along its currents in the dark. It was even then a place of enchantment, a penumbral world where anything could happen, and from its depths would come a continent whose immense, unstoried wilderness took your breath away.

3

THE KILLING OF THE CONESTOGAS: 1763

Black braids frame her face. She wears a colorful headband with an even more colorful feather, a brown dress, a choker strung with plump red beads. I was seven when I sketched her, in crayon, for the frontispiece of "My Indian Book," an illustrated collection of one-sentence stories about Native Americans who pray for rain, sing songs, build birch-bark canoes, and await the end of "hungry time." I was infatuated with Pocahontas and almost certainly had her in mind as I drew. Perhaps I imagined this young woman and I had been sisters in some prelapsarian world. More than forty years later her startled eyes look straight into mine, and she smiles as if to say, *It's all right, you may have my land. My bed. My home. My food. I understand.*

On the booklet's orange cover I drew what I took to be Indian symbols: a cloud fringed with lines of rain, a geometrical tree. Decades later I learned that shapes much like these are etched in giant schist rocks in the middle of the Susquehanna River at the southern end of Lancaster County, where I grew up. The carvings are perhaps a thousand years old and still visible, though you need a boat to get there, and the short voyage is not without its hazards. It takes muscle to get a purchase on a thigh-high ledge halfway up Big Indian Rock, then hoist yourself to the top of the huge boulder, whose surface is scarred with petroglyphs.

Perhaps you are wondering what this has to do with Yecker's Fulton Hall. There is, I believe, a connection, and it has to do with stone.

On the ground floor of the Fulton Theatre, around the corner from the lobby and just outside the women's room, a smooth interior wall parts to reveal a portion of a second wall, made of limestone, which dates back to the eighteenth century and belonged to the city jail. Downstairs in the theater's labyrinthine basement, further portions of the old jail wall wind through the greenroom, the dressing rooms, the bathrooms and ushers' quarters, under the stage and beside the file cabinets that hold financial and other records. When masons first coaxed these chunks of stone from the earth almost three centuries ago and hauled them here to build a prison, the town of Lancaster barely existed (it would not become a city until 1818). A pair of streets, King and Queen, met in a square that held a courthouse and market; a log cabin served as a Catholic chapel, and a stone building with a spire as a Lutheran one. There were a hundred or so private homes, most of them wood. Along the western wall of the new stone jail, a stream rumbled on its way to the Conestoga River, which fed into the Susquehanna, some ten miles distant, whose waters gave rise to mammoth rocks inscribed with sacred messages.

Pushing south from its crop of Indian petroglyphs, the Susquehanna empties into the Chesapeake Bay, mapped by the English Captain John Smith, of Pocahontas fame, in the early 1600s. Smith pronounced the area a revelation and called the Indians whom he met at the mouth of the river "Susquehannocks." They seemed to him giants, with calves that measured three-quarters of a yard around, though twentieth-century archaeologists would conclude that the average Susquehannock male stood just under 5'4". Of the Indians' language, which he did not understand, Smith wrote, "It may well beseeme their proportions, sounding as a voyce in a vault." The Susquehannocks wore animal skins and carried gifts, including swords and tobacco pipes. At their first encounter, they raised their hands to the sun, broke into song, and embraced Smith, who tried to push them away. They laid objects at his feet, and around his shoulders they placed a painted bear hide as well as other skins and a necklace of heavy white beads. They begged him to protect them from rival tribes.

Smith published his *Map of Virginia* in 1612, and for the next sixty years this document was the primary means by which British explorers understood the Chesapeake and its precolonial inhabitants. Among the Indians Smith identified was a group called the Conestogas. These too were Susquehannock people, whom French fur traders had labeled "Andastes" or "Gandastogues." They lived east of the Susquehanna River, many in and around what would become Lancaster County, and their footpaths criss-crossed the land. Smith and his compatriots anglicized their name and eventually used it to denote the places where these Indians dwelt.

I grew up in a suburban neighborhood in eastern Lancaster County, a few hundred yards from Stauffer's Run, a tributary of the Conestoga River and by extension the Susquehanna. Without realizing it, I was treading on Indian ground whenever I went outdoors to play. I was intrigued by arrow-heads, to be sure, and envied the few people I knew who'd found one. By rights I should have been among them; our neighborhood was under con-stant construction while I was growing up, with pits of earth ripe for exca-vation, but I wasn't interested. By the time I graduated from high school, the field across the street from my parents' house had become a grid of manicured lawns, two with swimming pools and one with its own tennis court. The Conestoga River meandered along a golf course on the far side of the neighborhood, and I often crossed it on a footbridge on my way to the country club to go swimming. I knew nothing about the origins of the word "Conestoga," except that it had lent itself to my high school, Cones-toga Valley, and a century before that to the huge red, white, and blue wagons that helped settle the American West. Other than "My Indian Book," I don't recall learning much of anything about Native Americans in school. History began with the Pilgrims, and I sketched them over and over again, cheerful faces in funny hats and stiff white collars. But at some point it catches up with you. Fall in love with a building, and the next thing you know, you're wondering what happened to the Indians.

The simple answer is: they vanished. The Conestogas who inhabited my county clung to the hope of peaceful coexistence with their European neighbors for more than a hundred years and signed treaty after treaty, several in the brick courthouse on Lancaster's main square. They met with William Penn, who pledged that the two groups "should always live as friends and brothers, and be as one body," but his heirs betrayed Penn's vision and continued to surge west, seizing Indian land as they went.

By 1745, when colonists in Lancaster began erecting a two-story lime-stone prison at the intersection of King and Prince Streets, one block west of the courthouse, European settlers had crossed the Susquehanna and were heading into the Alleghenies. The few Conestogas left in Lancaster County had taken up residence, along with the remnants of a half dozen other displaced and dying tribes, in a four-hundred-acre tract of land south of the city, known as Conestoga Town. Provincial officials authorized the area for use by the Conestogas—as the Indians who lived there were collectively known—"so long as they obeyed all the English conditions set forth therein." Here, on this hilly spot a dozen miles from downtown Lancaster, the stories of the Fulton Theatre and the Conestoga Indians converge.

In my own lifetime the acreage where the Indians lived would metamorphose into a scraggly farm owned by a widow in her eighties named Betty Witmer, who for a while served as the local trash collector and dogcatcher. In 1972, a team of archaeologists cleared the topsoil from a thirty-two-thousand-square-foot piece of land on her property and found a half dozen storage pits, three houses, and five small cemeteries crammed with funerary objects, which they took to the state museum in Harrisburg for safekeeping. A couple of years ago, I met up with a neighbor of Betty's who collects Indian artifacts, and with Betty's blessing he and I spent a muggy June afternoon walking up and down one of her fields. I came away with a fragment of clay pipe, less than an inch long and plugged with soil, which now sits beside my computer in a little ceramic bowl where I've also placed three pieces of stone from the Fulton basement. I often finger and sometimes smell them, and from time to time I touch my tongue to each in the hope of recovering something, I'm not sure what. The pipe tastes of chalk, the stones vaguely of salt.

Shorn of the wilderness that had previously sustained them, the Indians of Conestoga Town spent their last decades peddling baskets and brooms to the European immigrants whose farms surrounded their bleak reservation. No longer the noble Susquehannocks of Smith's day, nor even the buckskin-clad braves and squaws of "My Indian Book," they subsisted mostly on corn. It was not unusual to see them wandering the countryside in rags or begging alms in downtown Lancaster. In 1750, the Conestogas petitioned the governor of Pennsylvania to let them relocate. "Many of our old people are dead, so that we are now left as it were orphans in a destitute condition, which inclines us to leave our old habitations," they said. But nothing came of it.

Reading about the Conestogas, I'm not always sure what or whom to trust. Eighteenth-century provincial records chart a growing fissure between colonists and their Indian neighbors, but eyewitness reports are scarce; nineteenth- and twentieth-century historians shaped the story to suit their needs; the Indians themselves left no written account. But several thousand objects taken from Betty Witmer's farm and now in the basement of the State Museum of Pennsylvania—among them coins, bottles, tools, combs, slivers of mirror, gun parts, spectacles, and a dozen crosses, at least one with a figure of Christ—suggest the extent to which the Conestogas relied on Europeans for their everyday needs.

The outbreak of the Seven Years' War in 1754 set off a wave of violence across Pennsylvania. With the encouragement of their French allies, natives in the western part of the province attacked settlers and missionaries to the east. Colonists in Lancaster heard story after story of Indian atrocities: a woman stabbed to death while breastfeeding, a corpse with two toma-hawks sunk into its skull, natives who drank the blood of children "like water." Not far from Lancaster, four settlers were found scalped and butch-ered. There were rumors that "a great body" of Indians planned to launch a flotilla of canoes on the Susquehanna and invade Lancaster County. Locals talked of erecting a stockade. Vigilante groups sprang up through-out Pennsylvania province, spurred in part by a government offer of $130 bounty a head for Indian scalps. Forty miles northwest of Lancaster, near Harrisburg, members of a Presbyterian church in the frontier town of Pax-ton formed a posse of armed rangers under the leadership of a militant clergyman named John Elder.

At a treaty session in Lancaster in 1756, an elderly Conestoga told colo-nial authorities, "We have heard a great noise all about us and expected we should have been killed." He pleaded for protection.

Fewer than fifty Conestogas remained. They were penniless and starv-ing, but even so they inspired fear. Rumors spread that a young Conestoga named Will Sock was in cahoots with the French and had "murder in his heart." "In the immediate neighborhood, they were commonly regarded as harmless vagabonds," Francis Parkman would write of the Conestogas in his 1855 history of these events. "But elsewhere, a more unfavorable opin-ion was entertained, and they were looked upon as secretly abetting the enemy, acting as spies, giving shelter to scalping-parties, and even aiding them in their depredations." Aware they were in danger, the Conestogas stopped traveling long distances to sell their goods.

The Seven Years' War ended officially in 1763 with the Peace of Paris and subsequent consolidation of British control over North America, but relations between natives and colonists continued to deteriorate. The new British administration nullified previous treaties between Indians and the French, canceled long-standing rites, banned gift giving, halted the sale of liquor and weapons, and restricted trade. Natives across the Northeast retaliated. Led by a visionary Ottawa named Pontiac, who vowed to drive the English "into the sea," they attacked forts, cut communication lines, and terrorized colonists. By the summer of 1763, Pontiac's War had claimed more than a hundred British lives. The citizens of Lancaster, as elsewhere, feared "the extermination of us all," as Lancaster County magistrate Edward Shippen put it.

That September, nearly four dozen white settlers were murdered in eastern Pennsylvania. Paxton's John Elder implored the governor, John Penn, grandson of William, to remove the Conestogas from Lancaster and replace their log huts with a garrison. Penn replied that the Indians of Conestoga were "innocent, helpless, and dependent upon the Governor for support," and he could not remove them "without adequate cause." In October, Elder's rangers found the mutilated corpses of nine colonists along the upper Susquehanna River, and Elder again called for the area to be cleared of Indians.

Just over twenty Conestogas were left. They included an old man named Sheehays, whose father was said to have negotiated with William Penn. In late November, the Conestogas sent John Penn a letter reminding him of the friendship they had enjoyed with his grandfather and again seeking help: "As we have always lived in Peace and Quietness with our Brethren and Neighbours round us during the last and present Indian Wars, we hope now, as we are deprived from supporting our families by hunting, as we formerly did, you will consider our distressed situation, and grant our women and children some cloathing to cover them this winter." The letter reached Penn on December 19, five days too late.

Elder's rangers struck at dawn on Wednesday, December 14, 1763. Armed with hatchets, swords, and flintlocks, between fifty and sixty of them rode through the countryside from Paxton to reach Conestoga Town by daybreak. Deep snow covered the sleeping Indian village, and more snow was falling. Only seven Conestogas were home that morning; the rest had left to peddle wares to farmers in the neighborhood. The Paxton men broke into the Indian cabins and murdered six of the Conestogas—a seventh escaped—then plundered the threadbare village and burned what was left of it to the ground.

The ratio of killer to victim was nearly ten to one, and the butchery must have been extreme. Benjamin Franklin, who was miles away in Philadelphia at the time of the massacre but later decried it, claimed the Paxton "boys" scalped and "otherwise horribly mangled" their victims. The killers rode off in the snow with their bloody weapons, and no one stopped them. When local officials arrived on the scene, they found a smoking ruin strewn with charred corpses. One of the dead was Sheehays, who had so trusted the descendants of William Penn that he once declared, "The English will wrap me in their Matchcoat and secure me from all Danger." Also dead was his son, Ess-canesh.

As they winnowed the debris at Conestoga, officials reportedly found a bag containing two wampum belts and several documents, one of them Penn's original treaty with the Conestogas. Drafted and signed in Philadelphia in 1701, it promised unending "Friendship and Amity as one People." Like so much else, this document too would disappear.

Nine miles away from the Indian village, in the borough of Columbia, the children of Quaker sheriff Robert Barber Jr. learned of the killings and were heartstricken. Barber's children had often played with the children of the Conestogas and were so attached to one Indian boy they thought of him as a brother. Seventy years later, Barber's adult children were still unable to talk about the event.

Fourteen Conestogas survived the slaughter in their village. Officials promptly rounded them up, took them to Lancaster, and locked them inside the city's workhouse for their protection. Eight of the jailed were children; six were married adults.

To build a limestone wall in the eighteenth century, you first had to bore holes into a stretch of bedrock, then insert iron wedges into those holes and gently drive them deeper into the earth's surface, and finally, with the sharp edge of a sledgehammer, "strike hard on the rock in the line between every wedge," as a Pennsylvania stonecutter described the process, until the limestone cracked and eventually opened, like a fruit. In this manner quarriers worked their way down the crust of the earth, axes and hammers ringing. They used iron levers and bars, and sometimes sledges or stoneboats, to haul massive chunks of rock up ramps that led to the top of the quarry, where masons waited with chisels. Once hewn into rough blocks, these souvenirs of geologic time were carted off to construction sites in nascent American cities, laid side by side in long rows, one on top of the next, and secured with lime-sand mortar, the recipe for which dated back to Vitruvius.

In 1745, the commissioners of the newly incorporated town of Lancaster, Pennsylvania, had hired a mason named James Webb to construct a series of such walls on a half acre of land bounded by King, Prince, and Water Streets. The property had been given to Lancaster by the town's founder, Andrew Hamilton, a Philadelphia lawyer and the eventual designer of Independence Hall, for the purpose of erecting a jail to house "felons, vagrants, and loose and idle persons." A log prison had stood on the site for fifteen years, but the people of Lancaster wanted something stronger, so Webb went to work. By 1746, he and his fellow laborers had completed a stone jail; some years later the building was expanded to include an adjoining workhouse. It was to this compound the fourteen Conestogas were brought on December 14, 1763.

I don't know when I first learned about the connection between the Conestoga Indians and the Fulton Theatre. I remember seeing a movie version of *The Mikado* at the Fulton in elementary school, when the theater was a rundown firetrap. Maybe I learned about the Indians then. By the time I went to work in the Fulton a decade later, I knew. Sitting in the greenroom, surrounded by stone, stories swirled: Do you know what happened here? Can you feel it? The place has a chill, and it's not just the thermostat setting. Spend time in this room, as actors inevitably do, and you get sucked into the saga. Hear that noise? It's the rumble of wagon wheels on the dirt road outside the prison, it's the clang of the jailer's keys.

Authorities claimed they were incarcerating the Indians for their safety, but it's equally clear they were protecting themselves. The county magistrate, Edward Shippen, reasoned that had it not been snowing on the day Elder's rangers raided Conestoga, the Indians who survived the attack might well have embarked on a murderous rampage against their white neighbors. Shippen had long feared tensions with the Indians would lead to a civil war. A businessman and slave owner with a predilection for Renaissance literature and religious texts, he had briefly been an Indian trader and harbored his share of bigotry. Shippen and other Lancastrians urged provincial officials to remove the fourteen Conestogas from Lancaster and confine them on an island outside Philadelphia, where more than a hundred displaced Delaware were already being housed. Even the Conestogas begged to be taken to Philadelphia. But they stayed in Lancaster.

Outside the prison complex, colonists in their wood and brick houses were preparing to celebrate Christmas. Inside, the Indians were alone except for a jailer who fed them and built them fires. It's not hard to imagine their plight: cold, helpless, deprived of "necessaries and apparel," in mourning for their murdered companions and afraid of what lay ahead. I'd like to think some charitable citizen came around to the jail with a gift of food or apparel, or remembered the Indians in his prayers, but there's no record of it.

On December 19, Governor John Penn ordered the capture and arrest of the men who had attacked Conestoga Town, but before his proclamation could be published Elder's men attacked again. Edward Shippen was attending services in the sanctuary of Saint James Episcopal Church in downtown Lancaster on Tuesday afternoon, December 27, when the doors to the building burst open, and he heard shouts outside: "Paxton boys!" "Murder!" "The prison is attacked!" "They are murdering the Indians!" Shippen had been warned a few nights before that a "parcel of Rioters" from Paxton was in the area, and he had dispatched a pair of constables to investigate. (The jailer had been sufficiently worried that he'd armed himself and sent his children away from the prison.) But Shippen's men reported no signs of trouble.

Now the magistrate hurried to the workhouse. It was only a few blocks away, but by the time Shippen got there, the attackers had escaped and all fourteen Conestogas were dead. The killings had taken less than fifteen minutes. On their way out of town, the fifty to sixty men who'd carried out the assault rode around the Lancaster courthouse on horseback, "hooping and hallowing" and firing their guns into the air.

Roused by the commotion, Lancastrians streamed to the prison complex. Inside, they found what Shippen, invoking the Renaissance language he loved, termed a "Tragical scene." Beside one door lay the bodies of Will Sock and his wife, and on top of them the corpses of two children no older than three, whose heads had been split open and scalps peeled off. Another Indian was sprawled against the west wall of the workhouse. He had been shot in the chest, his legs sliced and hands amputated, and a rifle discharged in his mouth. "His head was blown to atoms, and the brains were splashed against, and yet hanging to the wall, for three or four feet around," said a shopkeeper's son who raced to the scene. "In this manner lay the whole of them, men, women and children, spread about the prison yard: shot, scalped, hacked and cut to pieces." In minutes, the Paxton frontiersmen had slaughtered the last collective body of indigenous people to inhabit Lancaster County while the land was still a wilderness.

Residents carried the Indian corpses from the workhouse into the street and eventually buried them in a Mennonite cemetery a few blocks from the workhouse. Days later, jailer Felix Donnally submitted a bill to the county for his services feeding and maintaining the Indians from the 14th to the 27th of December, and for the "Trouble and Expense of having the said Fourteen Indians carried to the grave and interred."

"My Indian Book" does not relate this part of the story. The booklet ends with a vision of bluebirds singing and a sun god painting the sky "beautiful shades of red and gold." I suppose that's what I was taught. The history of Indians in America was one of high drama and some suffering, but in the end things worked out the way they were supposed to. This was ten years before the founding of the American Indian Movement and the occupation of Wounded Knee, some twenty years before the Native American Graves Protection and Repatriation Act, and forty years before the opening of the National American Indian Museum in Washington, D.C. Although my stepchildren would learn about the Paxton killings in their eleventh-grade American history class in Ann Arbor, Michigan, I was not taught that the history of aboriginal extermination on this continent had its origins in my hometown, much less in a building on which I would come to pin my adolescent hopes.

In the aftermath of the murders, Edward Shippen went to vast lengths to absolve himself and his fellow magistrates of blame. Paxton's John Elder did the same. In a letter to John Penn, Elder insisted he'd tried to prevent both attacks on the Conestogas. "I expostulated, but *life* and *reason* were set at defiance, and yet the men in private life are virtuous, and respectable; not cruel, but mild and merciful." He accused others of having mutilated the Conestogas' bodies in order to blacken the image of the Paxton rangers. Penn ordered Elder to suppress further insurrections, and he stripped the minister of his office as a colonel in the provincial military. The governor commanded Shippen to get the names of the Paxton ringleaders, and he issued a proclamation, with a bounty, calling for the killers' immediate apprehension. No arrests were ever made.

A reconstituted Paxton gang set out in late January 1764 to attack the Delaware under Penn's protection in Philadelphia. The rangers were stopped just outside the capital by Benjamin Franklin, among others, who

arrived with five hundred armed men and a delegation of provincial officials and clergymen. Leaders of the two sides met in a tavern to hammer
out a settlement, and the Paxton men backed down. It scarcely mattered:
smallpox soon ravaged the barracks where the Delaware were held, and
fifty-six Indians died.

The slaughter in Lancaster deepened tensions between Quaker authorities in Philadelphia and their non-Quaker constituents—many of them
Scots-Irish Presbyterians—on the Pennsylvania frontier. It also gave rise to
a pamphlet war. Franklin weighed in with *A Narrative of the Late Massacres
in Lancaster County*, in which he argued that just because some Indians
had murdered some settlers, other settlers had no right to avenge those
deaths by killing blameless Indians. The Philadelphia printer and essayist
had visited Lancaster County on several occasions and was familiar with
the Conestogas. He could imagine the scene in the workhouse: "When the
poor Wretches saw they had no *Protection* nigh, nor could possibly escape,
and being without the least Weapon for Defence, they divided into their
little Families, the Children clinging to the Parents; they fell on their
Knees, protested their Innocence, declared their Love to the *English*, and
that, in their whole Lives, they had never done them Injury; and in this
Posture they all received the Hatchet!" No civilized nation in Europe
would commit such an atrocity, Franklin observed. "Do we come to
America to learn and practise the Manners of Barbarians?"

During the next months, upwards of sixty pamphlets and squibs for
and against the so-called Paxton rebellion were printed and distributed, or
read aloud, in taverns and coffeehouses throughout Philadelphia and as far
west as Lancaster—a quantity sufficient to move Philadelphia ahead of
Boston as the colony's top publisher. Several pamphlets took the form of
dialogues—primitive American theater. It's as if the ground where the
Conestogas died was fated to become sacral space. A friend who works at
the Fulton remarked by e-mail when I told him about the dialogues, "It
almost makes the building of a theater on the site of the massacre a touch
of destiny and a haunting sort of justice."

ANDREW TRUEMAN: Whar ha' you been aw this Time, Tom?

THOMAS ZEALOT: Whar I have been! Whar you should ha' been too,
Andrew, fechting the Lord's Battles, and killing the Indians at Lancaster
and Cannestogoe.

TRUEMAN: How mony did you kill at Cannestogoe.

ZEALOT: Ane and Twunty.

TRUEMAN: Hoot Man, there were but twunty awthegether, and fourteen of them were in the Gaol.

ZEALOT: I tell you, we shot six and a wee ane, that was in the Squaw's Belly; we sculped three; we tomhawked three; we roasted three and a wee ane; and three and a wee ane we gave to the Hogs; and is not that ane and twunty you Fool.

On the sixth and seventh pages of this slender tract, entitled *A Dialogue Between Andrew Trueman and Thomas Zealot, About the Killing of the Indians at Cannestogoe and Lancaster*, the pious Trueman speaks for those, like Franklin, who denounced the workhouse carnage: "I am afraid all this is wrong. I am a Presbyterian, you know, as well as yourself. But I wold fain hope that I am a Christian also."

Every theater has its ghosts, and every performance raises the specter of past performances, but the Fulton strikes me as uniquely haunted. A plaque marking the scene of the Paxton massacre hangs outside the theater, on Water Street. For several years a second plaque hung inside the Fulton greenroom on one of the stone walls James Webb built. It read in part, "They were not guilty of any crime other than being at this place during that turbulent time." Eventually the plaque was moved upstairs to the theater's administrative offices, so now you have to go to the third floor of the building to see it, but people do. We're drawn to the sites of savagery—Gettysburg, Little Big Horn, Ground Zero—even though we're sometimes disappointed by the banality of what we find there. Life, as they say, goes on.

In its own day, the Lancaster workhouse and jail became a tourist attraction. One year after the Paxton killings, the British astronomer and surveyor Charles Mason visited the massacre site. "What brought me here was my curiosity to see the place where was perpetrated last Winter the Horrid and inhuman murder of 26 Indians, Men, Women and Children, leaving none alive to tell," he wrote in his journal. The inaccuracy of Mason's numbers suggests the extent to which the facts of the case had already begun to morph into myth. Mason went on: "What was laid to the Indians charge was that they held a private correspondence with the Enemy Indians; but this could never be proved against the men, and the women and children (some in their Mothers wombs that never saw light) could not be guilty."

Mason seems to have spent just a day in Lancaster, and it's unclear whether his fellow surveyor, Jeremiah Dixon, went with him. Thomas Pynchon speculates that he did, and that at the murder site Dixon felt like a "nun before a Shrine." Both Dixon and Mason had witnessed barbarity before—public executions, whippings, torture—but the Lancaster jail was somehow different, maybe because it signified a fundamental betrayal of the idea of America. "Is it something in this Wilderness, something ancient, that waited for them, and infected their Souls when they came?" Pynchon has Dixon ask.

Pynchon imagines the streets and corners around the jail brimming with activity during Mason's visit: guides hawking tours; tourists with sketchbooks, easels, and specimen bags eager to document the crime scene, all drawn by "the same queer Magnetism." By this account, the Lancaster workhouse was already on its way to becoming theater.

Mason jotted down his notes and went on his way plotting the line that would separate Pennsylvania from Maryland and eventually cleave a nation into North and South. Weeks after he visited Lancaster, five Cherokee were murdered as they slept in a barn in Virginia. Mason may have heard about these and subsequent killings in Detroit, Fort Pitt, New York, and Ohio. By the time he and Dixon finished charting their line in 1767, dozens of natives had been murdered and countless more were fleeing west. The two surveyors may have wondered what their boundary defined.

No one from the Paxton gang was ever punished for the murders of the Conestogas. John Elder retained his job as a Presbyterian minister until his death in 1792 and is today lionized on websites as the "fighting pastor of Paxton," whose battle-ready parishioners killed the Conestogas "against his advice." The pretty limestone church where he preached with a rifle beside him in the pulpit holds services every Sunday.

The Conestoga Indians themselves, as I have said, vanished. Even their bones disappeared—unearthed, reburied, and ultimately lost in Lancaster's efforts to construct a downtown railroad line in the late nineteenth century. A few years ago, when I visited the State Museum in Harrisburg to see some of the artifacts excavated at Betty Witmer's farm in Conestoga, a curator told me that while members of other Indian tribes often called about objects in the museum's holdings (the day I was there a Delaware phoned), she had never received a call from anyone claiming to be either a Susquehannock or a Conestoga. It's as if they'd never existed.

Some of the petroglyphs in the Susquehanna River were altered in the 1930s by the construction of a hydroelectric dam just upstream. Officials removed several dozen sections of inscribed rock before the dam went up, but other parts of the site were submerged. Seven boulders remain visible. Paul Nevin, the de facto curator of the petroglyphs, makes an offering of tobacco every time he visits the site. "Native Americans referred to rocks as grandfathers, because rocks contain the stories of Mother Earth," he told me one evening as I watched him scatter copper-colored leaves onto the surface of one of the big stones. It was late October, and we had sailed out in Paul's battered aluminum dingy. Hawks coasted overhead. At my feet I could make out dozens of shapes: thunderbirds, crosses, circles, footprints, both animal and human.

Inside the Fulton basement, actors lounge in the greenroom, trading jokes and cough drops as they wait to go onstage. They're half-dressed— bathrobes and T-shirts over crinolines and tuxedo pants. You could be forgiven for thinking James Webb's prison walls still house "loose and idle persons."

If you look closely, you can see how Webb worked: tall blocks of lime-stone alternate with stacks of short blocks to create long rows he then plumbed with lines and bobs. He must have been proud of his craftsman-ship, the thousands of stones laid end to end, edges squared, thin bands of mortar laboriously applied with a trowel. Two of his walls extend all the way up to the stage, where they've been painted black.

It's a few minutes before eight. From her podium behind the prosce-nium, the stage manager calls places. Actors drift onto the set. They stretch and pirouette. Some check props. A soprano, warming up, utters kittenish yelps. "Standby lights one," the stage manager whispers into her headset. For an instant everything is suspended—actors, orchestra, audience, the redheaded boy, still as a statue, whose gloved hands grip the rope that controls the curtain that shelters this make-believe world. I watch his face. Very possibly he's the same age James Webb was when he went to work on the building whose walls gave rise to this theater. The boy listens for his cue. He's dressed in a flannel shirt and jeans, work boots, the kind of prac-tical attire I imagine Webb wore. This young man too is about to unleash a story. In another moment he'll swing into action, the Fulton's red curtain will lift toward the heavens (or more accurately, toward a wood grid rein-forced with steel), and Webb's walls will slip into shadow, or at least it will seem that way for a while.

SACRED SPACE

I made my stage debut when I was four, as an angel in a Christmas pageant in my grandparents' church. I wore a white taffeta sheath with a pair
of sheer white wings edged in tinsel. My mother fussed with them right
up to my entrance, but they flopped anyhow. I had no lines. My parents
tell me I clung to the altar rail and bobbed up and down.

My next role was Mrs. Claus in a second-grade skit, followed by a small
singing part in an operetta about flowers. By age eleven I was stagestruck.
That year our music teacher informed my sixth-grade class that she and her
colleagues were casting a Nativity tableau and needed a Mary who could
sit very, very still for long periods of time. We girls shut up for days, but in
the end the role went to an eighth-grade brunette who looked the part. I
was crushed. Two years later I was cast as Lady Macbeth, a role for which
I seemed better suited. "Out, damned spot," I intoned, thrilled by my
profanity. At sixteen I joined an evangelical Christian theater troupe, and
we traveled the country giving overwrought performances of *A Man Called
Peter* in sanctuaries and social halls. In one church we used an empty bap-
tism tank as the entrance for a maid.

I'm not sure what I believed back then. Faith was a way of doing theater,
so I accepted Christ and memorized John 3:16. I even handed out tracts in

Brooklyn one weekend. At a revival meeting I watched a pair of missionaries set a matchbook on fire and hold it under the fingers of someone they hoped to convert. "This is what hell feels like," they murmured. "Do you want to *burn?*" I was bewildered by their histrionics, so different from the tame Episcopal rites I'd grown up with.

I joined a Christian choir and learned dozens of gospel tunes ("Love is surrender / Love is surrender to His will!"). One night we gave a concert at the Fulton Opera House (as it was then known), my first appearance on that stage. We wore floor-length skirts of fuchsia and royal blue with big sashes and bright blouses. I stood off to one corner and swayed, much as I'd done when I was four. Henry Harrison, a singer from Harlem known as "Amen Henry," stole the show with his rendition of "Amazing Grace." There were drums and a synthesizer, swirling light effects, and a crowd of mostly family members who clapped in time to the music. Offstage we talked, as we almost always did in those days, about sex. The choir director's wife confessed that she and her husband had done it at least five times on their wedding night—she'd been too sore to remember. My friend Margaret and I swore to each other that we would not die virgins, even if we were diagnosed with a terminal disease the next day.

When I turned seventeen, my Christian theater troupe produced *The Diary of Anne Frank*, and I played Anne. We opened it in my high school auditorium, took it briefly on the road, and then rented the Fulton for a week and ran it there with my name on the marquee. The production was terrible—full of scenery-chewing and ad libs, for which our director, a sometime preacher, had a special bent. But I knew enough about acting (I'd begun studying Stanislavski) to try to impose some discipline. I spent months reading about the Franks, imagining what it was like to live crammed in an attic for two years, forced to tiptoe all day long. I conducted sense- and emotion-memory exercises, trying to conjure tears, and sat for days in a radio studio recording passages from the diary. *In spite of everything, I still believe that people are really good at heart.* The sentence became a mantra.

The night we moved into the Fulton we scoured the backstage for props to transform our plain gray set into the Franks' Amsterdam annex. We hauled a bucket of paint onstage, a Mexican flag, utter junk. But I painstakingly put up pictures of movie stars on the wall in Anne's room and came into the theater well before call each night to sit on her narrow mattress and summon her spirit. My devotion to Anne was a combination of ego and homage: I wanted to be as famous as she was. At the same time I felt immense pity for her, for all of them.

I had a crush on Anne's Peter, too. In my case he was a sweet Mennonite boy with blond hair, a wispy moustache, and a beautiful singing voice. Our director so worshipped him (Mann's Tadzio comes to mind) that he refused to let us rehearse with one another and instead conducted private sessions in which the director played all other relevant parts. The first time Peter and I ran our scenes together was onstage in front of an audience. I awaited his kiss as eagerly as the original Anne must have. Bathed in blue light, he leaned into me, and I felt the soft hairs of his mustache and then his rouged lips on my mouth, and afterward I floated out of his room as if on air.

Early the next morning my mother burst into my bedroom waving the local paper. "Anne Frank Is a Gift from Leslie Stainton," the headline read. For a day I again floated on air, and then it was over, our short run, the marquee billing, the star's dressing room. I went back to my life. Alive, golden-haired, insecure. I waited for another Anne Frank, but she never came.

In those moments before performance each evening, when I sat alone in Anne's room and thought about the night ahead, I felt for the first time the uncanny power of that space. The Fulton was mostly empty: maybe a house or stage manager in the wings, but there were no other actors, just me and the character I desperately sought to invoke. I doubt I ever got her. I doubt my Anne was a gift to much of anyone (there's a reason I no longer act), but something did take place in that groping, in my desire to be her, to take on Anne Frank's suffering at a time in my life when already I'd outlived her.

For the length of our run the Fulton stage became that iconic attic space. Theater exists in the moment when action becomes metaphor, a friend reminds me. I knew then that this place was somehow holy (I would eventually learn Grotowski's phrase), and I had come to worship. Perhaps the sparse audiences we attracted did too, though I suspect they were there primarily because we'd dragooned them into coming. One night the director, who also played Otto Frank, asked me to ad lib the name of a friend of his who was in the audience that evening, and I did, ashamed but obedient.

Anne for me was real, and I tried desperately to make her so. The power of the actor, Michael Goldman writes, is dangerous, and we harness it at our peril. I was giddy with authority: my name on the theater, my body onstage. The spotlight, the wig, the yellow star I'd sewn by myself onto my sweater. The gesture was heartfelt: I wanted to bring Anne back to life. Anyone who takes on that role is hoping to resurrect the dead.

Anne Frank was my last production with that company. I never got together with the boy who played Peter, but I did date his brother. The director went on producing Christian plays for another three decades, until one day he was charged with corrupting minors and arrested. Two teenage boys accused him of holding nude acting classes in his basement. The director pleaded no contest and was fined and put on probation, and a few months later he killed himself.

Theaters hold emotions, a ghost hunter named Rick Fisher told me one morning as we stood on the Fulton stage together, and "that emotion, that energy, stays here." I'd asked Rick to show me how he worked, and he'd turned up at the opera house with an infrared camcorder, a digital tape recorder, a thermal scanner, an electromagnetic field meter, a motion sensor, and one assistant. The three of us walked through the basement together and then went upstairs to the stage. It was a summer morning; a couple of crew members were on the pin rail hanging lights. Rick and his friend snapped away, and after a minute or two Rick called out, "Looks like we got a little friend here." I looked at his camera. There on the screen, beside me, was a white orb, faint but visible. I'll never know what it was. My former self? Anne Frank? Another actor? Someone who had once felt as I had standing here on this wooden stage, waiting for the lights to dim? Invincible. Reverent. Possessed by a god I am still trying to find.

5

MR. HAGER BUILDS A HALL: 1852

In his 1827 preface to *Cromwell*, Victor Hugo wrote that the place where
a catastrophe occurs becomes forever afterward a "silent character" in a
tragic tale. It is doubtful Christopher Hager thought much about tragedy
or character as he ordered workmen to begin dismantling Lancaster's old
jail and workhouse in the summer of 1852, although he did hire a sometime church architect to design the hall he intended to build on the site—
an unconscious nod, perhaps, to the gravity of his undertaking.

Hager's portrait hangs upstairs in the offices of today's Fulton Theatre,
and I've studied it more than once, trying to see in the Hapsburg nose and
pinched mouth the template for the Hager men I have known in my own
lifetime: Christopher's great-grandson Nat, who did much to save the Fulton from the wrecking ball in the 1960s, and Nat's son Chris, my old college classmate and friend, who has done his share of backstage work at the
Fulton and is the seventh generation of Hager to have served on the vestry
of Trinity Lutheran Church. The family's long sojourn in Lancaster began
on September 26, 1764, nine months after the slaughter of the Conestogas,
when young Stoffel Heger, a butcher from Hessen-Darmstadt, arrived in
the city after crossing the Atlantic with a shipload of fellow immigrants
and swearing allegiance to King George the Second. Fourteen years later,

Heger—by then Christopher Hager—signed a second oath, renouncing his allegiance to the king and swearing loyalty to the new and independent Commonwealth of Pennsylvania.

The butcher Hager had three successive wives and eight children, including a boy named Christopher, born in 1800 and baptized, like his siblings, at Trinity Lutheran Church. This second Christopher Hager, the eventual builder of Fulton Hall, was eighteen when his father died and was buried in a small yard adjoining the stately brick sanctuary where two centuries later members of the Hager family would continue to worship. (Not long ago I watched my friend Chris play Jesus in a vacation Bible school pageant at Trinity Lutheran.)

In 1821, three years after his father's death, Christopher Hager Jr. opened a store near Lancaster's market and jail and began selling dry goods, queensware, and groceries. His prices were fair, and his buying trips to Philadelphia yielded bargains: a shipment of coffee drenched but not damaged by seawater, a hundred barrels of molasses. Business bloomed. He began extending credit to his customers, and farmers started to invest their cash surpluses with him, making Hager a banker as well as a merchant. He issued loans to friends and family, expanded his store, bought real estate, and perfected a baroque signature not unlike John Hancock's. In time Hager became president of the Farmers National Bank, president of a volunteer fire company, county treasurer, a manager of the city gas company, a trustee of the local college, an officer in the Lancaster County Colonization Society, and a founder and early manager of the Conestoga Cotton Mills, Lancaster's midcentury leap into the Industrial Revolution.

Hager wore his sideburns low and his dark hair swept forward onto his face. His nose was long and pronounced, his eyes brown, and when he had his portrait painted shortly after his wedding to the former Catherine Sener, he donned a creamy yellow waistcoat and black jacket. Over the course of their forty-six-year marriage, Christopher and Catherine Hager had ten children, three of whom went into business with their father. When I was a kid, Christopher's great-grandson Nat was still running Hager's Department Store.

Christopher Hager grew up in a subsistence culture and helped create an urban one. The Lancaster of his youth—capital of Pennsylvania from 1789 to 1812, and briefly a candidate for the nation's capital—was a mostly agrarian community whose six thousand inhabitants, half of them German, half English, lived in one- and two-story brick homes on unpaved streets shaded by trees and watered by tributaries of the Conestoga River. In its size and scope, the place was almost medieval. The chief industry in the surrounding county was flour milling. Lancaster itself had a market and courthouse, a dozen or so churches, and at least as many taverns, where itinerant players sometimes put on shows. (In the year of Hager's birth, a Pennsylvania actor named John Durang performed an "Indian War and Scalp Dance" for the state governor at the Sign of the White Horse, on King Street, a stone's throw from the workhouse where the Conestogas perished.)

By the time Hager reached middle age, the town of Lancaster had become a city with a population of more than twelve thousand and what one resident remembered as "nothing but bustle and confusion, arrivals and departures of cars, stages, carriages, hacks, drays, and wheelbarrows, with hundreds of people, and thousands of tons of merchandise." Paved streets, lit by gas, were home to multistory banks, stores, churches, a telegraph office, and the city's first lager brewery. Rail lines and a new canal, plied by a steamboat called the *Conestoga*, linked the inland city to Philadelphia and Baltimore. There was talk of building a bigger courthouse and a new jail. The old colonial prison on Prince Street had run out of space, and besides, the citizens of Lancaster were tired of having inmates in their midst—criminals petty and grave, debtors, drunks, Negroes fleeing slavery. Children on their way to school used to see prisoners gazing forlornly from the building's grated windows, and everyone agreed that was too much. So work began on a new and much larger jail on the city's east end.

The new facility, a massive sandstone fortress that looked like a castle, opened in the fall of 1851, and the following spring, officials put Lancaster's now-vacant "old Bastile" up for sale. Christopher Hager submitted the highest bid—$8,400, roughly $250,000 in 2013 currency. Within a month of purchasing the prison complex, he announced his intention to erect a four-story public hall in its stead, to be used for meetings, conventions, lectures, exhibitions, concerts, and plays—a secular place of congregation for the residents of the city whose prosperity was so vital to his and his family's interests. He also disclosed the name of the building he intended to construct on the site of the old prison and workhouse: Fulton Hall, in honor of the late Robert Fulton, the Lancaster County–born engineer and inventor whose inventions were fueling Hager's century.

In early American villages, the meetinghouse "determined the character and limits of the community," Lewis Mumford writes in his early twentieth-century survey of American architecture, *Sticks and Stones*. "Around the meeting-house the rest of the community crystallized in a definite pattern, tight and homogeneous." As the American village morphed into a city, its need to retain a sense of community grew. Town halls—the nineteenth-century equivalent of the colonial meetinghouse—were crucial to that effort.

Although he left no public explanation of his reasons for wanting to build Fulton Hall, the canny Christopher Hager seems to have grasped instinctively what Mumford, citing Plato's *Republic*, teaches in his book: that "an intelligent and socialized community will continue to grow only as long as it can remain a unit and keep up its common institutions. Beyond that point growth must cease, or the community will disintegrate and cease to be an organic thing." Hager saw that his expanding city required a new gathering place where members of the community could forge bonds that were neither religious nor legal but rather social, cultural, and political, and that, furthermore, such a building could, in its very appearance and configuration, be an instructive and edifying force.

Enter Samuel Sloan of Philadelphia. Thirty-seven, brash and opportunistic, a quick learner who had begun his career as a carpenter and risen to architect, the man Hager chose to design Fulton Hall possessed no formal training but had what both men believed the profession required: taste, sensitivity, discrimination, and a vast fund of practical knowledge of the sort that defined so much of nineteenth-century American enterprise. Sloan understood masonry, joinery, carpentry, plastering, and painting; he knew why Grecian moldings were superior and that if you were to avoid lawsuits, you had to sign an airtight contract.

His models, like those of so many of his peers, were European—Palladio, Inigo Jones, Christopher Wren. When it came to style, Sloan preferred the Italianate. "Its great pliability of design, its facile adaptation to our wants and habits, together with its finished, elegant, and picturesque appearance, give it precedence over every other," he explained in one of the numerous books and articles he published in an effort to educate American consumers. "It speaks of the inhabitant as a man of wealth, who wishes in a quiet way to enjoy his wealth. It speaks of him as a person of educated and refined tastes, who can appreciate the beautiful both in art and nature."

I can imagine Hager's delight at seeing himself in just this light, a man of means and polish, a first-generation American who had reached the heights of civic leadership and could now extend his good taste to the community. It's little wonder he and Sloan hit it off. (A year later, Hager would help hire Sloan to design an ornate new pulpit at Trinity Lutheran.) To the architect, Hager was an ideal client: a man of independent thought and strong opinion, one of those thrusting, inquisitive personalities who were reshaping the cultural life of the United States.

The two would first have talked about what Hager wanted: a multipurpose building flexible enough to accommodate the communal needs of a flourishing populace, a place of elegance, European in feel and look. Sloan would have drawn up floor plans, then elevations measured to scale, and finally a sketch showing the hall as it would look "in nature" from a given perspective. That drawing, now on display in the office of the Fulton's managing director, reveals a square edifice whose milky façade rises in ever more delicate layers toward an airy cupola. Hager must have exulted when he first held the sketch in his hands. The front of Sloan's hall is symmetrical but not monotonous, a pleasing blend of angles and arches, reason and sentiment. The heavy stone blocks of its first two floors give way to smooth plaster and a pitched roof with deep eaves held up by the Grecian cornices Sloan loved. The architect was designing for posterity: "We Americans are not ashamed that we have nothing now venerable in years," he wrote in 1852, the year he designed Fulton Hall, "but we may fear that our descendants will have cause so to be, and have few buildings to point out, saying, this is the work of our fathers."

Sloan and Hager agreed that the stage inside the hall would face east, as altars traditionally do, and that the side and back walls of the building would be constructed of economic brick. They also agreed to retain as much of the old prison complex as necessary to support the new structure. The architect knew stone to be the best foundation for any building, and the jail walls had already withstood nearly a century of wind, heat, rain, and ice without cracking, so he left whole stretches of James Webb's masonry intact, including a two-story extension, with a vaulted double door, at the rear of the building on Water Street.

At the opposite end of the site, toward Prince Street, Sloan installed heavy log piers to help buttress his hall. The property itself was wildly uneven. Architect Dick Levengood, who took part in a late twentieth-century renovation of the Fulton Theatre, speaks of the "large-grade differential from the front of the building to the rear"—the site drops as much as fifteen feet from Prince Street to Water—and says the lot is "very challenging. It turns all the way around the corner, it drops both ways." Webb had already figured out how to build on the site "so you don't mess with it."

Hager took out a permit to construct Fulton Hall in early May 1852, and work began at once. He told reporters the new building would be ready in four months. It was hot, and at least one worker was felled by sunstroke. Teenage boys hung around the construction site, hoping to catch sight of the dungeon, where a prisoner was said to have starved to death. (The rumor could well have been true: in a late eighteenth-century petition to the Lancaster court, prisoners inside the jail complained that they were fed "but one single pound of bread" a day, "which is scearsly suffitient to keep us alive.")

Hager himself kept a close eye on the building and made frequent trips to Philadelphia to consult with Sloan. There were endless details to select: paint colors, window fastenings, plaster molds, ventilation, plumbing, light fixtures, doors. The press kept avid track of the project. "The new city hall, in Prince Street, is progressing finely," the *Lancaster Saturday Express* noted in July. "Mr. Hager is pushing the work as rapidly as possible towards an early completion. It will be one of the finest public halls in the state." Hager later calculated he spent $22,000—some $650,000 in 2013 dollars—on the venture.

Across America, people were doing just as he was, building shrines of culture festooned with muses and lyres in towns that a few years earlier had been little more than frontier outposts. The country was refining itself, as Sloan hoped it would. Part of that process was a newfound tolerance for the dramatic arts. William Penn and his Quaker peers had frowned on theater, and the first Continental Congress had banned it outright, but by 1850, major cities east of the Mississippi all had stages, and the suddenly popular art had spread to California, where men were digging for gold. Stock companies prospered. An American style of performance was emerging, raucous and physical. This had something to do with the freewheeling nature of the country itself, it seemed, with evangelical preachers who danced and barked and erupted in convulsions, with politicians who courted voters through bombast, and audiences addicted to sensation.

The whole enterprise had once smacked of the tawdry and louche, and itinerant companies—mostly English—hovered on the margins of respectable society. The city of Lancaster had shunned playacting until the Revolution, when a local brewer turned his beerhouse into a short-lived theater so that British soldiers held captive in the town could put on Shakespeare. It's likely young Robert Fulton, who was fond of sketching the enemy in his midst, attended. But after the war, the chary town resumed its old ways. "There is no theater, no assemblies, no literary society, nor any other public entertainment, except an itinerant exhibition of wax works or a puppet show," a visitor in 1810 grumbled. Taverns sometimes brought in theatricals and panoramas, and there were sporadic attempts in the 1830s and '40s to open a genuine theater, but nothing stuck.

Not so in 1852. In addition to its nine banks, sixteen places of worship, fifty-seven common schools, and nine newspapers, Lancaster would soon enjoy a public hall. As the walls of Sloan's brick-and-stone concoction rose, excitement grew. "The first floor room is intended for political meetings, county conventions, etc.," the *Examiner and Herald* reported. "The second is to be fitted more elaborately and to be used for lectures and entertainments of a social nature. The third is to be occupied by societies." By fall, the paper added brightly, "we may have the pleasure of hearing Jenny Lind in Fulton Hall."

In September Hager opened the unfinished building briefly so that the local Odd Fellows, who had been struggling to build their own lodge, could hold a soirée. Covering the event, the pro-temperance *Saturday Express* issued the welcome news that Fulton Hall did not allow liquor on its premises. By early October, workers were putting the final touches on the new structure. That month, Lancaster's city council repealed an 1846 ordinance requiring a tax on "plays, shows, theatrical entertainments and circus performances." The pennywise Hager was surely pleased.

And then it was complete, Sloan's buttery palace, brilliant in the autumn sun, ready for business. The young city had seen nothing like it. Squint, and you'd think you were standing before a cathedral. In place of a steeple there was a lightning rod, and the tympanum above the front entrance showed not heaven and hell but a glass orb wreathed in flowers, but still, Sloan had wrought a thing of beauty, a paean to European taste and American ambition.

It rained on opening night, and Lancaster's streets turned to mud. Crowds came nonetheless, ladies in crinolines and shawls, men in tailcoats and gloves. Hager, his hair thinning, sideburns going gray, was there to greet them. He had distributed fifteen hundred free tickets, and nearly that number of people showed up. One by one, they ascended Sloan's handsome staircase to the second-floor saloon (from the French *salon*), lit by three gas chandeliers and thirty-two wall jets, and took their seats on wooden benches facing a small platform at the far end of the room.

The main speaker of the evening, Judge Alexander Hayes, who had recently succeeded Hager as president of the Conestoga Cotton Mills, praised his colleague's achievement and reminded listeners that cities across Europe had long ago recognized the need for theaters, gardens, promenades, orchestras, and galleries. Now, Hayes exclaimed, it was Lancaster's turn, the desire for recreation following "long continued effort, as naturally as night follows day." The local Philharmonic Society struck up a polka written expressly for the occasion and dedicated to Christopher Hager, and the crowd, roused by the brisk tune, burst into applause.

As I summon this enchanted evening I see a room bathed in yellow light and a mass of glowing faces. All of Lancaster has turned out, it appears—shopkeepers and haberdashers, ironmasters, gun makers, bankers, lawyers, teachers, women in curls and chignons, young men with tidy beards. Christopher Hager stands in their midst, eyes creased in merriment as he accepts the congratulations of his neighbors and friends. Off in a corner the stentorian Judge Hayes is holding forth about the genius loci of this hall, how it will "kindle the social affections, adding length as well as happiness to life." That this was recently the site of the local jail and workhouse—and witness to a massacre whose notoriety persists—is momentarily forgotten.

Now the strains of Hager's polka give way to the oom-pah-pah of a brass band, and I catch sight of a middle-aged woman swaying in time to the music. Fair-skinned and gray-eyed, she might be me. One foot taps gently against the floor. She wears a taffeta gown with a lace collar and long sleeves, and beneath it a corset and petticoats stiffened with whalebone, although she is not thinking now of the ocean life that gave rise to her fashionable silhouette. She seems oblivious to anything but her own enjoyment this night. Later she will scrawl a note in her diary—*a great and attractive crowd filled Mr. Hager's new hall, we stayed past 9:30*—and in time she will buy a small volume in which to record her impressions of the plays she sees here.

Her boots are damp from the rain outside. When the band pauses, she can hear the thrum of water against the windowpanes. The sound pulls her briefly out of her reverie, and she thinks back to this afternoon, to the small leather case she received from the Daguerrian Gallery on Queen Street. The studio opened in May, but it was not until last week that she ventured to sit for her picture, curiosity finally conquering fear. The camera operator had put her head in a vise, and she'd sat for three minutes, unsmiling, while the exposure took. Opening the case this afternoon, she discovered a silvery image inside a gilt frame, and for the first time beheld her own likeness. *I saw my face as I had never seen it before,* she wrote in her diary, *and strange thoughts flowed through my mind.*

The proprietors of the gallery had promised her a "lifelike and enduring" portrait, but in fact she looked like a ghost. If she tilted the image in one direction or another, she found, her face vanished, and the effect was unsettling. *In my estimation it is better to make the hearts of your friends the plates upon which to impress our pictures, than steel, brass or any inanimates,* she wrote, and then closed the little case, vowing not to dwell further on the matter. But she couldn't help herself. Dipping her pen back into the ink, she scribbled, *My first picture! When will my last one be taken? Let the future answer.*

Now, inside Mr. Hager's hall, the band has resumed playing, and the bright present again quells the afternoon's odd sensations. The woman in the taffeta gown turns with pleasure to the spectacle around her. The room is vast and smells of fresh paint; there is a tiny balcony at one end, and there are tall windows along each wall. Mr. Hager has pledged that this will be the site of so much she has dreamed of: dancing lessons, balls, lectures, fairs, concerts, prayer meetings, and of course plays, tales brought to life by performers who will travel hundreds of miles for her sake, so that she can come to this room, and sit in the shadows, and lose herself in their sorcery.

Thunder begins to rumble, and someone gasps, but Mr. Hager laughs and announces in a triumphant voice, "My friends, there is nothing to fear, nothing at all, for Mr. Sloan"—he points to the dapper man at his left—"Mr. Sloan has thought of everything, and we are quite safe tonight. Quite safe indeed."

It is true. Should lightning strike, a man beside her whispers, it would hit not this building but the ingenious wrought-iron contraption first designed by Mr. Franklin, which sits on the roof and runs down the side of the hall, deep into the ground, carrying electricity with it. You are entirely safe, he assures her, and smiles.

She looks up at the ceiling and imagines the tall rod above it that guards her life and the lives of everyone around her. The rain continues to fall, but here in Fulton Hall everything is dry and warm, and although she knows better, she allows herself to believe that nothing can break the spell of this prodigious building, this temple of art, here in the center of the tranquil inland city she calls home.

6

"WHAT HAS THE NORTH TO DO WITH SLAVERY?": 1852–1861

We ask two things of the structures we erect: that they shelter us and that they communicate "whatever we find important and need to be reminded of," writes John Ruskin. Christopher Hager's town hall did both. Its soaring lines and airy façade spoke of the civilized society to which Lancastrians aspired. Enter, the building's exterior seemed to suggest, and behold your better self. Its interior spoke of darker matters.

Two days after the grand opening of Fulton Hall, the first ad for a show in the new space appeared in the Lancaster press: Kendall and Dickinson's Ethiopian Minstrels, a band of white "serenaders" particularly admired for their "delineation of negro character." Banjo, tambourine, fiddle, bones—the simulated sounds of plantation life in the American South—soon filled Lancaster's new town hall. Songs about darkies in the kitchen and slaves on the block, *the poor nigger's fate is hard, the white man's heart is stone*: even a building as fine as Hager's could not muffle the beast that stalked American life in 1852.

The passage by Congress, two years earlier, of the Fugitive Slave Law— under which every U.S. citizen, regardless of personal belief or religion, could be forced to participate in the capture of blacks fleeing slavery—had plunged Northerners into a moral swamp. "If our resistance to this law is not right, there is no right," cried Ralph Waldo Emerson. His neighbor Bronson Alcott asked, "What has the North to do with slavery?" The answer was clear: everything.

Hager's hall was itself complicit. Despite passage of a gradual abolition act in 1780, the state of Pennsylvania had continued to cooperate with Southerners seeking the return of their "property" until well into the nineteenth century, and freedom-seeking slaves who crossed the Maryland border into Lancaster County were routinely incarcerated in the jail whose walls would become the foundation of Fulton Hall. "Negro" Isaac; "Negress" Phillis; Jacob Bott, "a runaway from Baltimore"; Venus Levan, daughter of Lidy Profit, "woman of Color," and servant of Thomas Neal; William Toogood (alias Abram Boston), "colored man"; James Craten, "negro," and who knows how many other enslaved people from the American South spent days, weeks, sometimes months locked inside Lancaster's prison while bounty hunters and slaveholders compiled and submitted the legal documents necessary to remove them from the state and return them to bondage—or abolitionists tried through judicial means to free them.

Meanwhile, men like Christopher Hager, who ran cotton mills and whose banks invested in them, supported the industry that kept African Americans in chains. When Hager and other city leaders opened Lancaster's first cotton factory in 1847, even Congressman Thaddeus Stevens—who voted against the Fugitive Slave Law and defended Pennsylvanians who violated it—endorsed the enterprise, for the mills meant jobs and prosperity in a town struggling to move from an artisan to a factory economy.

So Fulton Hall was built, at least in part, with cotton money, and in his opening-night address, Judge Alexander Hayes paid tribute to the mills that had brought "new life and activity into our own too quiet city" and helped spur a building boom. Witness the new gasworks, new jail, new churches, two new cotton mills, and a thousand new homes that had gone up in just the previous year, Hayes said. Construction was also under way on a new courthouse, designed by Samuel Sloan, who in the summer of 1852 helped lay the building's cornerstone. Into it went a Bible, an almanac, and a copy of President Millard Fillmore's message to Congress endorsing the Compromise of 1850—which included the Fugitive Slave Law.

While the new courthouse was going up, trials and hearings took place in Fulton Hall. For a time, as well, the congregation of a local church used the space for Sunday worship—the first of many times the hall would host

Christian gatherings. Newly established Franklin and Marshall College held its first commencement ceremonies inside the Fulton in June 1853, with trustee James Buchanan presiding over the event. A "great desideratum," as more than one paper called Fulton Hall, had indeed been supplied. Soon Hager would turn the building over to a citizens' association, thereby fulfilling his pledge to create a truly public hall for the town he loved.

By night, the structure was the setting for concerts, panoramas, lectures, stock theatrical companies, an automaton band, bell ringers, and magicians. Next door, Colonel Frank Reigart set up a patent office where he sold, among much else, an engraving of Fulton Hall; to the north of the hall, Hager opened a hotel and bar. A few doors away, the Fulton Opera House Confectionary offered cakes and candies, and the Fulton Family Grocery sold food and other goods. Clothiers tapped the marketing power of the new facility: "The Philharmonic Concert at Fulton Hall was noted for the number of pretty women present, many of whom had adorned their persons with those beautiful shawls sold by Fahnestock," read an ad in the *Saturday Express*. "These shawls have a magical effect upon the purse strings of husbands and fathers."

In early 1854, workmen installed a seven-foot statue of Robert Fulton in a niche above the main entrance to the hall. Philadelphia sculptor Hugh Cannon had rendered the Lancaster native in cedar, the traditional material for ship figureheads, and Fulton—who had tinkered with submarines and torpedoes in the Seine and made history launching the first commercial steamboat on American waters—seemed poised to chart a journey aboard the building that carried his name. He looked east, toward the rising sun, one hand on his breast. Cannon had bolted planks of wood together to form Fulton's body and head, and although you couldn't see it from the street, he'd gone to the trouble of cross-hatching Fulton's trousers and drilling buttonholes into his cape. This Robert Fulton was all swagger and brio, an emblem of American drive. When a workman trying to install the sculpture griped to Hager that he couldn't get along with his temperamental foreman, Hager joked that they should petrify the foreman instead and put him above the door—but it was the visionary Fulton Hager wanted, a man contemporaries praised for his "calm constancy, his industry, and that indefatigable patience and perseverance, which always enabled him to overcome difficulties."

The same week that Fulton's statue was unveiled, *Uncle Tom's Cabin* played Fulton Hall for the very first time. For twenty-five cents, you could take in Harriet Beecher Stowe's "great moral lesson," and audiences did, in droves. This particular production, by George Aiken, had attracted huge crowds in Philadelphia, New York, and Boston, but dozens of other productions had begun touring American playhouses, and their numbers would soar. Aiken's play introduced the notion of single-feature entertainment as well as the matinee—launched in the 1850s to accommodate women and children.

When the first *Uncle Tom's Cabin* opened in New York in September 1852, *New York Herald* editor James Gordon Bennett assailed its "extravagant exhibitions of the imaginary horrors of Southern slavery." Bennett advised that the play be shut down "at once and forever. The thing is in bad taste . . . and is calculated, if persisted in, to become a firebrand of the most dangerous character to the peace of the whole country." But productions flourished, and the abolition movement surged—and with it opposition to the Fugitive Slave Law. Thousands who had shunned the theater as a coffer of sin, many of them working-class Americans, swarmed to the story of the beneficent slave who suffers on earth, dies, and ascends into heaven. "Now," declared the pacifist abolitionist Parker Pillsbury, "the Theater is openly . . . before and better than the Church." The production prompted some theaters to begin granting admission to African Americans, who sat in their own sections.

The images were unforgettable: Simon Legree whipping Tom, Eliza escaping with her infant across the frozen Ohio River, the death of Little Eva. These became, in effect, holy pictures for a rapt nation. In New York, the show enthralled a young Henry James, who later described Tom as a "wonderful 'leaping' fish" that flew through the air and landed "on every stage, literally without exception, in America and Europe." Moved by the drama, Stephen Foster composed "My Old Kentucky Home." "Tomming" became a way of life for countless actors and a mechanism by which Americans of all persuasions probed their assumptions about race. There were pro-slavery *Toms*, blackface lampoons, Irish parodies that critiqued white slave labor in the North, comic burlesques with happy endings.

The show that played Fulton Hall in March 1854 was more or less faithful to Stowe's novel and featured a seasoned cast, including Rose Merrifield, well known for her comic renditions of the child slave Topsy. The production ran for more than two weeks in Lancaster and drew big crowds, many of them churchgoing Christians, a sector ads worked hard to lure. It's likely audiences responded as they had the previous year in Washington, D.C., to a production of *Tom* featuring Merrifield: "Every allusion to freedom on the part of the colored *dramatis personae* was received with shouts of approbation, and every sentiment which counseled resistance to the slaveholder was echoed with yells of applause." The American theater had become a staging ground.

Merrifield frizzed her hair in wild disarray and came onstage barefoot in a bulky shift. She was white but wore blackface, as did others in the cast. T. D. Rice had popularized the practice and fathered minstrelsy when he began corking up as a dancing slave named Jim Crow in the early 1830s, an act he had brought to Lancaster in 1845. Watching *Tom* nine years later in Fulton Hall, Lancastrians may have remembered Rice and his high-jumping buffoonery and derisive songs. They were stock features of innumerable *Toms* and a popular part of Merrifield's Topsy, for she liked to lard her performances with minstrel tunes and "African" dance and even launched a side business giving Topsy concerts with her husband. "Nelly Bly, Nelly Bly," she would sing,

> Bring de broom along,
> We'll sweep de kitchen clean, my dear,
> And hab a little song.
> Poke de wood, my lady lub,
> And make de fire burn,
> And while I take de banjo down,
> Just gib de mush a turn.

By night, audiences laughed at Merrifield's antics and wept over Tom's fate; by day, men like Hager weighed the future of the country. The city's fledgling Republican Party began holding meetings inside Fulton Hall, and Hager, a former Whig, signed up, even though he and Democrat James Buchanan were neighbors and friends, and both were trustees of Franklin and Marshall College. Hager knew Republican Thaddeus Stevens, too, a regular speaker at Fulton Hall and a frequent target of the local press. "Lump, thump, / Thump, lump, / The old heathen took the stand," a reporter for the Democratic *Intelligencer* wrote after an especially vitriolic antislavery speech at the Fulton by Stevens, who was clubfooted. "A more disgusting, malicious and offensive harangue never fell from the lips of any decent man."

Buchanan came in for his share of scrutiny as well. In the summer of 1856, weeks after being named Democratic candidate for U.S. president, he joined Hager on the stage of Fulton Hall for Franklin and Marshall's commencement ceremonies. The two men listened politely as a graduate from Illinois gave a speech on "The Decline of Political Integrity." Midway through his talk, the young orator made reference to South Carolina Representative Preston Brooks, who had bludgeoned Massachusetts Senator Charles Sumner on the floor of the U.S. Senate that spring after Sumner, the Senate's most outspoken abolitionist, had given a speech decrying slavery. (It would take Sumner more than three years to recover from the assault.) So "destitute of moral courage" were some politicians, the student declared, his face flushed with excitement, "that men are found who applaud the attack of canine Brooks upon the noble Sumner for defending freedom."

The crowd inside Fulton Hall fell "still as death," a writer for the *New York Tribune* later reported, and then began clapping. After the student had finished speaking, he sat down next to Buchanan "amid thunders of applause" and a shower of bouquets. The presidential candidate, sixty-five but looking older with his white topknot and tilting head, turned to the boy and in a loud voice said that Brooks had had clear provocation for his attack, for Sumner's speech against slavery had been nothing but a "tirade of abuse." "My young friend," Buchanan continued, the others in the hall straining to catch his words, "you look upon the dark side of the picture." Eight months later Buchanan entered the White House, where the picture was no brighter.

Throughout Buchanan's four-year term as president, Fulton Hall continued to chart the nation's seesaw debate on the ethics and future of slavery. In 1857, Pennsylvania's first Republican candidate for governor, David Wilmot, gave a two-hour speech inside Fulton Hall, during which he defended the failed 1846 proviso bearing his name and blasted the South for its embrace of bondage. The Negro, Wilmot ventured, was the white man's equal "in all things." Wilmot lost the election but came back to Fulton Hall four years later to campaign for Abraham Lincoln and the Republican cause.

The election of 1860 brought both parties inside the Fulton for rallies and speeches and tumultuous demonstrations. Thaddeus Stevens presided over a "Big Republican Rally" at Fulton Hall in late September 1860. Within days of Stevens's rally, Democrat Herschel Johnson, Stephen A. Douglas's vice-presidential nominee, took the same stage. Johnson reminded Lancastrians that because the fractious Democratic party had split into two camps—each with its own presidential candidate—a vote for Southern Democrat John Breckenridge would be a vote for Lincoln.

Johnson was right. With just 40 percent of the popular vote, Lincoln won the presidency in November. In February, he traveled under heavy guard from Illinois to Washington for the inauguration, stopping briefly in Lancaster, where he told cheering crowds that in a few days he would "speak plainly in regard to the Constitution and the liberties of the American people." A panorama of legendary world sites was playing that night at Fulton Hall, and the coincidence appears to have prompted one reporter to suggest that in their punctuality, "the arrival and departure of Mr. Lincoln seemed like the shifting scenes of a panorama, to be remembered like a dream." But the remainder of Lincoln's journey to the White House was the stuff of nightmare. By the time he reached Lancaster, detectives had caught wind of a plot to murder him in Baltimore, so Lincoln made the rest of the trip in disguise, in an unmarked sleeping coach, with telegraph lines systematically cut behind him to halt news of his passage. The president-elect snuck into Washington at dawn on February 23, 1861, and the following week was sworn into office.

Two days after Lincoln's inauguration, James Buchanan came home to Lancaster in the company of a military band and was greeted by a thirty-four-gun salute and a parade through town in a horse-drawn barouche. He told his fellow citizens that on his last day in office he had said to his successor, "If, in going into the White House, you are as happy as I feel in leaving it and returning to Wheatland"—Buchanan's stately Lancaster mansion—"then, sir, I think you are the happiest man in the world."

Under his watch, seven Southern states had seceded, and Buchanan, a lifelong advocate of Southern interests, had done nothing to stop them. Even as Lincoln was making his way to Washington, Jefferson Davis was being sworn in as president of the Confederacy. Despite the fanfare with which Buchanan returned to Lancaster—the military band that accompanied him was duly fêted inside Fulton Hall—there was little to celebrate. A few weeks after his arrival, the Republican *Examiner and Herald* published a derisive sketch of the pilgrims who were lining up at Wheatland to rejoice with Buchanan "at the ruin and desolation he has brought upon the country."

On April 12, 1861, Confederate soldiers attacked Fort Sumter. Three days later Lincoln, who'd been in office for little more than a month, issued a call for seventy-five thousand militia. The next evening a throng of would-be soldiers packed Fulton Hall, where the Lancaster Fencibles kept their armory, and began drilling. They were young, fresh-faced, eager to serve. On the afternoon of Friday, April 19, the first regiment of Fencibles to go to war left the Fulton and marched through town on their way to the rail depot. An Episcopal minister blessed the troops, a band played, and the mayor gave a speech. Hundreds of people poured onto the streets to walk alongside the soldiers, and in many windows and doors women stood waving handkerchiefs and weeping. The *Examiner and Herald* pronounced this sudden exodus "the most impressive and affecting scene ever witnessed in Lancaster." The crowds were bigger than they had been for Lincoln.

More than a hundred young men were on their way to battle, among them Christopher Hager's eighteen-year-old son, Edward. "Friends, take care of our wives, and children, and sweethearts, and we will take care of our country," one buoyant youth told the crowd before he boarded his train. And then they were off, the radiant volunteers, gone on an adventure few thought would last more than a couple of weeks. Left to await their return were mothers and wives, fathers, brothers, friends, a whole city trembling with hope, and in its midst an ivory building not yet ten years old, proud symbol of the civilization these brave troops had sworn to preserve. Empty now of actors, lights dimmed, Fulton Hall readied itself for the drama to come.

1

INTERLUDE

I am sitting here beside Robert Fulton on a small ledge on the second story of the Fulton Theatre, looking out over the city where we both grew up. It is a substantial town, in my day much vaster than it was in Fulton's, and not nearly so rural. Hager's Department Store, just up the street, has been a condo for more than thirty years, and another department store, Watt and Shand, has finally been turned into a hotel and convention center after years of bickering. Construction stalled in 2002 when a cistern was discovered in a corner of the complex, behind what used to be Thaddeus Stevens's law office, at the precise spot where an escalator was supposed to go. Excavations revealed a small doorway connecting the cistern to the basement of an old brewery, and archaeologists concluded Stevens may well have used the site to harbor African Americans seeking freedom. The Historic Preservation Trust intervened, work on the convention center stopped, and developers redrew their plans to accommodate a proposed multimillion-dollar museum dedicated to Stevens and abolitionism.

Visitors to the eventual museum will likely tour Lancaster's Central Market as well, the oldest continuously used market space in the country (or so it claims). Were it not for the Hager building, Fulton and I could see the market's dark brick towers from our perch here over the marquee. Back in Fulton's day, Stoffel Hager rented a butcher stall inside the market, and in my own time I often ran into Stoffel's great-great grandson Nat as he worked his way through the building at lunchtime, pink-faced and waving to his many friends.

Fulton's landlocked town was more compact than mine, and I wonder what he thinks of the trafficked city below us, which his inventions did so much to spawn. The shops and smithies where he hung out as a kid, sketching guns and mechanical devices in dim anticipation of his brilliant career, yielded long ago to the hardware stores and booksellers of Christopher Hager's day and my own childhood before succumbing to the delirium of mall culture in the 1970s. We're gazing out over a city laboring to re-create itself. There are multiple signs of progress: a string of trendy galleries along Prince Street, a crop of new restaurants touting organic local foods, the refurbished theater where we sit, the aforementioned hotel and convention center on the site of the department store where in my twelfth year I shoplifted a three-ring binder and a leather purse.

In the year of Fulton's birth, 1765, John Adams wrote that "America was designed by Providence for the theater on which man was to make his true figure, on which science, virtue, liberty, happiness, and glory were to exist in peace." It was an optimistic moment—the Seven Years' War had just ended—and few of us have made figures of which we can invariably be proud, but Adams was right to envision the country as a stage. Haven't we always had one eye on our audience? Isn't acting at our core?

I think of the dramas, large and small, that have played out on these streets: the great treaty sessions of the eighteenth century, with their ceremonial exchanges of wampum and goods, their celebratory dancing; the sensational visit, in 1825, of the marquis de Lafayette, when the citizens of Lancaster erected a triumphal arch over King Street, near Christopher Hager's dry-goods store; James Buchanan's homecoming parade in 1861, spectators in every window, another arch spanning King Street, and seven years later his funeral along the same streets, then costumed in black.

I was nearly nine when I first saw this kind of metamorphosis in person. It was a Friday evening, and already the day was strange. We'd been dismissed early from school after being told the president had been shot in Dallas. My best friend's parents drove me home through town. As we neared the intersection of King and Queen Streets, I saw crowds of people milling around and newsboys hawking a special edition of the paper with huge black headlines. The image I retain of the scene is distorted, as if the boys were standing at the far end of an inverted telescope, or inside a magnifying glass, rimmed with fire. I remember the sobs of my friend's mother (did grownups really cry about people they didn't know?), and the thrill of having been let out of school early, coupled with a deep uncertainty as to how I was supposed to *act*.

Some twenty years later I was sitting in an office behind these very windows, filing records for the Fulton's development director, when NPR interrupted its programming to report an assassination attempt on Ronald Reagan by a man who was obsessed with an actress. Even if you hated our actor-president, you had to applaud his performance that day, asking the surgeon who was to operate on him if he was a Republican and invoking both Jack Dempsey ("Honey, I forgot to duck") and W. C. Fields ("All in all, I'd rather be in Philadelphia"). Again, the mood in Lancaster shifted as if in response to a stage direction: *Lights dim; townspeople gather silently around television monitors.* I recall thinking, This is what History feels like. Different, heightened, theatrical.

Our own president—Pennsylvania's only—was famously unable to act while in office, and afterward, here in Lancaster, spent his last years trying to rewrite the script of his unhappy life. Wheatland, the leafy estate to which James Buchanan retreated so gleefully in March of 1861, stands a mile from where Fulton and I sit. It's been a museum for years, lovingly tended by docents who do their best to redeem the reputation of its former occupant (Buchanan has long been a top pick for worst-ever U.S. president). During my junior year at Franklin and Marshall College, Buchanan's home was the site of an opening-night reception for the world premiere of John Updike's only work of theater, *Buchanan Dying*. I played the president's niece, Harriet Lane, in that production, which we staged at F&M. I'd desperately wanted the smaller but more interesting role of Buchanan's doomed fiancée, Anne Coleman, but I must have looked too virtuous for the part. Besides, the script called for Anne to reveal her breasts to Buchanan, a gesture I didn't think I could do in public. (As it turned out, neither could the girl who wound up with the role; much to the annoyance of the actor playing Buchanan, she faked the move with her back to the audience.)

Then in his forties, but seeming far older to my twenty-year-old eyes, Updike came to an early rehearsal and watched politely as we staggered through his wordy text. We were all struck by how nice he seemed. "I'm flattered that you take my lines so seriously," he told Peter Vogt, our

Buchanan, after Vogt confessed that a particular passage stumped him. Go ahead and change the line, Updike urged.

What we really wanted to ask him about was *Couples*, of course, all that middle-class American adultery. I was just coming off my own affair with a married stage-design professor, and was anything but the innocent White House hostess I was impersonating onstage—bosom wedged into a muslin corset, waist cinched, waltzing with my bachelor uncle on inauguration night. I'm guessing Updike would have been amused to know the circumstances of my dangerous offstage liaison: I'd lost my virginity the previous spring in the very theater where he was sitting, on a stack of black velvet stage curtains in the lighting booth. Surely this earlier *pas de deux* was closer to Updike in spirit than the genteel dance Buchanan and I were executing onstage that evening.

I've since learned the playwright was in the middle of his own divorce at the time; it became final shortly before we opened his play about an American president who can't hold the Union together. Updike donned a tux and came to our premiere, and afterward joined us at Wheatland for a gala reception in his honor. If he and I exchanged words, I don't remember it. Fueled by adrenaline and alcohol, I was busy pretending to be Harriet Lane, inviting people up to "my" bedroom and sliding down Buchanan's banister.

"All the world is not, of course, a stage," writes Erving Goffman, "but the crucial ways in which it isn't are not easy to specify." My life at that juncture was all about performance. I'd left F&M the previous fall to go to New York to get a BFA in acting, then abandoned the idea after a few months and come home to resume the more dramatic role of *enfant terrible*. At twenty I moved back into my parents' house, where my father, trapped in a job he loathed, sank into a daze most nights, and my sister, born with cerebral palsy, was struggling through a woeful adolescence; our mother could barely hold it together. My response was to act out: I became a bulimic, at war with my own transgressive body. One night I so enraged my mother with my secret gorging that she slapped me, and I fled the house and spent the next several hours wandering through the neighbors' backyards, sobbing.

I knew my Stanislavski well enough to think all this might be fodder for the roles I still hoped to play. It's as if he were goading me. "Always and forever, when you are on the stage, you must play yourself," he had written.

Midway through rehearsals for *Buchanan Dying*, I appeared at the Fulton in a short run of a play about the Lincoln-Douglas debates—yet another dramatic take on our foremost national drama. I played a Lady Democrat, and according to the review in my scrapbook, I sang a song. The stars of the show were actors on one of my favorite soap operas, *The Doctors*. As I sit here today with Robert Fulton, looking back on the small triumphs and colossal failures of those years, I think of the ways our existence is indeed like a TV drama. We plot our stories blindly, in scenes that often seem banal but later prove critical to the narrative, with small cliffhangers and periodic crises, commercial interludes and even theme songs. We hope our audiences will stay tuned.

I'm still scripting my saga; Fulton has finished his. Neither of us has full control over the story, of course. The statue beside me would have you believe he was a model of virtue and industry, just as Christopher Hager maintained. In truth, Robert Fulton was something of a fuckup. This spry Adonis with piercing eyes and tumbling locks spent much of his adult life in a *ménage à trois* with a married couple who called him "Toot" and for whom he served, in their words, as "the mediatorial part of the little holy trinity." Fulton carried on the affair—with both husband and wife, it appears—even after his own wedding. He owned at least one slave, a young woman for whom he paid $200 and whom he pledged to free after six years' service. In business dealings he was arrogant, combative, and vain, a mercurial genius who clutched at fame and blithely played adversaries—including governments—against one another to further his ends. (That he was not charged with treason is a wonder.) Fulton wrote wistfully of the "worthy" characters who would necessarily die as a result of his torpedoes, but he went on making the explosives. Indeed, of all his scientific pursuits, he said blowing up warships was his "favorite offspring." He viewed steamboats, by contrast, as "useful and honorable amusements."

Fulton's inventions accelerated transportation in this country and helped open the western frontier, and for that we revere him. Do his indiscretions matter? The wreckage, human and material, he left in his wake?

"We do not merely live but act," George Santayana has written. "We compose and play our chosen character, we wear the buskin of deliberation, we defend and idealize our passions, we encourage ourselves eloquently to be what we are, devoted or scornful or careless or austere; we soliloquize (before an imaginary audience) and we wrap ourselves gracefully in the mantle of our inalienable part. So draped, we solicit applause and expect to die amid a universal hush."

Perhaps the swashbuckling figure at my side is the real Robert Fulton. Perhaps, as Santayana suggests, the "archaic sculpture" Hager erected conveys Fulton's spirit "far more justly than the man's dull morning looks or casual grimaces" ever did. Fulton would approve of the pose, I'm sure: in it he is the "benign hero-benefactor" he sought to be in life but never quite was.

We'd both like to leave our salutary mark on the town below us. Its placid streets and sidewalks offer scant evidence that anything more dramatic than commerce has ever gone on here. It's in the nature of cities, I guess, as it is of sculptures and monuments, to hide the chaotic past and its imperfect players. Listen close, though, and you can hear the tempest.

THEATER OF WAR: 1861–1865

Note

From the start it was grand entertainment. Think of the audience at Bull Run—congressmen and their wives, news correspondents and the merely curious, arranged in their carriages, some with picnics and opera glasses, to watch the spectacle of what everyone assumed would be a Union rout, the first and last scene of a short-lived farce. But the battle between North and South near Manassas Junction turned out to be the opening exchange in an epic drama that would play out over the course of four years in the nation's towns and fields and river valleys, in its streets and hospitals, newspapers and halls. Even now, in the second decade of the twenty-first century, the tragedy that began as show in the spring of 1861, reached its peripeteia on the stage of a Washington, D.C., playhouse, and culminated in an artful *pas de deux* at Appomattox, still begets movie deals and Oscar awards.

In his treatise on war, published twenty-nine years before the first shots at Fort Sumter, the Prussian soldier and military theorist Carl von Clausewitz described a "theater of war" as "a portion of the space over which war prevails as has its boundaries protected, and thus possesses a kind of independence." "Such a portion," Clausewitz continued, "is not a mere piece of the whole, but a small whole complete in itself." Although local legend long held that from April 1861 through April 1865 Fulton Hall stayed dark, this figurative theater of war in fact played host to a stream of events through which the citizens of Lancaster came to understand, fund, debate, assess, champion, grieve, question, and escape the carnage unfolding on the country's battlefields (which in July 1863 came within sixty miles of Lancaster itself). Political conventions, speeches, graduations, fairs, lectures, concerts, fundraisers, exhibitions, boxing matches, laughing-gas demonstrations, prestidigitators, ventriloquists, and a "real-life" Southern refugee: all this and more came to Fulton Hall during the American Civil War.

Soldiers, too. On April 16, 1861, one day after Lincoln issued his first call for volunteers, troops gathered inside Fulton Hall, and from then on the theater took on yet another role, that of a rehearsal space for combat. The Lancaster Fencibles, Lancaster Rifles, Jackson Rifles, and Lancaster Guards all drilled here. Those who survived the fighting came back to the Fulton to mark anniversaries and mourn the dead. The hall was also the site of a near-riot in 1863 when local authorities announced a recruitment drive for black soldiers on its premises, with an appearance by Frederick Douglass. Officials canceled the event after protesters massed outside the building.

More than a century later, as I sat at the microfilm reader in the Lancaster County Historical Society (now LancasterHistory.org) working my way through nineteenth-century press accounts of the war, I was struck by the regularity with which reporters invoked theatrical imagery to describe events both at the battlefront and inside Fulton Hall. Perhaps it was wishful thinking: if you can conceive of human slaughter as play and the destruction of a nation as drama (witness *The Trojan Women*), then maybe what's happening around you has some larger meaning. As a student I learned that a play is not what's written in a script but what takes place onstage—let the mind's eye fill in the details we can only guess at. Hence the text that follows, a sequence of scenes to suggest the unimaginable. The script here dramatizes events, characters, and dialogue that are for the most part real, as the historical record attests. The Girl who appears throughout, with and without her canary, is inspired by an exchange in the *Life and Adventures of Signor Blitz*, by Antonio Blitz, who played Fulton Hall on April 8, 1865. Further notes appear at the end of the book.

*   *   *

SCENE I

Interior of Fulton Hall, downtown Lancaster, Pennsylvania. April 22, 1861; night. On screen: a Union flag. Trains whistle; voices shout ("Ten, hut!"). Ohio Volunteers *march onstage. They have been traveling for days and lack proper uniforms and equipment.* Volunteers *toss blankets onto the floor, remove their caps and boots, and collapse in exhaustion. So many volunteers have poured into the city that there is no place to house them save this public hall.*

As they sleep, light shifts and Girl *enters, holding a canary. The bird begins to sing, at first feebly, then with force. The sound is soon indistinguishable from that of a flute, and in fact is a fife, which one* Volunteer *has quietly pulled from his satchel and begun playing.*

Music gradually turns into a march tune as lights again shift, trains whistle, and voices bark orders. Volunteers *rise from floor, collect their belongings, and scurry offstage.* Girl *is left alone with the bird, which has begun to screech.*

SCENE 2

Exterior of Fulton Hall, July 1861. Train whistles; band strikes up march tune; guns fire salute. Townspeople *pour onstage, waving little Union flags and cheering.* Lancaster Fencibles *march across stage in parade formation. Unlike* Volunteers *from previous scene,* Fencibles *are sharply dressed in belted frock coats, white trousers, and tall caps with visors and chin straps. They have just completed ninety days of duty, unscathed.* Reporter *steps out from the crowd.*

REPORTER *(Approaching* First Fencible*)*: You look remarkably well, lad.
FIRST FENCIBLE *(Marching in place, face rigid)*: Thank you, sir. We're in fine spirits.
SECOND FENCIBLE *(Overhearing)*: Our only regret, sir, is that we had no opportunity of meeting the enemy.
FIRST FENCIBLE: But we're determined to try again.
REPORTER: How so?
FIRST FENCIBLE: Why, we're all going to re-enlist!
*(*Fencibles *turn, fall into line, march into Fulton Hall, site of their armory.)*
REPORTER *(To audience)*: I kept up with these gallant fellows as they marched through town. *(Scribbles on notepad)* Despite the gaiety of the occasion, I detected a note of solemnity among their friends and admirers. *(Lights shift.* Townspeople *drift in slow, wide circles around* Reporter.*)*

REPORTER: Many, I'm certain, were thinking of the dangers and horrors of war through which their friends had passed and must yet pass before this rebellion is crushed. *(Abruptly rushes from stage to file his story.)*
(Sudden explosion. Stage goes black, then red, yellow, purple, and black again. Flag vanishes from screen, replaced by battlefield images: corpses of Union soldiers strewn across the ground, buzzards circling overhead.
Girl *appears onstage, dressed as* Union Drummer Boy. *She runs like a madman, pounding on her drum, trying to escape the huge black birds, which now envelop the screen. Lights fade to black. Clatter of drum gives way to mournful violin rendition of "Yankee Doodle.")*

SCENE 3

Fulton Hall auditorium, September 1862. A podium draped in red, white, and blue stands on a small platform. The doleful "Yankee Doodle" of the previous scene has picked up tempo and become a snappy campaign tune played by a military band.

Thaddeus Stevens, 70, lumbers up to podium. He is clubfooted and wears a shapeless brown wig that does little to soften his hawklike features. To gaze at Stevens, *in the words of a contemporary, is to stare at a reptile. Dressed in a dark waistcoat over a white stock and bow tie, he speaks with what one biographer will term a "sepulchral" voice. The effect is both hypnotic and creepy. He is here to address the countywide convention of Lancaster's Republican Party, which has just renominated him as their candidate for U.S. Congress. As* Stevens *limps across platform, crowd, offstage, applauds.*

STEVENS: I had hoped to speak today about policy, but in the last hour I have hesitated whether to speak as I had intended . . . *(Pause)* . . . whether it were proper to criticize now, in this hour of deepest gloom, when we know not where our armies are, but know that they are nowhere successful.
(As Stevens *speaks, we see projected on screen a slow-motion sequence of stills by Matthew Brady and others of Union defeats at Bull Run, Shiloh, Williamsburg, Seven Pines. Photos show Yankee troops standing beside cannons, trains carrying supplies, soldiers with rifles cocked, wounded men clustered outside army hospitals, and scores of battlefield dead. Sound of crows and buzzards cawing.* Stevens *struggles to be heard.)*

STEVENS: But whether we advise the government or find fault with it, we must all do everything to strengthen the hands of our nation. Let us not despair—life is not all sunshine. *(Long pause; sotto voce)* Possibly we have not yet suffered enough. *(Voice rising)* But let no man falter in his loyalty to his government! For he who falters now is a traitor, not only to his country, but to humanity and to his God!!

(Delegates, all older males, emerge from shadows, cheering, and swarm around Stevens *until he is hidden. All at once,* Newsboy *breaks through crowd and rushes downstage waving newspaper.)*

NEWSBOY: Extra! Extra!! Terrible fighting at Antietam!! Twenty-three thousand dead, wounded, and missing in a single day! Read about it here!!

(He races around the stage as lights brighten to a harsh white, and a piercing wail sounds. Fade to black.)

SCENE 4

Interior of Fulton Hall, June 1863. Throughout this scene, we hear sporadic sounds of troops on the march. Lee's Army of Northern Virginia is on its way to Pennsylvania. Backdrop screen is blank.

Lancaster Fencibles, *no longer so nattily dressed as before, gather around a table laden with ham, pickles, cakes, pies, lemonade, whiskey, and beer. Gas lamps flicker. The* Glee Club *of the 122nd regiment, recently back from Chancellorsville, sings "The Soldier's Return." The* Fencibles *are celebrating their seventh anniversary. Small groups of battle-weary veterans stand here and there, talking; they move in exaggerated ways, feigning merriment. The scene has the air of a dumb show.*

Reporter *stands downstage center, his back to audience, scribbling on an oversized notepad.*

REPORTER *(Amplified voice)*: On every side, one well acquainted with the characters in this room can recognize representatives from every part of the theater of war.

(In the background, we hear a semblance of hurdy-gurdy music by the Fencibles Band; Fencibles *move dreamily in time with the tune, pantomiming conversation.)*

REPORTER: In different scenes, each one of an old association enacts a separate and distinct part in the same drama where life and death are in the balance. *(Pauses, surveys room)* In fact, wherever I look, some person or object recalls the history and progress of this monstrous rebellion. *(Realizing how few men are here tonight)* Death has made sad inroads into their ranks.

(Sound of wings flapping overhead; some soldiers look up. Members of Fencibles Band *launch into "The Battle Hymn of the Republic." A few soldiers hoist their glasses and sing, "Glory, glory, hallelujah!")*

REPORTER: Who knows, of the numbers present, how many will be able to participate in another such reunion one year hence, if treason still dares to raise its hand against the nation?

(Reporter turns toward audience, salutes, and begins singing. Lights fade.)

SCENE 5

Interior of Fulton Hall, June 15, 1863. Platform has been transformed into a stage with footlights and a crudely painted backdrop depicting the hills of Virginia, with a Confederate flag above them. A sign reads, "The Southern Refugee." Audience members sit on either side of platform.

Footlights brighten as Actor *steps from behind backdrop. He is in his twenties, with curly red hair, mustache, and goatee. He wears the gray uniform of a Confederate soldier and carries a rifle. He looks warily at his audience, reaches into his pocket, pulls out a harmonica, lifts it to his lips, grins, and begins playing "The Battle Cry of Freedom." Audience members titter as they hear the familiar Union tune.* Women *tap their fans in time to the music; a few* Men *sing.*

MEN: The Union forever, hurrah boys, hurrah!

ACTOR *(Southern drawl)*: Evenin', y'all! Allow me to introduce myself. *(Bows and doffs his cap)* Ladies 'n' gentlemen, I am a scout of the Shenandoah—a refugee from the South!—and upon my head the rebel government has placed a price!

(Audience murmurs.)

ACTOR: For although I have served in the rebel army many a day, I am *(melodramatic pause)* . . . a Southern Unionist!!

(Wild applause. Actor *puts harmonica back into his pocket, leans rifle against a chair, and hangs his cap from its bayonet.)*

ACTOR: I have stood by the old flag at the peril of my very life, in the midst of a community of traitors—

(Someone in the audience whistles.)

ACTOR:—who thirsted for the property and blood of every loyal man. *(Pauses)* I have come here tonight, for one night only, to describe rebeldom to you as it truly is. To tell you blood-tingling stories of the South, so that you here in the North, who live in absolute peace and safety, can know what it is to be a patriot where the rebel flag floats in triumph!! *(Long pause)* You will also have the chance to behold a rare and spectacular assortment of relics confiscated from the very perpetrators of the present rebellion.

(Actor slides backdrop to one side to reveal a set of brightly lit cabinets filled with Confederate paraphernalia—flags, uniforms, money, a pair of pearl-handled pistols, a bust of Jefferson Davis. Inside one cabinet, Girl, *dressed as a* Young Slave, *in blackface, stands motionless. Above her a sign reads, "Rebel Museum of Wonderful Curiosities."* Actor *plays "Dixie" on his harmonica as cabinets, backdrop, and platform roll offstage with audience in eager pursuit. Offstage, a voice emits a piercing rebel yell. Lights out.)*

SCENE 6

Lights up. On screen: Confederate flag. It is late June 1863, and Southern troops are threatening Lancaster. Spotlight up on Mayor George Sanderson, *50ish, center stage. Voices buzz.*

SANDERSON *(Amplified gavel)*: My fellow citizens! *(Waits for quiet)* As you know, General Lee's troops have reached Chambersburg and are heading east.

(Excited chatter.)

SANDERSON: At last account, all is quiet along the Susquehanna, but we must not rest idle. It's thought the rebels want to tap the rail line between Harrisburg and Lancaster.

(Cries of "No!" "Never!" Lights out on Sanderson. *Spot up on* Christopher Hager, *63, downstage left. Face pinched, he reads from a document.)*

HAGER: Be it resolved—*(Scans imaginary crowd)*—that in the event of the rebel forces approaching this city, it is the determination of this meeting to defend it to the last extremity. *(Pause)* Any demand for its surrender shall be peremptorily declined!

(Boisterous applause; shouts of "Hear! Hear!" Lights out on Hager. *Spot up on* James Buchanan, *72, seated in an armchair downstage right. The former*

president is dictating a letter to his secretary, whom we cannot see. Buchanan *wears a claret-colored dressing gown and leather slippers.)*

BUCHANAN: My dear niece—

(Spot up on Harriet Lane, *upstage center, in a homespun crinoline and shawl, surrounded by several women. All are rolling bandages.* Harriet *is played by* Girl. *She does not hear her uncle.)*

BUCHANAN:—under threat of Confederate invasion, Lancaster is in a state of agitation and alarm. *(He pauses, stares out imaginary window)* They have determined, on motion of Mr. Hager, to defend the city to the last extremity. *(Long pause)* I do not consider the danger great, so far as we are concerned.

(Blackout.)

SCENE 7

Downtown Lancaster, late June 1863. Stage is dark, screen black. Townspeople *flit back and forth in the shadows.*

MALE VOICE: The rebels are coming! They are at Columbia! Hurry! The rebels are coming!

(More Townspeople *run onto stage, lugging suitcases and trunks.* Boy *races out pushing a wheelbarrow, spins it wildly, and exits. Horses whinny.* Union Troops *march onstage in silhouette, drilling, then vanish, except for one* Union Soldier *who remains alone. He glances left and right, pulls a small box from his haversack, extracts a match, and lights it. The first of several small explosions erupts. The stage begins to glow yellow, then red. The* Soldier *bolts. A* Courier *runs onstage.*

COURIER: Union troops have fallen back across the Susquehanna! The bridge at Columbia is burning! Lancaster is saved!!

(Offstage crowd cheers. On screen: massive fire. Flames, then smoke and ash, consume screen, and it goes to black.)

SCENE 8

On screen: Union flag at half-mast. Mourners *stand upstage, backs to audience, singing, "Mine eyes have seen the glory of the coming of the Lord!" Shrouded figures cross the stage bearing the casket of Lancaster Major General John Reynolds, killed two days earlier at Gettysburg, less than sixty miles away.*

Bells toll. Downstage, Women *cross hurriedly in opposite direction with bandages and boxes of food. A* Boy *runs onstage, waving flyers.*

BOY: To men of color! A mass meeting of the able-bodied men of color will be held on Wednesday, July 15, at 8:00, Fulton Hall, Lancaster City, to promote recruiting for United States colored troops for the war.
(He presses flyers into Mourners' *hands.)*
BOY: Frederick Douglass and other distinguished speakers will address the meeting!
(Regiment of African American Soldiers *marches onstage.* Mourners *eye them warily.)*
FIRST MAN *(Hissing)*: Nigger soldiers!
SECOND MAN: That's the right way to get rid of the darkies!
FIRST MAN: I'd rather see them sent off to be killed than white men!
*(*Mourners *grow more agitated.*
Lights shift. Exterior of Fulton Hall, July 15, 1863. Night. Mourners *have turned into angry* Protesters, *mostly male, all white, primarily German. Brandishing draft notices, clubs, and hatchets,* Protesters *block doors to hall.* Boy *rushes up to them, waving new flyers.)*
BOY *(Reading)*: Postponed! The meeting of colored men called for this evening has been postponed!
*(*Protesters *grumble.)*
BOY *(Still reading)*: The recruiting agents for the colored regiments have already picked up nearly all the able-bodied Negroes in the city and county—
(Laughter.)
BOY:—a fact which was doubtless not known to the committee when they called the meeting.
*(*Protesters *disperse.* Sheriff's Posse *takes up positions around the stage as* African American Soldiers *continue drilling. Blackout.)*

SCENE 9

Interior of Fulton Hall, July 17, 1863. Lights up on "Doctor" Harry Lee, *35, with exaggerated Chinese features, on platform with six* Volunteers, *male and female, who sit nervously on chairs. Above them a banner reads, "Dr. Harry Lee's Grand Entertainment of Laughing Gas."* Audience *sits downstage of platform on benches.* Lee, *in a satin cloak, holds a metal canister with a long hose. As he speaks, he lifts and turns the device.*

LEE: Some sing . . . others laugh or dance! Still others declaim. It never fails to delight!

(Onstage volunteer, a Boy, around 13, giggles uncontrollably. Lee looks at him, turns to audience, grins.)

LEE: Witness its magic! I have not yet applied the potion, and see what has happened!

(Laughter; Boy stifles giggles.)

LEE *(To audience)*: When administered properly, Dr. Lee's laughing gas is a powerful anaesthetic agent by whose power teeth can be extracted more safely than by chloroform or ether! Without any pain whatsoever! *(Pauses)* And now—*(Long, dramatic beat)*—Do I have the first volunteer?

(Audience titters as Boy timidly raises his hand. Lee strides across platform, circles behind volunteers, and stops upstage of Boy.)

LEE: You're a brave young man.

(Polite applause.)

LEE: Now I must demand absolute silence or the mechanism will not work.

(Room falls still except for the muffled sound of horses and carriages on the streets below. Lee cradles Boy's head in his arm and slips a leather mask over his nose and mouth. Before the Boy can register what's happening, Lee has attached the hose to the mask and begun cranking the canister. Boy's terrified eyes flutter and close.

Stage lights flicker and dim as we, too, enter a hallucinatory world. On screen: burning letters spell "V-I-C-T-O-R-Y." Audience members rise from benches, as if sleepwalking, and in slow motion mime giddy celebration of war's end. Boy removes gas mask, rises from chair, and joins them. He begins to laugh hysterically. Soon everyone is laughing. Lee crosses downstage center and triumphantly bows. Lights fade to black; burning letters remain on screen.)

SCENE 10

On screen: flames continue to spell "V-I-C-T-O-R-Y." This time the bonfire, in downtown Lancaster, is real. It is April 10, 1865, and news of Confederate general Robert E. Lee's surrender at Appomattox has reached the city that morning. Jubilant Townspeople *pour onstage, waving hats and handkerchiefs, embracing and weeping.* Boy, *now 15, runs onstage, lets out a high-pitched laugh, furiously jiggles a small Union flag, then bolts offstage.*

Soldiers, *some on crutches, mingle with civilians.* Children *race pell-mell through crowd. Men in various states of inebriation spill from taverns. The*

Fencibles Band *plays "When Johnny Comes Marching Home Again." Crowd joins in the refrain: "Hurrah! Hurrah!"*

In midst of celebrations, Girl *wanders onstage with an empty bird cage. She moves purposefully through the crowd, as though searching for something or someone. Lights gradually fade.*

SCENE II

Inside Fulton Hall auditorium, that same night. Signor Antonio Blitz, *54, magician and ventriloquist, in tails and a top hat, stands on a platform decorated to suggest a Victorian parlor. He stands near a bird cage with several canaries.* Blitz *has a white beard and salt-and-pepper hair, which he combs over his balding pate.*

To his left, a small audience sits expectantly. Two young Soldiers, *both legless, watch enthralled from the front row as* Blitz *waves a handkerchief over a silver coin, and it vanishes.* Soldiers *clap and laugh with abandon, a sight that moves the magician deeply. "Their countenances beamed with pleasure," he will write in his memoirs, "and almost inclined me to wish that even I was not less discontented or aggrieved by misfortunes incidental to life."*

Girl, *also in front row, raises her hand.* Blitz *motions for her to come up to the platform. She does so, and hands the magician a folded square of paper.*

BLITZ: What does it contain, my little angel?

(Girl *says nothing.* Blitz *opens the paper to find a lifeless canary.*)

GIRL *(Fighting tears)*: He died last night. Please make him alive again. He always used to talk and sing to me, poor Dickey, did you not?

(*She smooths the bird's feathers. Audience murmurs.* Soldiers *in front row glance uneasily at one another. The* Girl *has cast a pall over the crowd.*)

BLITZ: Who told you to bring it to me?

GIRL: No one, sir. Only I loved him so much, and I have seen you put a bird to sleep, and look as if he were dead, and then when you spoke to him he would jump up and fly around and sing.

BLITZ: Very true, my dear. But he was trained to do so!

GIRL: Well, why not do the same with Dickey?

BLITZ: *(Pause)* I cannot.

(Girl *begins to sob. She takes the bird from* Blitz *and kisses it.* Blitz *tries to comfort her. Stifled weeping from audience.* Blitz *hits on an idea.*)

71

BLITZ: What would you say if I were to give you one of my own pet canaries?

(*Girl looks at him, incredulous. She nods. Blitz reaches inside his bird cage, pulls out a yellow bird, and hands it to her in exchange for the dead canary. The live bird begins to sing.*)

GIRL: Why, thank you, sir. (*Pets bird.*) I shall take Dickey home and bury him beneath the flowers in my Pa's garden.

(*Audience claps. Applause builds until it's clear we're no longer listening to this particular crowd but to an entire nation rejoicing. The spell is abruptly broken by the sound of a gunshot. Lights go out. In the darkness, screams.*)

VOICE 1 (*Shouting*): Sic semper tyrannis!

VOICE 2: Who was he?

VOICE 3: Hang him!

(*Blackout. Church bells toll.*)

SCENE 12

Inside Fulton Hall, April 15, 1865. On screen: eagle, with Union flag, draped in black. A few men and women mill about platform, which holds a translucent mural of a battle scene, lit from behind, showing victorious troops raising the Union flag amidst smoke and carnage. This is the Davies and Co. Polyorama, described by fans as a genuine "work of art."

A violin plays. Mural unspools to reveal more scenes of war: moonlit views of armies on the march, daytime images of soldiers in camp, and the pièce de résistance, a pictorial reenactment of the 1862 naval battle between the ironclads U.S.S. Monitor and C.S.S. Merrimac. A bass drum simulates cannon fire as the Merrimac burns.

Among the sparse crowd of onlookers is Victor Antonio Yecker, 9, and his father, Blasius Yecker, 31, a short, round-faced man with wavy brown hair and a close-cropped beard. The older Yecker stares at the polyorama, mesmerized. He slips away from the crowd and comes downstage, facing audience, lost in thought.

Lights shift. Drum continues beating, as in a funeral procession. A train whistles.

Blackout. End of act.

9

MR. YECKER OPENS AN OPERA HOUSE: 1873

The Fulton manager was tired of crowds so small you could count them on your fingers. God knew he'd tried. Since purchasing Fulton Hall six months after the war and turning it into a bona fide theater with a Venetian backdrop and weekly offerings by "artistes from the first-class Eastern Theaters" (as the *Lancaster Intelligencer* described the first troupe to play the refurbished Fulton Hall in 1866), Blasius Yecker had brought in minstrel shows, magicians, bell ringers, midgets, live Indians, bucking horses, more minstrel shows, even burlesque. He'd repeatedly tried to capitalize on the recent war, presenting not just *Our American Cousin*, the show Lincoln was watching when Booth shot him, but patriotic tableaux and panoramas, among them an interpretation of "the Invasion of this state by the Confederates under Gen. R. E. Lee." Barnum's Tom Thumb had inched his pint-sized frame across the Fulton platform. Acting companies had come and gone.

Yecker had made a little money leasing the building to groups for fairs and fundraisers, and five months after James Buchanan's death, in 1868, they'd auctioned off the late president's liquor collection inside Fulton Hall. It had seemed to many the end of an age. Old Buck, the last American president to wear a stock, was gone, and here were ordinary Lancastrians bidding on his bottles—$1,200 worth of brandy, port, champagne, sherry, claret, whiskey, and wine. The old man had succumbed in the early summer, one of a brace of kinsmen to vanish that season, for Christopher Hager had preceded him by a month, and Thaddeus Stevens followed in August of 1868.

That same year, Blind Tom, a twenty-year-old pianist and former slave, drew a respectable crowd to Yecker's hall, though who knew what attracted them—a love of music or the chance to gawk at a sightless black man whom the *Illustrated Annual of Phrenology and Physiognomy for 1869* described as "remarkably developed in the region of the perceptive faculties"? Whatever the lure, Tom pleased the audience with his virtuosic playing and uncanny imitations of a music box, a train, and a speech by the late Stephen A. Douglas.

The only time Yecker managed to sell out Fulton Hall was in early 1872, when a redheaded platformer by the name of Mark Twain came to town with his account of "roughing it" in California and Nevada. It was January, and sleet was falling, but in their zeal to see the lanky humorist with the nasal bark and windmill arms, Lancastrians bought up every ticket Yecker had to hawk.

The next month it was back to business as usual: a benefit for a local band, an evening of can-can by a troupe of dancing blondes. Sales slumped; the best companies shunned the place.

The little manager was almost forty and a father of six. His oldest boy, Victor, would soon venture west to help build the railroad that was reconfiguring the nation. You could now cross the continent in a week. The old wagon paths that had etched an earthen web across the prairie had morphed into iron tracks that bored through mountains straight to the Pacific. Hotels and churches stood on old Indian hunting grounds. As early as 1819, the Pennsylvania missionary John Heckewelder, who had lived among the natives and admired their hospitality, had written, "Alas! In a few years, perhaps, they will have entirely disappeared from the face of the earth and all that will be remembered of them will be that they existed and were numbered among the barbarous tribes that once inhabited this vast continent."

Yecker himself had seen their vanishing world. Shortly after reaching America in 1848, the Alsatian teenager had gone west to work in Oregon's timber mills. He had shadowed Lewis and Clark across the Great Plains and Rocky Mountains, past herds of buffalo and the tribes who depended on them—Sioux, Shoshone, Blackfeet, Crow. But the mills damaged his health, so Yecker had hurried back to the sheltered streets of Lancaster and signed on as an apprentice in Henry Pinkerton's saddle shop on Center Square, a block from Christopher Hager's dry goods store and the city jail.

While Hager was turning that jail into a public hall, eighteen-year-old Blasius Yecker was putting in twelve- and fourteen-hour days learning to make harnesses, followed by sessions of night school where he learned to speak English. In 1855, three years after Fulton Hall opened, Yecker donned a velvet jacket and brocade vest to marry Mary Schreck, a recent German immigrant. The two looked so much alike—brunette, round-faced, small-boned—they might have been siblings. A year later, Victor Antonio Yecker was born, and Blasius Yecker opened his own saddlery shop. He was twenty-one.

Business prospered—especially during the profitable war years—and before long Yecker took over the property next door to him as well. It was while running this "thriving enterprise," the local press would later report, that Yecker "conceived the plan of developing the amusement possibilities of Lancaster by purchase of Fulton Hall." By then Hager had turned over management of the building to a citizens' group, who gladly sold it to Yecker in late 1865. For a while the gamble paid off, then sales plunged.

Audiences in the early years of Twain's Gilded Age wanted pomp and spectacle, sumptuous decoration, hierarchical seating, state-of-the-art stage machinery, things Fulton Hall couldn't offer. In his 1871 treatise on the theater, Charles Garnier had written that most contemporary play-houses were "insufficient, poorly laid out, without character, without comfort, without grandeur and without art." Garnier's solution, as borne out by his lavish opera house in Paris, was luxury on a grand scale. Theater architects must address "a thousand and one" questions, he said, among them heat, ventilation, lighting, the stage curtain, acoustics, the arrangement of seats, and the storage of hats and lorgnettes. Two elements were paramount: the stage, which must be immense, and the auditorium, which must be crowned by a cupola or dome.

Fulton Hall had a temporary stage, no dome, faulty ventilation, poor acoustics, shoddy dressing rooms, uniform seating, a cramped entrance, and no balcony. It stank of beer. Despite Samuel Sloan's stately 1852 façade and the improvements Yecker himself had made to the building in 1866, it was at best a utilitarian place. Some felt it should be turned into a picture gallery.

Yecker—whom I like to imagine working his way through the worn interior of his storied hall, fingering the old jail walls, asking himself how much weight they could bear—thought otherwise.

He embraced Garnier's view that a properly decorated playhouse, like a cathedral, worked "unconsciously on the spirit" to elevate the moral sensibilities of an audience. "Like crosses on altars," the Frenchman had written, "lyres and masks in theaters keep thought oriented, by visual means, toward the central concern."

A practicing Catholic, Yecker understood how symbols could help people focus on what mattered. In his own life he had experienced the regenerative powers of the communion chalice and wafer, wedding ring and baptismal font. He found meaning in ceremony. All six of his children were christened within days of their birth, and when a seventh was born in early 1873, a daughter, Ida, she too was quickly baptized, and the dates of both events inscribed in German in the Yecker family record. Thus did metaphor anchor their lives.

Saint Mary's Church, where Yecker worshipped, stood one block south of Fulton Hall and had been built in the same year, 1852. Christopher Hager had, in fact, supplied the stones for its foundation from the jail he converted into Fulton Hall that summer, and it's possible Yecker relished this coincidence as much as I do. Hager was presumably making money selling excess rubble from his construction site, but the gesture resonates, and I am drawn to the image of these two buildings, one block apart, each devoted to the reenactment of stories, both held in place by ghosted rock.

After a fire nearly destroyed Saint Mary's in 1867, a church architect with a theatrical name was brought in from Philadelphia to rebuild the sanctuary. Yecker must have liked the results—the high ceiling and frescoed walls—because in the spring of 1873, five months after the birth of his seventh and last child, he hired the same man to renovate Fulton Hall.

Edwin Forrest Durang specialized in ecclesiastical structures: churches, rectories, parochial schools, convents, and orphanages. He was known for his gentility and attention to detail, for his ability "to unite beauty of design with substantiality and practicability," and for the speed at which he worked—"as quick with the pencil as thought is to the mind," a colleague said. Forty-four and debonair, with a dark, El Greco face, a sable mustache and wispy beard, Durang was a devout Catholic with a reputation for "inflexible integrity," and these qualities must have pleased Yecker, who asked the architect to examine Fulton Hall and recommend improvements.

As the two men walked through Yecker's building, they would have talked about structure and cost, about the luxuries American audiences had come to expect and the technical demands touring companies now made. Durang was used to accommodating the liturgical needs of churches, so it's probable Yecker's requests did not surprise him. Along the way the two men may have touched on their own affinities and on their common past, for nearly a century before Blasius Yecker traveled from Alsace to Philadelphia and then to Lancaster, Edwin Forrest Durang's great-grandparents had made the same journey. They arrived in the fall of 1767, and their first child, John—Edwin's grandfather—was born in Lancaster, possibly in a home behind the jail that became Fulton Hall.

Edwin did not know his grandfather, who died in 1822, but he would have known John Durang's story: his early love of dancing and panto-mime, his triumphant stint, at thirteen, as Mercury, in flesh-colored tights and feathered wings, in a victory parade celebrating the end of the Revolution. John Durang never outgrew his boyhood zeal for play. He became an actor, one of the first of that profession to call himself American, and he traveled up and down the Northeast doing clown acts and puppet shows and pantomimes. He entertained Benjamin Franklin and George Wash-ington, and in 1800 he performed an "Indian War and Scalp Dance" for the governor of the new state of Pennsylvania in a Lancaster tavern. John Durang claimed to have learned the art of native dance from a group of Indian chiefs, who in exchange for rum taught him the correct steps and sold him an authentic costume with knee bracelets that rattled like casta-nets. Audiences lined up to gawk at the jovial white man in savage pelts.

John Durang's oldest son, Charles, Edwin's father, was also an actor as well as a stage historian, manager, and ballet master. Dressed in a flowered gown, he used to caper about his Philadelphia home while playing the violin and counting, "One, two, three, hop!" as he taught pupils to dance. Edwin Durang grew up with the noise and paraphernalia of theater, with props and costumes and prompt books. He was named after an actor—his father's friend Edwin Forrest, the swaggering impersonator of Indian war-riors and rebel slaves, the first great American star—and he may have felt destined to wind up onstage himself. But in the end Edwin Durang chose a quieter profession and set up drafting rooms in his father's house, then signed on with a Philadelphia architectural firm. By the time Yecker hired him, he had racked up an impressive list of commissions, including at least one opera house.

Durang worked consciously from the past, braiding details from Roman churches and Gothic mansions into his nineteenth-century chapels and schools. As he stood outside Fulton Hall that spring, gauging the building's scale and calculating its geometry, he would have felt the tug of history. Here was the city where his great-grandparents' long flight from Europe had come to a safe end, where his grandfather had begun life. Lancaster's red-brick homes and shops housed people like himself, the children and grandchildren of immigrants who had come here in desperation and hope and chiseled towns out of the wilderness. In ways Durang may not have been able to pinpoint, Fulton Hall conveyed something of that experience— of the confidence with which new arrivals laid claim to the land and of the exhilaration with which they declared its independence. Close your eyes, and you could almost hear John Durang dancing.

His grandson's task was to enshrine that spirit, to turn Christopher Hager's multipurpose hall into a modern opera house devoted to performance, with a picture-frame stage where Blasius Yecker could parade celebrities and actors could earn their keep. It would take months, and they would need to gut the place—lower the ground floor, raise the roof, build a stage, add a balcony, fresco the ceiling, install a fly system—but think of the gains, the architect told the manager, and Yecker agreed. Durang didn't come cheap; the work would cost $15,000, but Yecker said that was fine, it had to be done. They were both in their forties, these brisk men of European stock, young enough to envision the next decades and old enough to be thinking of legacy.

On June 16, 1873, Durang's crew went to work. By the time they'd finished, nearly four months later, "scarcely a vestige of the old interior" remained, a reporter saw. Carpenters replaced the top floor of the hall with a dome to improve ventilation, lowered the auditorium by a dozen feet, and constructed a fifty-four-foot-wide stage with sunken footlights. Above it, Henry Young of Philadelphia's Walnut Street Theatre erected a massive system of pulleys and pins, with hemp ropes that crawled over a grid four stories tall and sandbags so heavy they could kill a man. A newspaperman described Young's backstage as a "wilderness" of ropes, drops, curtains, flies, lights, borders, weights, trap doors, and hinged grooves for shifting flats. New York scenic artist Richard Smith painted a drop curtain showing the Lake of Lugano, and a full set of backdrops—the usual English and continental landscapes and breathtaking vistas of a vast, uncharted America that most of Yecker's audiences could only imagine.

Out went the old benches of Fulton Hall, and in came numbered seats made of black walnut upholstered in red terry, with cushioned armrests, arranged in semicircular tiers. Above them Durang installed a swooping balcony with gilt-edged railings supported by twelve iron columns, each topped by a red-and-gold capital. With this new configuration Yecker could seat over a thousand people, with standing room for an additional three hundred. Overhead, a painter by the name of Reingruber frescoed a portrait of Beethoven and a quartet of women decked out as the four seasons, surrounded by stars. In such an exalted setting, Garnier had promised, audiences could feast on the spectacle of themselves in their finery and experience a "kind of magnetic shivering" as they observed and felt themselves observed, listened and perceived themselves heard. From a maroon recess over the stage, a plaster likeness of the god Apollo looked down on the quivering spectacle.

So many coves and curves crowded his new interior that Yecker declared he had bought out the local lumber yards "several times" and "nearly exhausted the hardware stores," never mind his own checkbook, but it was all good. Durang was concocting a space for dreaming. He had devoted his career, after all, to designing buildings meant to inspire devotional piety. The architect bricked in the old windows of Fulton Hall, and from the center of its domed ceiling hung a six-foot-wide chandelier with fifty-four gas burners, each backed by a reflector. Together with eight smaller chandeliers on either side of the proscenium, it cast so much light you'd think you were outdoors on a sunny afternoon. Backstage, perhaps thinking of how his actor grandfather and father must have suffered on the road, Durang installed two furnaces, ten dressing rooms, a pair of water closets, a greenroom, and a spiral staircase. He built an orchestra pit and ran speaking tubes between it and the stage and the dressing rooms.

The transformation of Fulton Hall was scarcely less miraculous than the one the nation had experienced in the previous decade. "On entering the place, the visitor is at once struck by the wonderful metamorphosis it has undergone," a reporter for the *Intelligencer* exclaimed in an article entitled "Fulton Hall—Its Reconstruction." The former armory and convention hall was now a shrine to the gods of culture, one of some four thousand such buildings to open between 1865 and 1900 in towns and cities across the newly united states. By 1885, nearly every town in the country had a theater or opera house.

The grand reopening of Fulton Hall—some now called it the Fulton Opera House—took place on October 2, 1873, with a performance by the Chestnut Street Theatre of Philadelphia under the management of Edward L. Davenport, a Shakespearean actor who a year earlier had refused to perform in Fulton Hall until it had better light. "We have now not only more light but one of the handsomest, if not *the* handsomest opera house in the United States," the courtly fifty-eight-year-old told the opening night crowd. "True, it is not so large as the Philadelphia Academy of Music"—a building Durang had also worked on—but "in architectural proportion and elegance of design" Fulton Hall surpassed the academy, and as such, Davenport gushed, was "another illustration of the old adage that gems and other valuable articles come in small packages. Fulton Hall is certainly a perfect little gem."

Davenport and his troupe performed excerpts from *Othello* followed by a short farce. Yecker donated the evening's proceeds to the Grand Army of the Republic to benefit the widows and orphans of slain Union soldiers. Durang would have appreciated the deed: his brother John had been wounded at Gettysburg, and Edwin himself would soon marry a woman left fatherless by the war. Few people sitting in the Fulton's newly upholstered seats that night were untouched by the calamity. Just up the street, stonemasons were at work on a granite column commemorating those who had fallen "in defense of the Union in the War of Rebellion." A portion of the structure's $26,000 price tag had been raised inside Fulton Hall.

The war was fast becoming myth, even to the veiled women and scarred veterans who populated Yecker's crowd that night. More than a thousand people, some from as far away as Baltimore, attended the grand reopening. To kick off the evening they stood and sang "The Star-Spangled Banner," a tune made popular by the Civil War, their voices rising in praise of a reunited America that was itself something of a myth. Out west, government troops were slaughtering buffalo and herding Indians onto reservations; the South had become a cauldron of racial violence; strikes and financial unrest plagued the North. Just two weeks earlier, the Philadelphia investment firm of Jay Cooke had collapsed, prompting the New York Stock Exchange to close for ten days and seeding a nationwide depression. In Lancaster County, work on a new rail line had stopped.

"The future of America is in certain respects as dark as it is vast," Walt Whitman had foreseen in 1871. "Pride, competition, segregation, vicious wilfulness, and license beyond example, brood already upon us. Unwieldy and immense, who shall hold in behemoth? who bridle leviathan?"

Certainly not Blasius Yecker, who longed to make a profit from his fancy new theater. He would have been pleased by the rush for opening-night tickets—seats in the parquette circle went for two dollars apiece. Everyone, it seemed, wanted to see the changes he had made. Into the hall they swarmed that gay October evening, a gaggle of tailcoats and celluloid collars, bustles and kid slippers. They swept past Yecker's ornate new box office, through doors as solid as rock, into a brightly lit auditorium whose crimson walls cast a pink glow on their astonished faces. Everything shimmered: the star-studded ceiling, the immense chandelier, the gilt-edged railings. At the front of this enchanted room the grandson of John Durang had constructed a two-story proscenium arch trimmed in gold and flanked by classical female figures holding gas candelabras. For the first time, the people of Lancaster had a dedicated stage.

Now the lights were dimming. A curtain rose, footlights brightened, and into Durang's oneiric frame stepped an actor. As it happened, he was Edward Davenport, playing the role of the villain Iago, but he could have been Thespis or Richard Burbage or a shaman casting spells, for he possessed their same uncanny energy, and in his presence the audience at Fulton Hall was transported. Here was a rite every bit as charged as the one Yecker and his wife observed weekly at church, a pageant by which a motley crowd turned into a community of believers.

Watching a play you both lose and find yourself. The boundary between light and darkness, actor and audience, communal and private experience keeps shifting. Onstage, performers are free to do as they wish; out in the auditorium there are rules. Yecker, for example, posted signs banning catcalls, whistling, spitting, and behavior injurious to furniture, but on his stage anything could happen. A man could goad a friend into killing his wife and be applauded for it, as Davenport did that evening, for that was the power of the theater: it licensed the forbidden. Yecker's crowd knew firsthand the destructive force of violence—this very building had been part of the machinery of war—and yet that night they took pleasure in watching it erupt before them. Such was the peculiar enchantment of plays.

What was real? One floor below the new Fulton auditorium, as the *Lancaster Daily Express* took pains to remind readers on the occasion of the grand reopening, lay the scene of an earlier drama, "a deed of horror which only needed the magic touch of a Shakespeare's dramatic pen to make it as

impressive as the plays of *Hamlet* or *Othello*"—the massacre of the Conestoga Indians in 1763. "Almost beneath the very spot where many of our
readers will sit, thrilled by Davenport's masterly rendition of the leading
characters in two of Shakespeare's wonderful creations, this horribly real
tragedy was enacted over a century ago."

To the audience upstairs, the story of the Conestogas probably seemed
more illusory than the plots Davenport was unspooling onstage that evening. Did no one question the propriety of erecting a theater on the site of
a mass murder? In his 1872 history of Lancaster County, biographer Alexander Harris suggested the Paxton gang's actions were largely the result of
"pent-up rage against the Indians for the atrocities committed on the
white settlers" and cautioned, "We should endeavor, therefore, to place
ourselves in imagination in their circumstances before passing too harsh a
judgment upon them." At a time when government troops were killing
Native Americans throughout the West, many Lancastrians would have
been inclined to agree with Harris. They wanted their Indians tame, like
John Durang's war dances.

In a few years, the Young Ladies' Guild of the local Moravian church
would present a *tableau vivant* of the Paxton killings on the Fulton stage,
along with fifty other historical scenes. Before a hall "crowded almost to
suffocation" the amateur group would impersonate a group of armed Paxton men with their victims, some "lying dead and others in attitudes of
supplication or terror." The *Intelligencer* pronounced the evening as a whole
"very beautiful" and said the Paxton tableau "had the advantage of being
presented on the very spot on which the massacre took place."

By transforming a bloody rampage into a living sculpture, the young
Moravian women were fulfilling one of the theater's most ancient func-
tions, the recycling of raw experience into metaphor. Yecker grasped the
fundamental human urge for this process—it's why he sank his fortunes
into redoing Christopher Hager's town hall. The people of Lancaster
needed a place where they could wrestle with memory. They called it entertainment, of course, as did Yecker, but it was also this. Durang had built a
sanctuary, a safe place halfway between waking life and dreaming, where
the residents of Yecker's growing town could reimagine their lives.

Those of us who fall in love with the buildings we call theaters never
quite get over our infatuation. Yecker would devote the rest of his life to
the Fulton; Durang would design another ten or so theaters and then
bequeath his affinities to his heirs. His great-grandson Christopher tells

me that when he was growing up in the 1940s and '50s, "I was told there were generations of architects in the Durang family, and before that generations of actors. So it was often said they wondered if I'd want to be an architect or in theater, and when I showed an early interest in theater, everyone thought that was fine and dandy. Which is interesting, given how other children sometimes are discouraged by their families."

My own mother urged me not to go into the theater, but to no effect. I was hooked. I don't know when or where it began—perhaps with the pink showboat I received for Christmas when I was six, though I suspect it was earlier. We spend our lives imitating others and thinking in scenes. Christopher Durang wrote his first play when he was in second grade and besotted with *I Love Lucy*, and he kept at it. Plays allowed him to make sense of his father's drinking and his parents' squabbling and his strict Catholic upbringing. They gave him the energy and distance, he says, to "relish" human suffering—"mine, others', the concept of. . . . This 'relish' is something that audiences do not always feel comfortable with, and I find that some people, rather than simply disliking my work, are made furious by it."

Yecker too would make people uncomfortable with some of the shows he brought to the Fulton. His descendants—who, like Durang's, took up the family trade—would tangle with priests and policemen and moralizing citizens. But the theater Yecker set into motion on the night of October 2, 1873, would stay open.

10

IN TRANSIT

I fell out of love with acting. I was twenty and briefly, ecstatically, in love with a stage manager I'd met at the Fulton. He had curly black hair and a blue van with a mattress in the back, and he called himself a free spirit, a term I hadn't heard before. (Read *The Razor's Edge*, he told me.) I was just coming off a dismal, short-lived fling with an actor from John Housman's Acting Company, who had played the Fulton that spring in a cast featuring Patti Lupone and Kevin Kline. They were all recent Juilliard grads. The actor and I had met in Lancaster and spent a torrid weekend in Manhattan, and I'd come home convinced my acting career and love life were both about to take off, and then he'd dumped me. I slashed my wrists and began thinking about existentialism.

From my journal, June 16, 1976: "I just keep thinking we're going to die anyway, why bother with trying to fill out the in-between time."

A week later, just starting rehearsals for a summer rep season at the Fulton, I wrote, "Oh God I'm ready to give all of this up." "This" was acting, my raison d'être since seventh grade.

I'd promised people I would be an actress—no, a *star*, as if only celebrity could justify my having been born. I had auditioned for the Fulton summer season intending to throw myself into rehearsals, as I'd done for years with every play in which I'd been cast, but suddenly I didn't trust what I was doing. I thought about how pointless theater was. The hours of rehearsal, the relationships cast members forge, the moments of real brilliance in a performance, "the thousands of thoughts surrounding each thing onstage. All that comes to an end and will never be re-created. Then multiply this experience by the many times it occurs during an actor's career. It seems fruitless—why bother?"

I had been cast as Amy in George Kelly's *The Show Off* and as Annie Oakley's kid sister in *Annie Get Your Gun*. The first was a deliciously big role for which I got to wear flapper dresses and a marceled wig. The second was a bit part in the chorus that had me trilling lines like "How do you rope a cow?" A local opera star by the name of John Darrenkamp sang the male lead in that production, and we hovered at the edges of the halo that enveloped him wherever he strode.

During auditions for the season, I'd been interviewed by a reporter for the *Intelligencer Journal* about my plans for the summer and life in general. The article, which came out under the headline "Leslie Stainton Dreams of Being 'Really Fine Actress,'" described me as "a 20-year-old hopeful with quite a bit of amateur experience behind her" and "some excellent performances to her credit." Missing was any mention of the bandaged wrists with which I'd started the summer, or my dawning misgivings about the theatrical enterprise. Instead, I was quoted as saying I had never felt more secure onstage.

A week or two later, a young stage manager with Irish good looks swept into my life. He was working for a local theater group and came to the Fulton to borrow something, and we got to talking, and the next thing I knew I was standing out under the stars on an abandoned highway overpass at four o'clock in the morning, kissing him. We spent the rest of the summer together. I was convinced he was It and we would marry. I was about to start my senior year in college and frantic to figure out the rest of my life, and here was the piece to complete the puzzle: the first man I'd been involved with who wasn't married or geographically unavailable or significantly older than I was. In his presence, I wrote in my diary, "I act unlike myself. Or maybe more like myself."

Suddenly life interested me more than the stage. Rehearsals became an inconvenience and performances a distraction from what really mattered, time with my guy. That he was self-absorbed and controlling escaped me. I followed him around like a puppy, took up his interests, listened enthralled to his thoughts on the nature of existence (he'd majored in philosophy). "How can I live up to your goodness?" I asked myself. "I feel miles below you." I began thinking maybe I'd like to stage-manage instead of act.

Where once I had been content to lose myself in scripted parts, I now lost myself in him. "We come into the world as individuals, achieve character, and become persons," writes Erving Goffman. We adopt masks that represent our ideal—Goffman uses the word "truer"—selves. I assume that's what I was doing, trying to live up to a role. My stage manager had grown up in Kenya, the son of missionaries, and suddenly I wanted to live overseas too, preferably in Africa. He liked to go rafting, so I took it up as well. I read Somerset Maugham. Was it just me, or is this what it's like to be almost adult and in search of a self?

And what was the difference, really, between my latching onto his persona by day and sitting in a dressing room at night adjusting my character's wig or putting on her cowboy boots? An actor before a mirror, that iconic figure beloved by painters, embodies a transaction we all recognize.

I wanted desperately to be someone other than myself. In Stanislavskian terms, I was building my character. The process was not unlike the one I undertook most nights at the Fulton. I had been taught to spend a half hour or so in the dark before every performance, summoning the feelings and perceptions of the role I was about to impersonate, so I'd sit somewhere in the basement by myself, feigning sensations. I failed to see what David Mamet would later articulate, that the "magic phrases and procedures" an actor invokes before going onstage are nothing more than "incantations to lessen the terror of going out there naked."

"Someone says character is the external life of the person onstage, the way that person moves or stands or holds a handkerchief, or their mannerisms. But that person onstage is *you*," Mamet writes in his brief guide for actors, *True and False*. "It is not a construct you are free to amend or mold. It's you. It is *your* character which you take onstage."

And my character that summer was a mess.

September came, the shows closed, I went back to college, and the love of my life left town and me. I thought I would not recover. Hoping to wean myself from my dependence on men, I enrolled in a course on women and culture. I took classes in dramatic theory and criticism, on the Irish Renaissance, and on modern drama. I became enamored of Lady Gregory and Chekhov's three sisters, for whom work (however unsatisfactory) was everything. I contemplated a career as an academic. Without knowing it, I was beginning to construct a self.

Identification is the "covert theme of drama," Michael Goldman suggests. This isn't simply a matter of actors identifying with roles but of "the making or doing of identity." You watch an actor, onstage or on screen, and wonder where her private life stops and the public, *performed* one begins, what parts of herself we see revealed in her role. Because this activity is so deeply engaging, so profoundly illustrative of the shaky negotiations we make with ourselves throughout our lives, but perhaps especially when we are young and still emerging from the cocoon of our parental homes, we return to it again and again, often paying huge sums for the pleasure. "It should not be surprising, then," says Goldman, "that the process of identification in this sense—of establishing a self that in some way transcends the normal confusions of self—is remarkably current as a theme in plays of all types from all periods, from *Oedipus* to *Earnest* to *Cloud Nine*."

Not long after my summer of heartbreak, Elizabeth Ashley published a memoir of her life as an actress. Her account of wrecked love affairs, broken marriages, and redemption through art resonated so powerfully with me that I memorized whole chunks of the book. "All the things that are negative in me as a person—the incompetence and despair and weakness and pain—are like a gift from God in a performer," Ashley wrote, and I repeated to myself. "If you don't hide them and if you stop lying to yourself about what you are and are not, there is a ring or a tent or a stage where you can take them and use them to make something beautiful. Because drama is made up of what people most fear and deny in themselves. The taboos. The secrets. The devils and the demons. The only reason they let us live, I suppose, is because somebody has to confront what those things are like and tell other people about them."

I wasn't out of the woods yet. Before I'd finished college, I embarked on yet another doomed affair, this one with a graphic designer ten years my senior who was still involved with his previous girlfriend. In the midst of it I took up acting again, and one night during rehearsals I swallowed a bottle of aspirin and was taken to the ER. I spent the next twenty-four hours in a psychiatric ward, where I gained a new appreciation for what it means to take on roles. My favorite theater professor—a man who had played Lear to my Cordelia two years earlier—picked me up after I was discharged and drove me home to my parents. "You've peered into the abyss," he said to me as we left the hospital.

Actors occupy a liminal space somewhere between self and character, life and death. It is a condition of their employment that they pass repeatedly back and forth among these states. No wonder they unsettle us.

"Actors used to be buried at a crossroads with a stake through the heart," Mamet reports. "Those people's performances so troubled the onlookers that they feared their ghosts."

I was not cut out for the actor's transitory life, a fact I began to realize just as I was preparing to take up that life. Not for me the makeshift families and rented rooms, the constant quest for work. I could mime that existence onstage as Annie Oakley's sister, touring with Buffalo Bill, but I lacked the temperament to do it for real. One night after a performance of *Annie Get Your Gun*, I left the Fulton so distraught I drove out of the parking lot in the dark with my lights off. A police car materialized out of nowhere— maybe they shadowed actors after all—and pulled me over. When the cop realized I was not drunk but sobbing, he softened.

"Are you sure you're all right?" he asked.

"Yes," I wept. But I was not; everything was a jumble. I remember looking back at the dark building I had just left and thinking it had betrayed me. It was no different, really, from a psych ward—you went inside and poured your guts out and then walked away pretending you were whole when you weren't, when you'd left entire parts of yourself back in that ravenous space. The Fulton was devouring me.

Theater does not last. Anyone who goes onstage must make her peace with that fact. Plays, said Federico García Lorca, who spent much of his short life creating them, "last as long as the performance lasts, and nothing more." The beauty of the theater, he added, is that, "scarcely created, it vanishes. It is the art of the moment. It is built upon sand."

"These our actors, as I foretold you, were all spirits and are melted into air, into thin air," Shakespeare wrote in a play I helped direct shortly after I stopped wanting to act. Listening to *The Tempest* night after night, I struggled to reimagine my tiny spot on the globe. I'd broken my own staff that summer and was groping, like the blinded Gloucester in another play I'd once inhabited, for terra firma. "We are such stuff as dreams are made on," I heard Prospero say, and for the first time in my life I understood what he meant.

Within the image:

V: _Maſſawomeck_ omecks

Signification of theſe markes,
To the croſſes hath bin diſcouerd
what beyond is by relation ✠
Kings howſes 2
Ordinary howſes 2

The Saſqueſ ahanougs are a Gyant like peo=ple &
Vtchowig thus a tyred

SASQVE HANX OVGH

Attaock

Teſinigh

Quadroque

FIG 1
Susquehannock. The seven-
teenth-century English captain John Smith described
the Susquehannocks whom
he encountered around the
Chesapeake Bay as "giants."
Among the Susquehannock
people Smith identified were
the Conestogas, who lived
in and around what would
become Lancaster County.
Courtesy of the William L.
Clements Library, Univer-
sity of Michigan.

FIG 2
Lancaster jail, ca. 1745. A nineteenth-century depiction of Lancaster's colonial jail and workhouse, site of the December 27, 1763, massacre of fourteen Conestoga Indians. From I. Daniel Rupp, *History of Lancaster County* (1844). Courtesy of LancasterHistory.org, Lancaster, Pa., 2050121.

FIG 3
T. D. Rice as Jim Crow. Performer T. D. Rice fathered minstrelsy when he began corking up as a dancing slave named Jim Crow in the early 1830s, an act he brought to Lancaster in 1845. Courtesy of Special Collections, Sheridan Libraries, Johns Hopkins University.

FIG 4
Samuel Sloan, drawing of
Fulton Hall, 1852. When it
came to style, the architect
Samuel Sloan preferred the
Italianate for its "finished,
elegant, and picturesque
appearance." Courtesy of
the Fulton Opera House
Foundation.

FIG 5
Street scene showing Fulton
Hall, ca. 1852. When Christopher Hager built Fulton
Hall on Prince Street in 1852,
he created "one of the finest
public halls in the state,"
according to the *Lancaster
Saturday Express.* Courtesy
of the Fulton Opera House
Collection, LancasterHis-
tory.org.

FIG 6
Christopher Hager. A
merchant, banker, volunteer
fireman, trustee of the local
college, and founder and early manager of the Conestoga
Cotton Mills, Christopher
Hager (1800–1868) spent
more than $22,000 to build
Fulton Hall in 1852. Courtesy of LancasterHistory.org,
Lancaster, Pa., 2160928.

FIG 7
Sculpture of Robert Fulton,
Fulton Theatre. In 1854,
workmen installed a seven-
foot cedar figure of engineer
and inventor Robert Fulton
above the main entrance to
Fulton Hall. The Lancaster-
born Fulton (1765–1815)
launched the first commercial steamboat on American
waters. Courtesy of Lan-
casterHistory.org, Lancaster,
Pa., 1020151.

FIG 8 (*above*)
Blasius and Mary Yecker, ca.
1855. German-born Blasius and
Mary Yecker were married in
Lancaster in 1855, eleven years
before he purchased Fulton Hall.
The first of their seven children
was born in 1856. Courtesy of
Paul E. Yecker Sr.

FIG 9 (*below*)
Fencibles drilling in down-
town Lancaster, Pennsylvania.
During the Civil War, Fulton
Hall served as a home base
and armory for the Lancaster
Fencibles, who also used the
building for military drills—as
did the Lancaster Rifles, Jackson
Rifles, and Lancaster Guards.
Courtesy of LancasterHistory
.org, Lancaster, Pa., D070359.

FIG 12
Edwin Forrest Durang. A specialist in ecclesiastical structures, Philadelphia architect Edwin Forrest Durang oversaw the renovation of Fulton Hall in 1873. Edwin was the the son of actor and stage historian Charles Durang and the grandson of Lancaster-born John Durang, one of the first American actors. Courtesy of Athenaeum of Philadelphia.

FIG 13
Joseph Keppler, *Mark Twain, America's Best Humorist.* When Mark Twain brought his raucous account of "roughing it" in the American West to Fulton Hall in 1872, the theater sold out. Courtesy of the Library of Congress, LC-USZC4-4294.

PUCKOGRAPHS—NEW SERIES, NO. I.

"MARK TWAIN,"
AMERICA'S BEST HUMORIST.

FIG 14
Water Street, showing the rear
of the Fulton Theatre, ca. 1873.
The construction of a rail line
on Water Street in the 1870s
meant stagehands could unload
shows directly onto the Fulton's
second-story loading dock. The
stone portion of the theater's rear
wall originally belonged to the
Lancaster jail and workhouse.
Courtesy of LancasterHistory.org,
Lancaster, Pa., LC011146.

FIG 15
Blasius Yecker, studio portrait,
ca. 1873. In a matter of decades,
Blasius Yecker (1834–1903) went
from being an immigrant harness maker to a civic leader and
model of bourgeois respectability.
As a theatrical manager, he was
known for his "genial manners
and square dealing" and his "rare
discrimination." Courtesy of Paul
E. Yecker Sr.

FIG 16
Advertisement for *Uncle Tom's Cabin*, Fulton Hall, 1878. The single most-produced play in the history of the American theater, *Uncle Tom's Cabin* played the Fulton nearly seventy times between 1866 and 1927. Courtesy of the Fulton Opera House Collection, LancasterHistory.org.

FIG 17
Advertisement for Buffalo Bill and His Mammoth Combination at the Fulton Opera House, 1881. A bullet fired by William F. Cody—better known as Buffalo Bill, who played the Fulton six times—was long rumored to be lodged in the molding above the Fulton stage. Courtesy of the Fulton Opera House Collection, LancasterHistory.org.

FIG 18
Buffalo Bill in Lancaster,
Pennsylvania. Buffalo Bill
often preceded his perfor-
mances by parading through
Lancaster with his entourage.
Riding behind him here is
Iron Tail, the Oglala Lakota
chief whose profile appears
on the buffalo or Indian-head
nickel. Courtesy of Gordon
Wickstrom.

FIG 19
Edwin Booth as Hamlet.
Wherever Edwin Booth went,
he drew huge crowds, but
Booth knew they came as
much to see the brother of
Abraham Lincoln's killer as to
see him. Predictably, Edwin
Booth's 1886 appearance at
the Fulton, as Hamlet, was
a sellout. Courtesy of the
Library of Congress, LC-
USZ62-53046.

FIG 20
Minnie Maddern Fiske. In 1895, Fulton manager Blasius Yecker staked a small claim to theatrical history when he presented the popular American actress Minnie Maddern in her first professional appearance as "Mrs. Fiske." Courtesy of the Library of Congress, LC-USZ62-90017.

FIG 21
Yecker's Fulton Opera House, ca. 1897. A local amateur troupe poses in front of "Yecker's Fulton Opera House." Advertisements from Blasius Yecker's bill-posting firm frame the entrance to the theater. Courtesy of Barbara Dorwart Lehman.

FIG 22
Blasius Yecker and family, ca.
1902. Charles Yecker (*bottom
right*) would become manager
of the Fulton after his father's
death in 1903. Courtesy of Paul
E. Yecker Sr.

FIG 23
Bert Williams in blackface.
With his partner, George
Walker, Bert Williams played
the Fulton five times from 1901
to 1907. Of their first Fulton
appearance, in the blackface
musical *Sons of Ham*, a reviewer
wrote that they were "unusually
black and comical." Courtesy
of the Library of Congress, LC-
USZ62-64929.

FIG 24
Fulton Theatre, ca. 1908. In
the early years of the twentieth
century, manager Charles
Yecker sought to counter the
seductions of moving pictures
by enlarging the Fulton's stage,
adding a second balcony, and
installing box seats, marble
floors, carpeted floors, and
other luxuries. Courtesy of the
Fulton Opera House Collection, LancasterHistory.org.

FIG 25
Fulton Theatre, ca. 1966.
By the 1960s, the Fulton was
mostly a movie house, and
there was talk of razing the
theater to build a parking
garage. Courtesy of Leslie
Stainton.

FIG 26

John Updike (*right*) with actor
Peter Vogt at opening celebration
of *Buchanan Dying*, Lancaster,
Pennsylvania, 1976. Author and
Pennsylvania native John Updike
attended the world premiere of
his only play, *Buchanan Dying*, in
Lancaster in 1976. The play examines the life of President James
Buchanan, a Lancaster resident
who periodically turned up at
Fulton Hall. Courtesy of Archives
and Special Collections, Franklin
and Marshall College.

FIG 27
Fulton Theatre interior, 1995.
After a group of citizens
saved it from destruction in
1964, and the U.S. Depart-
ment of the Interior desig-
nated it a Registered National
Historic Landmark in 1969,
the Fulton resumed its earlier
role as a home to live theater.
Courtesy of the Fulton
Opera House Collection,
LancasterHistory.org. Photo:
Lori Stahl.

11

BUFFALO BILL AND THE AMERICAN WEST: 1873–1882

When he first went onstage he was so frightened he couldn't speak, and someone had to prompt him. At the start of one show, he turned to his wife and pleaded, "Oh, Mamma! I'm a bad actor. Does this look as awful out there as it feels?"

Apparently it did. Reviewers mocked his "absurd attempts to act," his "wild and ineffectual struggles" on the stage. "Nothing could be worse from an artistic point of view," one wrote. Never mind the lines he was asked to declaim, "Then burn, ye cursed Dogs, burn!" "I'll not leave a Redskin to skim the Prairie!"

By the time William Cody played Fulton Hall late in 1873, a scant year after making his stage debut, the reviews were better—Lancaster's *Intelligencer* praised the "sensational acting" of his troupe—but the quality of his performances was never the point. People flocked to his shows for the novelty "of seeing those who in life have enacted the scenes which they depict upon the mimic stage," wrote the *Intelligencer*, whose ads promised "The Originals! Living Heroes! Links between Civilization and Savagery!"

Yecker's theater filled up. In the two months since he had reopened Fulton Hall, the manager had brought in acrobats and pantomimists, *opéra bouffe*, an encore run by E. L. Davenport and his company, and a concert (his third in Yecker's hall) by the pianist and former slave Blind Tom. Cartoonist Thomas Nast, who had recently helped bring down New York City's Tweed Ring, gave a lecture on his exploits, and Lotta Crabtree, the "fairy star of the Gold Rush," brought her banjo-picking and clogging act all the way from the mines of California to the Fulton, and with it a whiff of the American West, that fabled territory so central to the country's newfound sense of self.

Now Yecker was offering the real thing: a cowboy with shoulder-length hair, mustache and goatee, fringed jacket and thigh-high boots, a man who had fought Indians and driven wagon trains. Gaze at him and you beheld the West, or what was left of it. Not yet twenty-eight and already a star, he had a handsome face and regal carriage that made women swoon. This larger-than-life phenomenon, this "Buffalo Bill," as he called himself, arrived in Fulton Hall one week before Christmas with a retinue of actors and a "Tribe of Wild Indians" in a frontier drama called *Scouts of the Plains*, and the crowds came.

The play itself was tawdry. "The characters are mainly Indians and trappers, who repeatedly amuse themselves by fierce and fatal combats," a reviewer said of an early version of the drama. There was no plot to speak of, just a sequence of fight scenes culminating in tableaux. Dim-witted monologues alternated with tirades calling for the extermination of Native Americans and temperance lectures by the play's author, Ned Buntline, a hard-drinking bigamist and writer of dime novels. Although the show's promoters promised "genuine red men of the woods," the Indians were played by extras with stage names like "Grassy Chief." They died by the dozens on Yecker's stage that December night—whipped, burned, knifed, and shot, their red-flannel scalps brandished in the air.

Critics across America had dismissed the show as "a nondescript dramatic piece miscalled a play" (New York), an "incongruous drama" with "execrable acting" and an "intolerable stench" (Chicago), a "brutal, commonplace, and disgraceful" exercise whose audiences were "the great unwashed" (Boston). But *Scouts of the Plains* was a hit. Credit that mostly to its star, who later said of his theatrical career, "I didn't try to act. I did what I used to do on the prairie, not what I thought some other fellow might have done if he felt that way."

He played a frontiersman playing an actor playing a frontiersman, and in that complex tangle lay his appeal. The "great unwashed" put up with the corny postures and wooden lines because they knew that underneath

them stood a man who had actually done what he was pretending to do—
Barnum without the humbug.

Born William F. Cody, he called himself Buffalo Bill after the hundreds
of animals he had slain on the Great Plains so that the crews building
America's railroads could eat. Take almost any job available to a young
man in the West in the 1860s, and Cody had tried it: soldier, scout, mes-
senger, guide, horse thief, gold prospector, teamster, and hotel operator,
the latter with his wife, Louisa, a girl he had met in St. Louis. He'd shown
off his frontier skills in horse races, buffalo-shooting competitions, and
safaris for American businessmen and European aristocrats.

In 1869, the year he turned twenty-three, he had met Edward Zane
Carroll Judson, better known as Ned Buntline. They were an incongruous
pair—the tall, swashbuckling Cody and the short, slouching Buntline, an
army veteran in his forties with a mass of coiled black hair and a walrus
moustache, whose résumé included a couple of jail sentences, one riot, two
wives, a pair of duels, a failed lynching, and several lawsuits. Buntline had
been a writer since his twenties and by the time he met Cody was earning
as much as $20,000 a year manufacturing fiction for the firm of Beadle
and Adams, which cranked out books on an assembly line. He had been
searching for a new adventure hero, and in Cody he found one. *Buffalo
Bill, the King of the Border Men*, the first of Buntline's serial novels about
the dashing scout, began appearing later that year in the *New York Weekly*.

The earliest fans of dime novels had been Civil War soldiers, both
Union and Confederate, to whom their respective armies shipped blood-
and-thunders "by cords, like unsawed firewood," according to a contemporary. After the war, the books drew a mostly eastern and male readership
who thrilled to the battles and gore that packed their cheap little pages. If
war had torn the nation into North and South, dime novels helped stitch
it back together again with their depiction of a West that didn't much matter to anyone except as a backdrop for killing Indians.

This new America, unbounded and whole, became the repository of a
ferocious longing, and theaters like Yecker's were its immediate beneficia-
ries. Buntline's hero quickly made the transition from book to stage. The
first Buffalo Bill drama debuted in 1871. When Cody went to New York to
see it, the manager of the theater made him go onstage at intermission and
take a bow. The next year Cody agreed to play himself in a new Bill show—
the specter of big money proving irresistible—and man and myth became
one. The play opened in December, Cody's off-season, and for the next

decade he kept to this schedule, spending his winters onstage and his summers out west scouting and hunting.

Lancastrians loved him. From 1873 to 1882, Cody played Fulton Hall six times and only once failed to draw a sizable audience. At one performance, Yecker opened his doors to find "a mass of yelling and surging humanity, all anxious to see the hero of the plains." The noisy crowd swarmed into the vestibule, through the oilcloth doors shielding the entrances to the parquette and parquette circle and up the staircase into the balcony. Yecker's red-and-gold auditorium was "literally packed from pit to dome with as noisy a crowd of persons as we have ever had the misfortune to see at any performance," the *Daily Examiner and Express* reported gloomily.

Cody and his troupes served up kidnappings, knife fights, gun battles, prairie fires, live animals, scenes of Mormon life, and reenactments of actual events such as the Mountain Meadows Massacre. The bullets and horses were authentic, and after a time so were the Indians. "The delineations of frontier life by this company are very real and startling," the *New Era* reminded Fulton theatergoers before one show.

After their first season together, Cody had dropped Buntline, formed his own combination troupe, and found better scripts, but the plot line that made his shows such a hit remained essentially the same: white men battled and vanquished their Indian tormentors. "It was cheerful to contemplate the way in which virtue was rewarded and villainy punished," read an 1881 review in Lancaster's *Intelligencer*, "and in the denouement nothing was wanting to complete the satisfaction of right-minded people nor to point the moral with which this thrilling tale is adorned."

When he first began hiring genuine natives to play themselves, in 1878, Cody ran into trouble with the U.S. government, which objected to the removal of Indians from the reservations into which they'd been herded. Cody replied that he felt he was "benefitting the Indians as well as the government, by taking them all over the United States, and giving them a correct idea of the customs, life, etc., of the pale faces, so that when they returned to their people they could make known all they had seen." Such was his clout that the government allowed the actor to take a band of Pawnee Indians on tour with him so long as he supplied bonds to guarantee their safe return at the end of the season. The once-ferocious Pawnees submitted to the arrangement because they'd been pushed off their lands in Nebraska and needed work. As part of Buffalo Bill's entourage they recovered a measure of the freedom their ancestors had taken for granted.

Soon they were joined by other Plains natives, who found in Cody's shows a way both to earn a living and to perpetuate the traditions federal troops were bent on annihilating, the songs and dances and games that kept their cosmos intact.

In exchange they agreed to let Buffalo Bill and his sidekicks curse and wound and slay them onstage. Night upon night, in city after city, they sprawled their limp bodies across the floor and listened to their killers trumpet another victory. Many of them had experienced the same humiliations in real life, and that was part of the draw. Cody's maudlin parodies of what was happening to Indians throughout the West—of what had happened more than a century earlier to the Conestogas—enthralled audiences in the East, who saw the glamorous cowboy as a model of virtue, a good American.

Before his fourth appearance on Yecker's stage, in 1880, Cody paraded through Lancaster with his company, and people lined the streets to gawk at the spectacle, much as they had in the previous century during the city's great treaty sessions. Young boys in knickers trotted alongside Cody and his Indians, who wore massive headdresses and carried tall spears trimmed in feathers. A military band played, and there was Cody himself at the head of it all, long hair billowing onto his shoulders, gloved hands gripping the reins of a stallion, his gaze fixed just above the crowd. "I'm not an actor," he once told a journalist. "I'm a star." One of his partners said Cody saw himself as "a Tin Jesus on horseback."

This particular show, *Knight of the Plains*, featured a "Band of Genuine Indians in their War and Medicine Dances," with the added pleasures of a young Pawnee chief, a "Jew money lender, Shyster Judge," a fop, and a border heroine. Cody, as always, displayed his "Marvelous Shooting with the Rifle." In this and other shows at Fulton Hall, he shot apples and potatoes from ladies' heads and cigars from men's mouths, often holding his rifle upside down or firing backwards with the help of a mirror.

When I learned to give tours of the Fulton in the early 1980s, I was told to point to a small indentation at the top of the proscenium and say that it came from one of Buffalo Bill's guns. I never quite believed the story, but that didn't stop me from repeating it, or from wanting to believe that Cody—debonair, fearless, larger than life—had indeed left his mark on our theater. But of course he had done that to the country at large, given America a vision of the West that became our idea of the West. And he did it with panache, blurring the line between performance and life in ways that fired the imagination. Other border dramas came and went—and they came to the Fulton in abundance in those days, plays about Davy Crockett and Jesse James and Daniel Boone, about pioneers and rangers, miners and sharpshooters and Mormons with "one hundred wives"—but Cody's shows were true in a way the rest weren't. Audiences put up with his contrived plots and crude stage effects because the man at their center was authentic. Cody walked through the doors of the Fulton and brought the West with him. You could smell it in his gunpowder and on his clothes.

This singular American actor played only himself. He never dabbled in Shakespeare, never went through the rituals of "becoming" someone else, made up or real. He never risked getting lost in a role, because he *was* the role. When he fought and killed a Cheyenne chief named Yellow Hair out in Wyoming in the summer of 1876, less than a month after the death of George Armstrong Custer, Cody reportedly wore a stage costume—a black velvet Mexican vaquero outfit with silver buttons—and carried out the murder in the presence of a U.S. cavalry brigade, who cheered the actor as they rode past the scene. Cody then toured the East in a drama about the killing, which he called *The Red Right Hand; Or, Buffalo Bill's First Scalp for Custer*. For a time he put Yellow Hair's actual scalp on display, until members of the clergy and press cried *enough*.

To an extent audiences found exhilarating, Cody framed his life as theater. He took part in events he knew he could later market to the public onstage. As my friend and former theater professor Gordon Wickstrom writes, "He was an actor and more than an actor: a kind of prophet/preacher in an extraordinary pulpit, the incarnation of his message with a shaman's power to evoke in the consciousness of his audiences the very presence of the western prairies." Cody never lost track of the fact that he was acting, nor did his admirers. *Oskate Wicasa*, some of Cody's Sioux friends called him: *He Who Performs*.

Through his plays and later the grand outdoor extravaganzas he called Wild West Exhibitions, which he brought to Lancaster repeatedly, long after he'd stopped appearing inside theaters like the Fulton, Buffalo Bill inspired young men to follow him out to the frontier. Blasius Yecker's sons Victor and Benjamin both went west to help build the American railroad, and in the spring of 1886 their father joined them for a visit. As he stood at the station in Lancaster awaiting his train, the fifty-two-year-old manager wore a "placid smile," reporters saw. He had yet to become an American citizen, even after three decades in the country, but, like thousands of others, he felt a sense of curiosity and entitlement when it came to the vast landscapes west of the Mississippi valley. The Lancaster papers were full of accounts by locals who had done just as Yecker and his sons were doing, crossed the continent to take in "What May Be Seen on the Plains," as one front-page article put it. In another few years that same experience would lead the Wellesley English professor Katharine Lee Bates to write a poem celebrating the amber waves of grain she saw from the windows of her train as it crossed Kansas, the spacious skies and purple mountains and countless "pilgrim feet," hers and Yecker's among them, that were beating a "thoroughfare for freedom . . . across the wilderness."

The completion of the railroad was devastating to the indigenous inhabitants of the North American wilderness. Trains drove the buffalo off the plains and the Indians from their hunting grounds, and that made it easier for the government to force tribes throughout the West onto reservations. William F. Cody, hired by the government to keep order on the frontier and by the railroad to feed its workers at a rate of twelve buffalo a day, played a leading role in this sorry drama. He liked the Indians, and many were friendly with him, but he helped destroy their way of life. Between 1872 and 1874, nearly four million buffalo perished in the West, most at the hands of white hunters and soldiers who left the carcasses to rot. Asked to justify the butchery, U.S. General Philip Sheridan said, "Let them kill, skin, and sell until the buffalo is exterminated, as it is the only way to bring lasting peace and allow civilization to advance."

At the end of Arthur Kopit's play *Indians*, written in 1969 in response to another government misadventure, Buffalo Bill surveys the slaughter at Wounded Knee and tells the ghost of Sitting Bull, who had once toured with him, "For awhile, I actually thought my Wild West Show would *help*. I could give you money. Food. Clothing. And also make people *understand* things . . . better."

SITTING BULL (*Slight smile*): Your show was very popular.
(*Pause.*)
BUFFALO BILL: We had . . . *fun*, though, you and I.
(*Pause.*)
Didn't we?

SITTING BULL: Oh, yes. And that's the terrible thing. We had all surrendered. We were on reservations. We could not fight, or hunt. We could do nothing. Then you came and allowed us to imitate our glory. . . . It was humiliating! For sometimes, we could almost imagine it was real.

BUFFALO BILL: Guess it wasn't so authentic, was it?

(*He laughs silently to himself.*)

SITTING BULL: How could it have been? You'd have killed all your performers in one afternoon.

Cody's genius had been to substitute imagery for the real thing, to package Indians as harmless showmen and the West as a romantic destination eastern spectators could enjoy. An ad in the *New Orleans Daily Picayune* assured audiences that in Cody's Wild West Show they would "see Scenes that have Cost Thousands their Lives to View." Like the black actors who plied the minstrel trade, Indians signed on with Cody because it was one of the few ways they could still be themselves. By the time Buffalo Bill stopped performing, just two months before his death in 1917, his was the only Wild West in existence: the real one had vanished. The Census Bureau declared the American frontier officially closed in 1890, the same year Indian police murdered Sitting Bull at the behest of the federal government.

Did the Pawnee and Nez Percé and Sioux and Cheyenne who accompanied Cody to the Fulton in the 1870s and early 1880s realize they were treading ground that had once been the frontier? The murder of the Conestogas was merely a curtain raiser in a tragedy that subsequently played out across America. One by one, Delaware, Cherokee, Choctaw, Chickasaw, Shawnee, Cheyenne, Sioux, Chippewa, Navajo, Apache, Modoc, Nez Percé, Comanche were pushed off their land, bribed, duped, starved, shot, raped, jailed, tortured, killed, mutilated. Eyewitness accounts of the genocide read just like William Henry's description of the Paxton massacre: "I saw one squaw cut open with an unborn child, as I thought, lying by her side"; "I found quite a number of women shot while asleep"; "The wounded who were unable to get away had their brains beaten out"; "One infant of some ten months was shot twice and one leg hacked nearly off." The killing went on for more than a hundred years.

After removing the Navajo from their ancestral lands in New Mexico in 1865, U.S. General James Carleton remarked that their exodus was "a touching sight." When at last the Indians realized it was their "destiny . . . to give way to the insatiable progress of our race, they threw down their arms, and, as brave men entitled to our admiration and respect, have come to us with confidence in our magnanimity."

Shortly before 1880, the year Cody made his fourth visit to Fulton Hall, the bones of the Conestoga Indians were unearthed for the second time since their interment—in both instances to make way for new rail lines. This time their remains were put into an unmarked packing case and buried under a rail embankment and subsequently forgotten. No one today knows with certainty where they are. That same year, Indians throughout the West were performing ghost dances in a vain effort to vanquish their white assailants and to lure both the buffalo and the Native dead back to life.

One could say that Cody was also summoning the dead each time he strode into Fulton Hall. I can see him onstage, the dark eyes and smooth, almost feminine face, the cascade of brunette curls. "I'm afraid that even with the stories of his prowess on the plains, Buffalo Bill would not have been Buffalo Bill without that long hair," his wife wrote after his death. In his last years, Cody took to wearing a wig in order to preserve his famous looks, and once, as he swept off his hat, the wig came off too, but reporters and fans pretended not to notice.

A century later, there we were on the same Fulton stage, pretending he walked among us. We called our ghost dance *Annie Get Your Gun*, and we too painted our faces and gathered at night to dance and sing in an effort to conjure the dead. We aimed our fake rifles at the same spot on the proscenium where the real Bill had supposedly lodged a bullet, and we fired, and the theater filled with the acrid smell of smoke, as it had in Cody's time, and before, during the war, when the Fencibles practiced their marksmanship inside Fulton Hall, and earlier, when the Paxton gang came crashing through the basement doors to vent their fury on fourteen human beings huddled in the cold.

One nineteenth-century critic wrote of Buffalo Bill's Wild West exhibition, "It is not a show. It is a resurrection." Historian Joy Kasson terms his Wild West "a passion play for the American frontier." In the person of William F. Cody, Americans found the hero they needed in order to live with the crimes they were committing. The city of Lancaster, Pennsylvania, had played its part in the malfeasance through the manufacture and sale of rifles to be used "in pursuance of treaties" with western Indians "for lands purchased" by the government, as one press account had it. And so when Buffalo Bill appeared in his chaps and Stetson before the citizens of Lancaster on the stage of Fulton Hall, with his white horse and a troupe of willing Indians, people were reassured. It was as if none of it had ever happened, none of it at all.

12

MEMORY MACHINE

Think of the buildings that anchor your life: not merely the homes, which may be many and ancestral, but the public buildings to which you migrate out of habit or devotion, the buildings that ground your existence. The temples, libraries, museums, theaters, schools, halls, fortresses, monuments, shrines where you have lost yourself and been lost, sought and found, remembered and forgotten. You enter such a place after years of being away, believing it is in some measure *yours*, even though common sense tells you it belongs to others, which is to say to no one. Nostalgia couples with hope; you try to slice through time to retrieve (or at the very least touch) the person you were when you first came here. Or more accurately: you seek to retrieve your own astonishment. Can the walls still speak? Their scent elicits a slight gasp of recognition. Here I am again, you say to yourself. Still alive. This assemblage of wood, plaster, stone, brick, steel, doors, ceilings, steps, windows, closets, thresholds, hearths, chambers, floors, echoes, pattern, air, figure, light resides in you as much as you reside in it. Are we *here*, Rilke asks,

perhaps just to say:
house, bridge, well, gate, jug, fruit tree, window—

at most column, tower . . . but to *say*, understand this, to say it
as the Things themselves never fervently thought to be.

The buildings that embody our deepest dreams are forever summoning
our past and gnawing into our future; they contain us as nothing else does,
not our human companions, not our grandparents or children. Even when
they disappear they hold us tight. Gaston Bachelard speaks of the sites we
cherish as "eulogized space." "Space that has been seized upon by the imagination," he writes, "cannot remain indifferent space subject to the mea-
sures and estimates of the surveyor."

This is not to say such places are without their darkness. Although it is
tempting to cling to the brighter parts of the buildings we love (the white
façade, the shiny roof), to truly dwell in a site you must acknowledge its
depths. You must go down into the cellar and touch the old trees that hold
the floors in place and crouch in the shadows they cast; you must visit the
crypt.

The first permanent dwellings our nomadic ancestors stopped to construct were burial sites for the dead: caverns, barrows, mounds. "It is not
only places, then, but also nations and empires, which repose on such
human—call them humic—foundations," Robert Pogue Harrison writes
in his treatise on death and burial, *The Dominion of the Dead*. Sometimes
this is literally the case, as in 1852 when workmen digging the foundations
of Fulton Hall unearthed the remains of a human skeleton and its coffin.
(The discovery prompted a reporter to ask, "Who buried him (or her)
there, and why was an obscure corner of the jailyard selected as the tomb
of a secret?")

"Humans bury," Harrison suggests, "not simply to achieve closure and
effect a separation from the dead, but also and above all to humanize the
ground on which they build their worlds and found their histories." It is
no accident that so much of the world's architecture is funerary: we are
afraid of forgetting the people who are precious to us. But a dwelling need
not be consecrated to the dead to remind us of their presence. To enter
some buildings is not merely to cross a line from exterior to interior but to
trespass on the deceased.

Step from a corridor into a room, and the sigh of the rug beneath your
shoes reminds you of a voice you last heard in college. A chair by a window
brings back a glimpse of your grandmother sipping coffee before dawn and
waiting for the birds to come to her feeder. The dim glow of an empty

auditorium reminds you of a woman you loved, who has been gone these ten years but is abruptly here beside you, her translucent face floating above your shoulder. In time you reach a point when the pleasures of these hauntings outweigh their terrors, when a building becomes dear to you as much for what it has lost as for what it contains, and you wander its halls even though you are thousands of miles away.

Practitioners of the classical art of rhetoric understood the peculiar power of architecture to stimulate memory. Orators mentally stored the components of their speeches in the different rooms of specific buildings, and when called on to recite a given text thought their way through its associated building, room by room. Churches were preferred for this activity because they were quiet, but the ingenious sixteenth-century Italian philosopher Giulio Camillo came up with the idea of using a theater as a machine for remembering. He built a wooden amphitheater large enough to hold one or at most two visitors, and he filled it with images and little drawers. Spectators who stood inside the space beheld a profusion of icons, each capable of provoking thought.

"He calls this theater of his by many names, saying now that it is a built or constructed mind and soul, and now that it is a windowed one," wrote a colleague who traveled to Venice to see Camillo's invention. The remarkable structure triggered both personal and collective memory, and I can only guess that to experience it in person was like going to a play: you were flooded with images that stirred your heart and fired your brain cells. Here was the ancient Greek *theatron* incarnate, a place for literal as well as figurative *seeing*. Camillo himself said he called his device a "theater" because it made visible what was otherwise "hidden in the depths of the human mind."

A century later an Englishman named Robert Fludd picked up where Camillo had left off and designed a stage whose various entrances served as mnemonic prompts. Fludd's theater, like Camillo's, was a repository of cosmic knowledge, a small world that epitomized the larger one. In his two-volume discourse on the topic, Fludd placed his image of a memory theater opposite one of the zodiac, so that when his book was shut the heavens covered the stage.

The earliest theaters really did open to the heavens, but even those stages that are shut to the external world hint at its dualities: sky and earth, firmament and grave. My own first theater, the showboat I received for Christmas when I was six, had "windows in the back and all the other things on the side and in the middle is the stage," I wrote exuberantly to an aunt that year. It was my private universe, a tiny arena where I could bring to life people and events that did not in fact exist, and although I've long since outgrown that first stage of my theatrical life, its echoes reverberate every time I walk into a playhouse.

Perhaps in this way we truly come to possess the places we received as children. Of a childhood spent largely in church pews (and occasionally in movie seats), Michael Mitchell, artistic director of the Fulton from 1998 to 2008, said, "That's really where I probably had my first exposure to theater."

> And these things that live,
> slipping away, understand that you praise them;
> transitory themselves, they trust us for rescue,
> us, the most transient of all.

When I gave tours of the Fulton in the 1980s, I liked to take people into the crawl space beneath the auditorium. I still go there when I can. It's a long, dim tunnel with a low ceiling whose few lights cast thick shadows, but once your eyes adjust to the dark, you can see the logs and bricks and stones that tether the theater to the ground. This is literally the case, because the flooring on either side of the cement aisle that bisects the room is soil, Harrison's humic foundations. You can touch it with your hands. *To be here is much*, Rilke writes. Maybe that's why I come: to scratch at the dirt and brave the night, even in the fullness of a spring afternoon. To feel the walls dissolve and the lost world pour in, as sure as the earth beneath my fingers.

13

THE MINSTREL'S MASK: 1852–1927

The process was easy: you set fire to a cork, let it burn, moistened the black ash with water, greased your face with cocoa butter, then spread the ash on top. You outlined your eyes and mouth in white chalk and put carmine on your lips, the better to imitate the gaping stares and bright grins of the plantation darkies. Add a fright wig, baggy pants, oversized shoes, a swallowtail coat with a flashy boutonniere. Pick at a banjo, clap *dem bones, de dancing nigger dey call Jim Crow.* Shuffle and slur your way across the stage, *turn about an' wheel about an' do jis so.*

Twitch your arm, then your shoulder. Laugh. Jiggle your leg. Be the butt of a joke. Go on, let them bait you. Let them peel you like a potato, *chaw* you like a plug of tobacco—

> Natur planted a black baby,
> To grow dis weed divine,
> Dat's de reason why de niggers
> Am made a 'baccy sign

Listen to the crowd bellow. There goes Bones, clicking his sticks. His arms are flailing, watch him skitter, *ah, hoo, ah, hoo.* Sam here beside you, he's singing a coon ditty.

On de Mississippi Riber, I used to cook de pork and beans,
Chief cook aboard a steamboat dat run to New Orleans.
I recomember well it was in de month of June,
Darkies, take de banjo down, and gib de boys a tune—

Well, you is de hungryest nigger eber I saw, you cry out to him. *You'r neber satisfied widout your tinken bout bean soup all de time.*

The folks out front are roaring. Go for another. *Say, Sam, why is a nigger's nose placed in de middle of his face?*

Dunno.

Because it's a scenter.

Reach over and pick up the banjo, wrap your hand around its long, skinny neck, start plucking. Keep time with your toes. That's it. The fiddler's just warming up, hear him squeak? Bones is pounding his foot on the floor now and making all kinds of noise, *ra, raka, taka, tak.* Tambo's thumping away, holding his instrument up in the air, jingling it nonstop. Nothing goes with anything else in this scratchy, scruffy, cackling band of yours. It's all twang and clatter, but the folks out there can't get enough of it. Listen to them clapping time, clumping the floor with their boots.

Now it's time for something soft. You look at one another and nod, slow down, suck in the air, let the song come. It's just you on the banjo now, your voice and theirs sweetly mingling, the crowd momentarily stilled, clutching at the words—

'Twas on the old plantation, not many years ago,
Our work was done at set of sun, we quit the spade and hoe;
And on the green were darkies seen, in many a happy row,
Dancing to the music of the bones and ole banjo.
Our hearts were light, the moon shone bright, kind massa he
    was dere,
For nothing did him more delight, our joys and sports to share.

Later in the evening, after the crowd's gone home and the buzz in the hall has dimmed, after the jokes and speeches, the Women's Rights Lecture (*I tink de ladies oughter vote*), the Radish Girl and Molly Malone, after Dandy Jim and the beautiful Miss Lucy Long, the Live Injin and plantation skit, after the props have all been packed away, the clock and table and pistol and clubs and carpet bags and brooms—afterward, backstage in the dressing room that Mr. Yecker has thoughtfully provided, you pick up a cake of cocoa butter and rub it gently over your face, and with a dry piece of cloth you wipe the black away.

OLIO

To redheaded Sam Clemens, not yet ten, the minstrels who pulled into Hannibal, Missouri, were a "glad and stunning surprise." The boy laughed at the coal-black faces and hands, the patchwork clothes and lips so red and thick they could have been "slices cut in a ripe watermelon." He especially liked it when the Negroes quarreled.

—Stop looking at me dat way or I'll chuck you in de jaw.
—Go way, boy.
—Just come around de corner and I'll give you more trouble dan you can store away in a coon's age.

Only they weren't Negroes like the slaves all around him in Hannibal, they were white men with black faces, which was half the fun. They jittered and whooped just like the slaves, though, and they told tall tales—*He swallowed two small rail roads wid a spoonful of ice cream*—which the boy loved.

By the time he was old enough to be spinning his own tales, the war had ended and the slaves were free. But the shows kept coming, and now the blacks were real. They corked up just like the white folks and told jokes on themselves and sang sad tunes about how they missed the cotton fields. *Oh! darkies how my heart grows weary, far from de old folks at home.*

By then he'd taken to calling himself Mark Twain. Soon he too was touring, playing the same halls as the minstrels did, Hartford and Philadelphia and Albany and Toledo and Lancaster, lecturing on his adventures and getting the same crowds to snicker. A reviewer in Chicago told how Mr. Twain "bestrode the stage as if it were a steamboat" and spoke in a nasal snarl, "punctuating his tardy fun with the most complicated awkwardness of gesture. Now he snapped his fingers; now he rubbed his hands softly, like the catcher of the champion nine; now he caressed his left palm with his dexter fingers, like the end minstrel-man propounding a conundrum." (*Why is Sunday de strongest day, Sam?—Because de others are all weekdays.*) The papers in Lancaster, Pennsylvania, reprinted the remarks of the

Chicago reviewer just before Twain spoke at Fulton Hall in early 1872, and the theater filled with people eager to clap eyes on the tall westerner whose ninety-minute talk, they agreed, was the sensation of the season.

He had grown up with blacks and considered them friends, the differences in their status notwithstanding, and he would soon embark on a book about a white boy and a runaway slave in which he succeeded in illuminating "the parasitical nature of white freedom," as Toni Morrison has expressed it. As a boy in Hannibal he had seen his father beat the family's one slave and later sell her down the river, young Sam Clemens in tears, and one day he'd happened to glimpse a dozen black men and women chained together, waiting to be shipped to New Orleans. "Those were the saddest faces I have ever seen," he remembered.

To come of age in the United States at that time was to grapple with the contradictions of a land where people trumpeted liberty but sold and bought human beings whom they considered a separate, uniquely debased species. "Thus," explained Louisiana physician and "Professor of Negro Diseases" Samuel Cartwright, who often testified in slave cases, "they break, waste, and destroy everything they handle; abuse horses and cattle; tear, burn, or rend their own clothing."

The minstrel troupes who played Hannibal, Missouri—who played Fulton Hall from its inception in 1852 until the century turned—mimed such tomfoolery. Sloppy and dumb in their big shoes and tattered pants, they wisecracked and clowned about and tricked and thieved. They mocked the Irish, the Germans, the Chinese, the Indians, the black dandy of the urban North, the ladies who would be their equals—

> When woman's rights is stirred a bit
> De first reform she bitches on
> Is how she can wid least delay
> Just draw a pair ob britches on.

They mangled operas and misspoke Shakespeare (*Friends, Romans, countrymen! Lend me your ears. I will return them next Saturday*). They put on dresses, played the wench and prima donna and funny ol' gal, clogged, strutted, jigged, performed instrumental solos, and sang ballads in which they occasionally mourned their lot but mainly embraced it: *Dis being free says ole Mammy Winny, / Is worser den being a slave*—

Oh! darkies all take warning,
Never 'tempt to roam,
For de Abolition folks won't support you,
Den you'll wish yourself at home.

In an essay he called "Change the Joke and Slip the Yoke," Ralph Ellison described minstrelsy as a "ritual of exorcism," an outgrowth of white Americans' "Manichean fascination with the symbolism of blackness and whiteness." To a white America straining to deal with what Morrison has termed "the racial disingenuousness and moral frailty at its heart," burnt-cork performance introduced a new language, one that spoke in codes:

> Ethiopian minstrelsy has become one of the standard amusements of the American people, and will continue to be such, so long as the heart is moved by simple melody, or the risibles can be excited by real wit, and though many have decried this style of amusement as being vulgar, or not exactly refined, still it has continued to gain ground in favor of the masses; for while it does not furnish the obscenity of the Moral Drama, it simply portrays, in a jocular manner, the peculiarities of a race we all have a common interest in.

> —*Matt Peel's Banjo: Being a Selection of the Most Popular and Laughable Negro Melodies, as Sung by the Renowned Peel's Campbell's Minstrels*, 1858

> In the march of time there has been a marked improvement both in the negro and the character of the entertainment designed to portray his peculiarities.

> —*Bones—His Gags and Stump Speeches; Nigger and Dutch Stories and Dialogues*, 1879

> Minstrelsy is the one American form of amusement, purely our own, and it has lived and thrived even though the plantation darkey, who first gave it a character, has departed.

> —*The Witmark Amateur Minstrel Guide and Burnt Cork Encyclopedia*, 1899

Three months after Twain appeared in Lancaster, the all-black Original Georgia Minstrel Slave Troupe played Fulton Hall. Hailed in the local press as "a company of negro 'Nigger Minstrels'" whose every member "seemed to be a gentleman—more than we can say of some 'white nig-gers,'" the Georgia troupe offered the usual mix of skits and songs, topped by a "characteristic representation of plantation life," which Northern theatergoers particularly enjoyed. In different configurations and under various managers and names—Callender's, Haverly's, Sprague's—all-black companies calling themselves "Georgia Minstrels" returned to the Fulton more than a dozen times in the 1870s and '80s, along with scores of other minstrel acts.

To white audiences the Georgia minstrels represented "the darky as he is at home, darky life in the cornfield, canebrake, barnyard, and on the levee and flatboat," said company manager Charles Callender, a white man. To the African American artists who joined the troupe and corked up nightly in the dressing rooms of theaters such as Yecker's, blackface offered favorable wages and a chance to display their talents. "It is something gained, when the colored man in any form can appear before a white audi-ence," said the former slave Frederick Douglass, who nonetheless despised the racial stereotypes minstrelsy perpetuated.

The men in the Georgia troupe were hugely gifted: bones soloist George Danforth was one of the best in the business; you could count on singers Dick Little and Sam Lucas to bring down the house with their renditions of character songs like "Shivering and Shaking." (Lucas had the distinction of being the first black actor to play Uncle Tom, in 1878.) Company mem-bers were so good they received invitations to perform in churches and on the concert stage, and some toured with legitimate African American shows like the Hyers Sisters Combination and the Fisk University Jubilee Singers, both of which came to Fulton Hall. On these occasions the enter-tainers appeared unmasked, in their own clothes and skin. *Go down, Moses,* they keened, *way down in Egypt land. Tell ole Pharaoh, Let my people go.* W. E. B. Du Bois praised the Fisk singers for introducing the world to "the Negro folk-song," which he thought "the most beautiful expression of human experience born this side of the sea." But because they earned less money performing as themselves, most black singers and dancers contin-ued to work the minstrel stage.

They were captives of the form. Whites who took part in minstrel shows, many of them immigrants waging their own battles against dis-crimination, passed through the mask of blackface "into an assimilated world," writes theater historian Thomas Postlewait. Blacks who corked up "remained enclosed in the codes of darkness." ("But what does it mean," Postlewait asks, "that one must become black in order to become American?")

Minstrelsy also, paradoxically, freed African Americans to shed the masks of deference and reserve they were expected to don offstage. "We put on blackface," a twentieth-century black actor quipped, "when we had something really *crazy* to say." The stock African American figures of the nineteenth-century stage—Sambo, Zip Coon, Jim Crow—ate, sang, danced, and clowned around. They were, argue cultural historians Yuval Taylor and Jake Austen, "far freer than any slave ever was, and far freer than the black members of their audience, who had to constantly bow to the authority of whites, and be on their best behavior no matter their station."

The golden age of minstrelsy coincided with the collapse of Reconstruction, the departure of federal troops from the former Confederacy, an ascendant Ku Klux Klan, the passage of the first Jim Crow laws, lynchings and mob attacks on African Americans in communities across the South. "Only a 'nigger' killed by mistake," Twain wrote bitterly in 1869 after reading press accounts of an innocent black man who had been lynched in Memphis. "Surely there is no good reason why Southern gentlemen should worry themselves with useless regrets, so long as only an innocent 'nigger' is hanged, or roasted or knouted to death, now and then."

This too was the world of the Georgia minstrels who soft-shoed their way along the Fulton stage to the joy of spectators who relished their antics as much as young Sam Clemens once had. The songs and choruses of blackface performers, said the man who spent his life masquerading as Mark Twain, "were a delight to me as long as the negro show continued in existence." The gaslit stage, the dopey smiles, the clattering shoes: it was magic. Young Sam Clemens had even dreamt of being a minstrel, and in a sense he became one, strutting his stuff in places like Fulton Hall just as they did. He must have enjoyed it when reviewers compared him to an end man. "If I could have the nigger show back again in its pristine purity," he reminisced toward the end of his life, "I should have but little further use for opera."

PLANTATION SKETCH

I don't know what Blasius Yecker thought of black Americans. It's possible he took part in the near-riot in front of Fulton Hall in July of 1863, two weeks after the battle of Gettysburg, when a crowd of German Americans swarmed the theater to protest a draft rally for black soldiers scheduled to take place the following evening inside the hall, along with a speech by Frederick Douglass, whom the *Intelligencer* denounced as a "foulmouthed Negro orator." Fearing a repeat of the draft riots that had bloodied Manhattan that same week, Lancaster authorities canceled Douglass's talk and postponed the rally, and the demonstrators went home.

After the war, after he'd bought and renovated Fulton Hall and turned it into an opera house, Yecker padded his seasons with minstrel shows, often two or three a month. Tommy Mack's, Carncross and Dixey's, Sprague's Famous Georgia, Haverly's Colossal Colored Carnival and Genuine Colored, Dockstader's Mammoth, Baird's New Orleans Minstrels: these and more delivered a steady supply of "ludicrous originalities," "a continual roar of laughter." Some nights the seats inside Yecker's theater sold out, and the aisles filled "to suffocation" with sweating crowds whose feet kept time to the music. People couldn't get enough. When the all-white Lafayette College Glee Club sang at Fulton Hall in 1882, fewer than twenty spectators showed up. "But if it had been a 'nigger show,'" someone suggested, "what a crowd there would have been."

Crowds turned out for blackface productions of *The Octoroon* and *Uncle Tom's Cabin*, which played the Fulton nearly seventy times, in dozens of different renditions, between 1866 and 1927. Stowe's antebellum denunciation of human bondage became a postwar excuse for burnt-cork gaiety. Ads for an 1874 production of *Uncle Tom's Cabin* at Fulton Hall promise slave laments, a plantation slave melody, a plantation festival, and a quartet of slave minstrels, "The Jolly Four Coons." In an era of sometimes bewildering social and technological change, it was reassuring to look up at the Fulton's shiny gold proscenium and see darkies back in their plantation homes strumming the banjo. By the 1890s, as many as five hundred *Tom* companies were touring the country yearly. Audience members saw the show five, six, a dozen or more times.

Every couple of months Yecker brought in a new *Tom*. "Each successive representation of this ancient and absurd play is considerably worse than its predecessor," a local critic complained in 1882. "This is about the tenth *Uncle Tom's Cabin* company that has visited us this season," a colleague wrote some months later, "and no more are wanted." But audiences, ever "loud in their praise and approval" of the play, kept coming. Never mind that the bloodhounds who chased Eliza across the ice were more often

than not underfed mutts, or that the most convincing actors in some productions were the donkeys. After P. T. Barnum and J. A. Bailey merged
their circuses in the early 1880s, double *Uncle Tom's* companies became the
rage, and suddenly there were two Toms, two Topsies, two Simon Legrees
whipping his slaves. One actor spoke or sang while the other mimed or
played the banjo, as if you were watching them through a stereoscope.

The spectacle was exotic, especially in Lancaster, where the city's relatively few African Americans kept largely to themselves in a neighborhood
southeast of Fulton Hall. Most were poor and ill-educated and worked
menial jobs, which was still the case eighty years later when I was growing
up. As a kid, I seldom crossed paths with blacks in Lancaster except for a
short period when I was very young and we had an African American
cleaning lady named Katie, who lived in a row house south of King Street.
Once a week my mother would pile us into the station wagon and drive
into town to get her. One day I was sitting in the front seat of the car, with
Katie behind me, and I turned around and stared at her. She had silver hair
and deep brown eyes, and she smiled at me with exquisite calm as I studied
her. When we got home and she was out of earshot, my mother shook her
finger at me and told me never to do that again, it was rude and I had no
business staring at Katie just because she was black. To this day I don't
know what I was looking at—I recall only Katie's kind face—but I suspect
my mother's instincts were right. I was curious about Katie's skin.

Both of my grandmothers employed black women to cook and clean
and iron for them, and if you went back a hundred years on my mother's
side of the family, you came across slaveholders in Georgia and North
Carolina. My maternal grandmother, born in Brunswick in the last years
of the nineteenth century, said of the Civil War, "There are some things we
don't talk about." I sometimes wondered if she resented her Yankee grandchildren. "Virginia is as far north as I'll ever go," she once told me, and it
was true. She and my grandfather had retired to a small town in the
Northern Neck, where I spent two weeks every summer, and where their
African American cook and housekeeper, Carrie Johnson, taught me to
churn butter and bake rhubarb pies and steam the crabs we trapped in the
Rappahannock.

You don't have to dig far to tap into the murky currents of race that
flow through this country—even when you're the product of a white sub-
urb north of the Mason-Dixon line. I was always, in some sense, peering
over the car seat, trying to fathom what it felt like to be black. We watched

the Civil Rights movement unfold on the tiny black-and-white Sony on our kitchen table, but it was as foreign to me as the war whose images blipped across the same screen. I was young and oblivious, and the lens of whiteness distorted my view. Even now I'm startled to learn from Leroy Hopkins, an African American historian who grew up in Lancaster in the 1940s and '50s, that when he was a boy, his family "never ate out. There was just a feeling that most places we were probably not wanted and besides we had no money to waste." There were unwritten rules. If a black person tried on a hat in a downtown store, like Hager's, "it was theirs whether it fit or not," Hopkins told me. Some of the city's German American residents were "notorious" for not liking blacks, and Hopkins heard tales of people being attacked. But when he and his family went to the Fulton on Sunday afternoons to see a movie, no one bothered them.

African Americans who found their way into Yecker's theater in the late nineteenth century most likely sat in the balcony. An 1887 Pennsylvania law made it a misdemeanor for any theater, restaurant, hotel, or railway manager to refuse admission to someone "on account of race or color," but that didn't mean Yecker had to seat blacks beside whites once they were inside his building. (Nor did everyone obey the law: a whites-only amusement park opened in Lancaster in 1887 and stayed in business until 1966, when its owners chose to shut down rather than integrate.)

You couldn't go from one end of town to the other without being reminded of the war that had been fought in part to free black Americans. A towering gray memorial to Lancaster's Civil War dead, built from the same Rhode Island granite used to build the national monument at Gettysburg, went up in Center Square in 1874. Its uniformed figures gazed out at the passing city, at shoppers and newsboys going about their business, at the Wild West combinations and minstrel troupes and Tommers who paraded through town, horns tooting, on their way to Fulton Hall. The boys and girls who skittered in their wake were predominantly white, as was their city, the number of African Americans in Lancaster having plunged from nearly six thousand before the war to fewer than two thousand by 1900, thanks largely to joblessness and discrimination, which so often went hand in hand. You could be forgiven for thinking this was the natural order of things.

A popular nineteenth-century theory held that America's "second-class" races, notably blacks and Native Americans, were doomed to extinction. Scientists who pushed the concept based their understanding on

Darwinian principles and a eugenic faith in the ascendancy of the "superior" races. Even a man as enlightened as Walt Whitman subscribed to the idea of racial attrition. "The nigger, like the Injun, will be eliminated," he told his biographer. "It is the law of races, history, whatnot: always so far inexorable—always to be. Someone proves that a superior grade of rats comes and then all the minor rats are cleared out."

Perhaps Yecker shared such thinking. He was, after all, an immigrant from northern Europe, and their numbers in Lancaster kept rising, some years by the thousands. Perhaps he felt, as I did growing up in our mostly white city, there was something essentially foreign about the dark-skinned men and women with whom we occasionally crossed paths. From his desk behind the box office in Fulton Hall, Yecker would have seen African American patrons approach the window and inquire about seats. He would have watched them purchase tickets and cross the vestibule to one of the two entrances that led upstairs to the balcony. Inside the auditorium, shielded from the crowd below, they would have taken their seats in chairs that were neither upholstered nor numbered, and they would have gazed out at the stage across the pale heads of their neighbors. When the curtain rose, as it so often did, on a white man's parody of a black man's life, I imagine Yecker's African American patrons would have laughed along with everyone else, much as the black performers onstage were doing and as their enslaved ancestors had done for two hundred years, for that was how you survived.

Frederick Douglass put it this way: "The remark is not infrequently made, that slaves are the most contented and happy laborers in the world. They dance and sing, and make all manners of joyful noises—so they do: but it is a great mistake to suppose them happy because they sing. The songs of the slave represent the sorrows, rather than the joys, of his heart. . . . In the most boisterous outbursts of rapturous sentiment, there was ever a tinge of deep melancholy."

CAKEWALK

His name was Bert Williams, and he was, W. C. Fields famously said, "the funniest man I ever saw, and the saddest man I ever knew."

> My hard luck started when I was born,
> Leas' so the old folks say.

With his partner, George Walker, he played the Fulton Opera House five times. Their first appearance, in 1901, drew praise from a reviewer who described the men as "unusually black and comical" and their production, the blackface musical *Sons of Ham*, as "snappy."

> Dat same hard luck's been my bes' frien'
> To dis vary day.

A year later Williams and Walker returned to the Fulton in their great innovation, a musical written and produced almost exclusively by blacks. *In Dahomey* perpetuated some stereotypes, subverted others, and proved that African Americans could act—none more deftly than Bert Williams. Across Yecker's stage he shambled, the hapless darky, butt of all jokes, pounding his Salvation Army drum and ruing his lot—

> When I was young, Mama's friends—to find a name they tried.
> They named me after Papa—and de same day papa died

The first time he'd blacked up, he sweated so much his makeup ran, and he ended up looking like a zebra. The second time he tried it ("just for a lark"), the results stunned him. "Nobody was more surprised than me when it went like a house on fire. Then I began to find myself."

> Fo' I'm a Jonah, I'm a Jonah man

In the dressing room of Yecker's opera house he dipped his fingers into the black paste again, smeared it onto his face, and wreathed his mouth in red. He put on a shabby suit and battered shoes, slid his graceful hands into a pair of dark gloves—

> My family for many years would look at me
> And den shed tears.

Upstairs, before the laughing crowd, he shrugged his shoulders and flapped his eyelids, wiggled his fingers, played what a reviewer called "the common everyday nigger" who had "only to open his mouth to bring laughs."

Why I am dis Jonah
I sho' can't understand

Born in the West Indies and raised in California, more white than black—
and seemingly more comfortable performing with and for whites than
blacks—he'd had to study the "Negro dialect" as if it were Italian. "I learned,"
he said, "not to be myself." Onstage he stretched a sentence like a piece of
elastic, slipped in and out of rhythm, hooted, deadpanned, drawled. Now he
was a drum, now a trombone sliding down an octave, now a gently belching
bassoon. "Mr. Williams has methods which are absolutely 'sui generis,'" a
critic effervesced. "There is not a white comedian on our stage who could
not profit by watching his methods." A Chicago reporter termed him the
"Mark Twain of his color"; Eleonora Duse thought him a great actor.

But I'm a good substantial, full-fledged
Real, first-class Jonah man.

Tall and urbane offstage, an amateur pianist, photographer, and baseball
player with a buoyant sense of humor and a taste for tailored attire, a lover
of books whose private library filled several rooms, he once said that while
he found nothing disgraceful about being black, "I have often found it
inconvenient—in America." On tour he was routinely turned out of hotels
and restaurants, threatened on the street, relegated to the coloreds-only
section of saloons. Once, in St. Louis, he tried to order a drink and was
told, "I'll give you a gin, but it's $50 a glass." Williams pulled a $500 bill
from his wallet. "Give me ten of them."

Fo' I'm a Jonah, I'm a Jonah man.

So long as he remembered his place, the press loved him, but when he and
Walker brought out a more nuanced version of *In Dahomey* in 1904, critics
griped. A reporter who saw the show at the Fulton in 1905 said the new
Dahomey gave the impression "that these two clever colored men, two of the
very cleverest comedians on the stage today, are not satisfied with making a
success in their own peculiar way, but aim to have a 'white man's' show."

It sounds just like that old old tale

Bert Williams envisioned a more beneficent future. "Let some Shakespeare arise and write a drama," he said, "the story of the Negro to rise from meniality and servility to a position of independence, portraying the difficulties that seem almost insurmountable, keeping always in mind a certain omnipresent prejudice against him." He foresaw a day when legitimate African American dramatic troupes would rival coon shows, and through the "presentation of proper plays, aid a more perfect understanding among the races."

But sometimes I feel like a whale

In 1922, the year of his death, Williams told a friend he'd been thinking "about all the honors that are showered on me in the theater, how everyone wishes to shake my hand or get an autograph, a real hero you'd naturally think. However, when I reach a hotel, I am refused permission to ride on the passenger elevator, I cannot enter the dining room for my meals, and am Jim Crowed generally." He wasn't complaining, he added, just wondering. "I would like to know when (my prediction) the ultimate changes come, if the new human beings will believe such persons as I am writing about actually lived?"

Why I am dis Jonah
I sho' can't understand,

The show was nearly over now, the cakewalk about to start. First came Walker, strutting and whirling across the stage, feet raised, toes pointed. (*Be sure to have a smile on your face / Step high with lots of style and grace.*) The crowd out front in Yecker's opera house went wild. Here came his partner, the great Bert Williams, "funniest Negro onstage today," stumbling after Walker like a drunk. Both men would go on to perform with George M. Cohan, and after Walker's death Williams would spend a decade with the Ziegfeld Follies—the first black man to perform with the troupe—playing alongside Fanny Brice and Eddie Cantor, and then one night, at the age of forty-seven, his heart failing, he would collapse onstage in Chicago and be carried off, still in blackface, never to recover.

But I'm a good substantial, full-fledged
Real, first-class Jonah man.

Here he was now, waving the sole of his shoe, flicking his cigarette, the funniest saddest man you ever saw. Yecker's audience howled. He was such a clown up there in his baggy pants and black gloves. Such a natural, so full of glee.

14

EMPTY SPACE

For years I have tried to picture how a real showboat works. It comes to me in daydreams: I am standing on the banks of a wide, mud-colored river in a small American town, surrounded by people who wear hats and wave handkerchiefs. A band is playing. It is early evening in the summer, and because it is a dream there are no mosquitoes, and I don't have to buy a ticket, and the only thing on the horizon is a slow-moving playhouse, wreathed in light, floating downriver in my direction.

My late godmother Mary Evans, who was born in Tidewater Virginia at the end of the nineteenth century, told me showboats still came regularly to town when she was a girl. Whenever one docked, people hurried to the waterfront. After much time and commotion a curtain would rise somewhere inside the boat, and my young godmother would look across the footlights at a costumed actor pretending to be someone else. She could recall few greater pleasures. She didn't tell me what happened next, but I can imagine it: the overwrought gestures, mistaken identities, laughter, applause, an intermission, more laughter, a revelation or two, further applause, a last curtain, and then the crowd scattering while the crew packed up the stage and the showboat moved on to another town, taking its stories with it. That image, of a tale-bearing vessel afloat on a river, stays with me.

Half a century later my godmother sat in a chilly sanctuary in the same Tidewater town where she had grown up and watched me bounce up and down as an angel in the church Christmas pageant. Of that morning I recall three sensations: the scratch of tinsel wings on my skin, the blur of my mother's hands as she straightened my halo, and the peculiar ecstasy of performing in front of people I loved.

My godmother did not see me onstage again until she was in her eighties, a few years before her death. I was twenty-four and had taken a job with a children's theater company at the Fulton. Mary Evans happened to come to Lancaster for a visit the week we opened, early in 1980. Our show was brief and small—we'd designed it to take on tour to elementary schools and day care centers—so we invited the audience to sit onstage with us inside the opera house as we performed. I played a talking dog. My godmother professed to enjoy every minute of our little play, and I again felt the exhilaration of acting in front of someone who had helped to raise me. (*Look at me*, the child cries. *I exist!*) During the party afterward, my godmother waltzed around the stage sipping punch and flirting with my friend Rob, the one gay member of our cast.

I was living at home again after two years of being away. Since college I'd worked as a governess in Manhattan and as a secretary in Oklahoma; I'd dabbled in stage management, stitched costumes for a summer theater company, and twice tried to get into a PhD program in theater criticism at Stanford, the second time successfully. I'd scarcely had time to celebrate when the stage-design professor with whom I'd had an affair four years earlier, and whom I hadn't seen in years, phoned to offer me a job in a summer stock company he was directing in upstate New York. I said yes.

Had I stuck to my prepared script, who knows how the plot might have unspooled, but I went east, not west, to a barn near the Finger Lakes that had been converted into a theater, and quickly fell back under the spell of my former teacher. He'd cast me as Eve in *The Apple Tree*, but he was the one whose temptations proved irresistible. By September I had backed out of graduate school, and he had left his wife and persuaded me to move to Florida with him and his five-year-old daughter. The adventure lasted four days before I came to my senses and fled north to Lancaster in a rented car and asked my bewildered parents to take me in.

My journal from those months is filled with words like *disintegration,*
terrors, unknown. Outside my parents' house the wind blew and trees shook,
and the ducks on the pond out back screamed at each other in the dark.
One night the air felt so sharp I imagined it piercing my skin, turning me
into a sieve. I took a job as a receptionist at a downtown law firm run by a
sometime slumlord who made me sharpen pencils for him at his desk
while his clients watched. When he wasn't around, I read Ibsen and Virginia Woolf and pored over the depositions of divorcing couples. I have
seldom been more adrift. Late in the year the Fulton posted auditions for
a children's theater company, and I jumped.

Two months later I was crawling around the stage of the opera house
on my knees, barking for my stagestruck godmother and a flock of children we'd brought in for our opening. I had painted my nose black and
dotted whiskers on my cheeks, and I wore brown sweatpants and a black
sweater with my character's name, Bravo, stitched in bright green letters
across the chest. Before joining the company I had known nothing about
children's theater, but in rehearsal we went over creative drama techniques and developed games and improvs to use with kids in workshops.
One exercise had us sitting on the floor in a circle, gently passing an
imaginary bird from one person to the next. When we tried it with actual
four-year-olds, they made cooing noises as they petted the air with their
hands.

I bought a book about children's theater called *A Space Where Anything*
Can Happen. Its main point was that theater could free kids to dream in
important ways about who they were and what they might become. ("If
we cannot imagine," Gaston Bachelard writes, "we cannot foresee.") A
poem on the book's opening pages spoke of

> A space
> I can change
> with the experiences of my life . . .
> the imagined,
> the feared,
> the loved,
> the hoped for,
> the possible,
> and the impossible.

The specific space could be anywhere, but in a larger sense it was always a stage—a place for playing, for acting out the myths and rituals in which, as the Dutch historian Johan Huizinga observes, "the great instinctive forces of civilized life have their origin: law and order, commerce and profit, craft and art, poetry, wisdom and science. All are rooted in the primeval soil of play."

Which is how I was unexpectedly spending my twenty-fourth year. My former professor was still phoning and sending letters from Florida begging me to change my mind. I resisted, numbed by his pleading. *This quest through nothing, for nothing,* I scribbled. At night I fought off demons, his and mine; in the morning I climbed into the Fulton's station wagon with my fellow actors, and we trooped off to another school to give our show and do a workshop. I had been told children were the most demanding of audiences, but I never felt less than welcome anywhere we went, maybe because most kids were giddy with pleasure at the arrival of these strangely costumed adults in their midst. It's one thing to *go* to the theater, another to have it come to you on a sodden March morning, to have it erupt in your cafeteria the way medieval pageants used to erupt in town squares.

We had little scenery and one change of clothes. I suspect we weren't far from the kind of enterprise Peter Brook had in mind when he said the only thing needed for an act of theater to take place is for a man to walk across an empty space while someone else watches him. Certainly the kids who sat cross-legged on carpet squares watching us perform didn't seem to distinguish between what we were doing and what took place downtown on the Fulton stage. "Red curtains, spotlights, blank verse, laughter, darkness, these are all confusedly superimposed in a messy image covered by one all-purpose word," Brook writes.

Theater, as I discovered that spring, required none of the apparatus we'd left behind at the opera house. We had no box office, no lobby, no lights, no stagehands, no drops descending from on high, no tickets, just ourselves and what we could carry in the back of a station wagon. We made our own sound effects and mimed most of our props, and our audiences didn't seem to care.

At a time when I had broken the rules of civilized behavior—when I had betrayed the values my godparents and parents had sworn to instill— I rediscovered the primal joy of make-believe. "I am happy in this work at theater," I wrote, as if theater were a time of day or a state of being, like peace. I'd never had a sillier role in my life, howling every morning for attention, but the dog Bravo turned out to be an agent of hope, skilled at retrieval.

The incubus that stalked my bed at night had no seat by day in the four-wheeled showboat we steered along the highways of southeastern Pennsylvania. We traveled from port to port, dropping anchor in community centers and playgrounds, churches and schools, and every evening we sailed back to our harbor in Lancaster and pulled up to the rear door of the Fulton on Water Street and unloaded our stuff and checked the next day's schedule. Then we got into our own cars and went to our separate homes. Mine, I noticed, was starting to feel full again.

15

Two gleaming bands of rail run side by side down the middle of the street. To my left, the towering back wall of the opera house. To my right, a row of one- and two-story houses, some dating back to the eighteenth century and so small, by our oversized standards, as to resemble dollhouses. They are the quintessence of home, the sort of structure a child would draw: a single window in a dormer, a front door designed for a Lilliputian. How must it be to live in such a place and gaze out on a building that despite the *house* in its name is in most ways the antithesis of home?

Terminus might be a more accurate word. Those who work this end of the Fulton, actors and stagehands mostly, tend to be transients, not dwellers. They come and go, leaving no trace of their presence save the stage doors through which they have passed, often late at night, like contraband. The vast brick-and-stone wall of the opera house back here on Water Street is pockmarked with doors, most of them locked, several bricked in, two floating a dozen feet above the sidewalk. These last served as the front entrance to the Fulton for years but were brought to the rear of the building in the early twentieth century, during one of the theater's many renovations, and installed at the opening of the second-story scene dock, where for decades they oversaw the transfer of trunks and sets and curtains and lights and animals from street to stage. They remind me of the doors on an Advent calendar.

This stretch of building speaks of transformations and journeys: a pedestrian passes behind the wall and turns into a prince, a scrap of upholstery into a doublet, lamps into moonlight. I have lost count of the number of times I've come here, by car, on foot, riding my bike, en route to a job which in many ways is more expedition than job.

How the mind travels in such a place! For example, just now I am on my bicycle, riding down the street on my way to rehearsal, working to avoid the tracks when without warning my front wheel catches the lip of the rail, and I topple to the ground and bang my head on the macadam. I lie here for an instant, grateful for my helmet, which is scratched but otherwise intact, and then I hear the train. Softly but inexorably it moves down the tracks, from my century into theirs. The sun goes sepia; the cars disappear. Ahead of me I see figures scurrying in the cold. They wear top hats and bustles. I pick myself up, brush off my hands, cross to the side of the street, and there at the end of the block, on this New Year's Eve, 1886, I see Blasius Yecker on his way to the opera house. He rounds the corner, glances in my direction, touches his hat, and continues walking.

He is in his fifties, like me, and in a hurry. He is a handsome man with a rectangular face and dark beard that remind me of the late Ulysses S. Grant, but beneath his good looks, I perceive a certain weariness. The eyes droop at the corners, as if weighted by invisible lead plugs. A few years ago he and his wife lost a son, Freddie, and more recently he has struggled to keep his theater profitable in a city rife with competition from the likes of Barnum, whose circus now visits yearly, and cheap variety shows. For much of the past year, a skating rink on King Street has bedazzled the town, and to Yecker's disgust the seats in Fulton Hall have often gone vacant, even for the best of attractions. Some shows draw such tiny crowds that companies bail, and he has to issue refunds. But lately the skating craze seems to have ebbed, and audiences are back. Last summer Yecker expanded his box office, and now the proprietor of the city's oldest hall has scored what everyone agrees is a singular coup.

The train rasps to a stop behind Fulton Hall, and Yecker's stagehands swing into action. They work quickly. Tonight's show has to be set up within hours, and when it's over they will pack it back onto the train, and tomorrow they'll go through the ritual again with another show. Yecker is lucky. Ten years ago, before the new tracks went in on Water Street, he had to pay to have his shows unloaded at the station on Queen Street and hauled by dray to the theater, but now the trains pull right up to the scene dock behind the Fulton.

He is a shrewd manager, part of a new class of businessmen who are changing the shape of American enterprise. He has founded his own advertising firm, Blasius Yecker and Co. City Bill Posters, which he runs out of an office on Prince Street, next door to the theater. The company controls most of the billboards in Lancaster, and wagons emblazoned with Yecker's name criss-cross the city. On either side of the front entrance to Fulton Hall (or, as the sign over the doors now reads, Yecker's Fulton Opera House) he has hung billboards where millinery shops and clothiers promote their goods. Heeding the example of Barnum himself (who advised, "Put on the *appearance* of business, and generally the *reality* will follow"), Yecker publishes a weekly guide filled with theatrical trivia and "news" items touting the Fulton's upcoming shows, and he has mastered the art of slipping favorable reviews and announcements into the local press. Just two days ago, the *New Era* reported that tonight's performance was nearly sold out, and warned, "If you have not secured your seats, go to Fulton Hall as soon as this paper reaches you and see whether you cannot secure some sort of accommodation. It will pay to be in *any* part of the Hall on Friday night."

Not that Yecker's record is perfect. Thanks to the rage for variety shows, he has had to pad his schedule with productions like *Fun on the Bristol* (parts of which the *Intelligencer* denounced as "broad, vulgar, and utterly unfit for presentation before a respectable audience") and last night's *Black Crook*, a musical extravaganza featuring dozens of young women prancing across the stage in armor and tights. (This time the *Intelligencer* remarked only on the shapely performers and nearly full house.)

Tonight's show is at once more refined and more sensational. Ads read simply, "Mr. Edwin Booth as Hamlet. Supported by His Excellent Company." Nothing more is needed. It is the first and only appearance in Lancaster by the man many esteem the country's finest actor, and even though Yecker has charged unusually high prices (two dollars for a parquette seat, as much as a pair of dress pants), the show is sold out.

Outside on the streets a mixture of rain and snow is falling, and people are scurrying about in the slush, wishing each other a happy holiday as they load up on sauerkraut at the market and comb through the Christmas bargains at Watt and Shand. Inside the opera house furnaces are straining to warm the dressing rooms where Booth and his entourage will turn themselves into members of the Danish court. The actor has played Hamlet for so many years that when his daughter and only child, Edwina, first heard the word "omelet," she cried, "That's Papa!" "You see, between ourselves, he *is* Hamlet—melancholy and all," Booth's late brother John Wilkes remarked.

Edwin is used to cold dressing rooms and drafty stages, to the stale hotel food and lumpy beds that constitute life on the road. He has been touring for nearly forty years, ever since his actor father, Junius Brutus Booth, hired him to be his dresser and aide. Except for a brief period after Lincoln's murder, when he retreated from public life and "lost the level run of time and events," Edwin has made his living as an actor, "the only trade for which God has fitted me." Eleven of the sixteen roles he keeps in his repertory are Shakespearean.

He is a small man with huge brown eyes that seem to radiate light. Where his half-mad, alcoholic father was all fury and sound, Edwin is somber and remote, more intellect than animal. "I am conscious of an interior personality standing back of my own, watching and guiding me," he has said by way of explaining his power as an actor. He is shy and often depressed. On the night of his birth, meteors tumbled from the sky above his father's Maryland farm, and some thought the heavens were bursting. Edwin arrived with a caul, prompting the slaves who worked the Booth farm to predict he would one day see ghosts. They also thought he would be guided by a lucky star. Locked in that strange prognostication, it seems, was a fated sadness, a sense Edwin himself has had, for most of his life, that nothing would turn out right.

He has lost two wives, one of them insane, and an infant son. He has gone bankrupt trying to launch a theater in Manhattan. He has been shot at while performing onstage. He has battled his own alcoholism and what he calls the "sad work" of "starring around the country," and he has endured the disgrace of being a Booth after the events of April 14, 1865. Wherever he goes Edwin draws crowds, at times so big his managers have to lock his rail car to keep voyeurs at bay, but Booth knows they come as much to see the brother of Lincoln's killer as to see him. As he puts it, "Each little piddling village has stabbed me through and through."

Even here in Lancaster, where the papers have gently refrained from mentioning the assassination, Booth knows it is part of his lure, perhaps even the reason that on this gloomy December evening, the last of the year, more than a thousand people will come out to see him, some to spend more than three hours on their feet in the aisles of Yecker's opera house. "Had it been raining pitchforks," the *Intelligencer* will report in a front-page review tomorrow morning, Lancastrians "could not have been kept away from the Booth performance."

He cannot remember how often he has stood backstage and scrutinized his image in the mirror: the square face and thin, unsmiling lips, the waves of graying hair. In his reflection he sometimes sees his father, the volcanic Junius Brutus, a man whose genius, wrote Walt Whitman, "was to me one of the grandest revelations of my life, a lesson of artistic expression." On the night that sixteen-year-old Edwin Booth made his stage debut in a walk-on role in his father's production of *Richard III*, the normally gruff and distant Junius came to his son's dressing room after the performance and "'coddled' me; gave me gruel," Edwin would recall, and to prevent the boy's catching cold "made me don his worsted night-cap." At the time Edwin understood his father's gestures to be ironic, but over the years he has come to believe those long-ago ministrations were "a genuine act of solicitude for the heedless boy who had drifted into that troublous sea."

Decades later Edwin Booth remains adrift, a wanderer in a strange town on a bleak winter day. Tonight, in the shadows of Blasius Yecker's opera house, he will slip into his tunic and fasten a miniature of his father on a chain around his neck and go onstage again, into the light that is his true home, the arena where his fans await him, they and his family's assembled ghosts.

When I picture Edwin Booth I see those American actors, most of them born in his century, who were destined to roam. I see Joseph Jefferson, condemned to tour the country as Rip Van Winkle for forty years until death freed them both. I see James O'Neill, trapped in the role of the Count of Monte Cristo, a part he and his son Eugene both came to despise. I see Minnie Maddern Fiske, doomed from the age of eight to a life in transit. I imagine the minstrel singers and vaudevillians and Tommers who plied their tricks from one town to the next.

The actress Fanny Kemble, writing in 1847 of her woes on the American road, complained of being made sick by auditoriums with walls as "thin as my stockings" and of her "wandering and homeless life," conditions little changed by the time Booth—and Jefferson and Fiske and James O'Neill and Frank Mayo and Lotta Crabtree and Bert Williams and the child star

George M. Cohan, among so many others—played the Fulton. Moths drawn to a fickle light, these men, women, and children moved from theater to theater along a route hewn by fellow players who couldn't afford to go home, or didn't know how, or had no home. Eugene O'Neill, born in a hotel room while his father was on tour, captured the paradox of their existence. The actor on the road, he said, "doesn't understand a home. He doesn't feel at home in it. And yet, he wants a home."

The rail system that spread like a spider's web across the United States in the second half of the nineteenth century carried all manner of human cargo: miners, bluebloods, soldiers, preachers, immigrants, and those supreme drifters, actors, their lives reduced to trunks and train schedules, the clatter of boxcars and the fleeting gratification of a night's paycheck and applause. "We do not ride upon the railroad; it rides upon us," Thoreau wrote when the American railroad was still in its adolescence. What actor—trapped in an unheated train compartment, tired, bored, ill, subject to summer pests and winter chills, crooked managers, filthy hotels, indifferent audiences, the sheer drudgery of living in transit ten months of every year—did not agree?

Dante had it no worse. "You shall leave everything you love most dearly," he observes in the *Paradiso*:

> This is the arrow that the bow of exile
> shoots first. You are to know the bitter taste
> of others' bread, how salt it is, and know
> how hard a path it is for one who goes
> descending and ascending others' stairs.

Without wayfarers like Booth, Yecker's opera house could not have functioned. Back and forth they went, the players, from New York to Poughkeepsie to Cleveland to Manistee to Milwaukee to Chicago, across the prairie to Leadville and Tombstone, on to California, up into timber country, back through the belly of the continent to Kansas City and Cincinnati, south to Galveston and Natchez and Charleston, north again to Baltimore and Philadelphia, to Lancaster and Allentown and East Haddam and Boston and Provincetown. Though even a spectator as avid as Whitman had his beef with a system in which stars flitted about the country, "playing a week here and a week there, bringing as his or her greatest recommendation, that of novelty," it was novelty Americans craved—that and a steady supply of mythic figures: Buffalo Bill, Jim Crow, Little Eva, Rip Van Winkle, Davy Crockett, Jesse James, Daniel Boone, the Count of Monte Cristo, Hamlet.

The blunt silhouette of the proscenium stage became a fixture in America's urban skylines. Thousands of theaters went up in the United States between the Civil War and the turn of the twentieth century. Behind its curtain each had the same factory-like warren of dressing rooms, shops for building and painting scenery, storage and prop rooms, pulleys, ropes, sandbags, pipes, pin rails, gridirons. On the public side of the curtain the look was increasingly that of a private home: lobbies had oriental rugs, tapestried walls, cabinets, clocks, console tables, fountains and ferns. Auditoriums had folding seats with racks for hats, overcoats, canes and umbrellas, and comfortable footrests—innovations Yecker would introduce to the Fulton in 1890, along with a Brussels carpet, ornamental railings, a newly frescoed proscenium arch, fresh lobby décor, and a plate-glass panel at the back of the house so that members of Yecker's staff could peek at the auditorium without disrupting the show.

The German manager was known in the trade for his "genial manners and square dealing" and admired in Lancaster for his "rare discrimination" and the scrupulous care with which he tended the reputation of his hall. Managers of the better American roadhouses went to Manhattan each summer to book shows for the coming season, and Yecker was surely among them, New York being just a day's train ride from Lancaster. He liked to screen the artists he brought to the Fulton. Despite his occasional lapses, the city so trusted his judgment that the mayor gave him a general license "for the exhibition of Theatrical Entertainments, Shows, Spectacles, etc.," for which Yecker paid $75 a year, in lieu of the special licenses he'd once had to secure every time he wanted to present something.

Years earlier stars had toured on their own, using resident companies to fill out their casts, but now combination troupes—star plus cast, hence "combination"—were the norm. Yecker typically rented the Fulton out to these companies, but when he couldn't get a better deal, he played on shares, meaning he agreed to furnish the theater and its stagehands for one-fourth the gross receipts of a show, or to supply both the hall and advertising for one-third the gross take. Sometimes the arrangement yielded a decent profit, and sometimes it hardly covered expenses.

"In a business that is so frequently invaded by sharps and tricksters," the *New Era* would primly report, "actors and patrons alike rejoiced in the confidence they always safely reposed in the management of the Lancaster house." Yecker could be relied on for timely payments and decent lodging a block away at the Stevens House, where local fans sometimes sat in the lobby, hoping to glimpse celebrities. His theater was orderly and for the most part clean. "Boys and young men are not allowed to whistle, holler or throw peanut shells about," signs read. When a patron crunched too loudly on his peanuts—as happened one night during a performance of *Rip Van Winkle*, just as the protagonist was waking from his twenty-year nap—the police evicted him.

Performers came back to Lancaster again and again. Blind Tom, Frank Mayo, James O'Neill, Kate Claxton, Oliver Doud Byron, Frank Frayne, Ole Bull, William F. Cody, Fanny Davenport, James Wallick, Ida Lewis, Joseph Jefferson III, Otis Skinner, Fanny Janauschek, Helena Modjeska, Go-Won-Go-Mohawk ("The only American Indian actress in the world") all played Yecker's house three, four, even five times. John Philip Sousa made eleven appearances with his bands. Junius Brutus Booth, another of Edwin's brothers, came twice. The world-famous magician and publicity hound Harry Kellar brought his tricks to the Fulton no fewer than fifteen times. Rounding out Yecker's seasons were itinerant lecturers (Horace Greeley, Henry Ward Beecher, Victoria Woodhull), minstrel acts and freak shows (the Great Kentucky Giant, the Siamese Twins Millie and Chrissie, Tom Thumb), panoramas and stereopticons, political meetings and church fairs and revivals and art exhibitions and boxing matches and spiritualist acts and glee clubs.

One-night stands were the norm. Patrons went to the Fulton two and three times a week. Many kept diaries of what they saw, accounts of how full the house was, whether they liked the show, how much they paid to see it. Students at Franklin and Marshall made Yecker's hall the centerpiece of their social lives. A Lancaster teenager by the name of Milton Hershey snuck off from his job making candy at Royer's Ice Cream Parlor to join his friends in the Fulton gallery.

Perhaps inevitably, the grind of running such a big operation took its toll on Yecker, and for a time in the late 1880s he turned over the daily management of the theater to a pair of men named Proctor and Soulier, who added electric lights to the auditorium, reconfigured the main floor, and announced their intent to book companies for three-night stands and to offer matinees every Wednesday and Saturday for the "ladies and children who could not otherwise attend." But the fare at Proctor's Opera

House proved inferior (when it wasn't downright objectionable), and to everyone's relief, the experiment ended after just two years.

The place needed Yecker after all, and he it. In a letter heralding his return to the Fulton in August of 1890, he told producers and agents he meant to book "first-class companies" and reminded them that he enjoyed "the confidence of theatrical managers and others in the profession, as well as that of the playgoers and citizens of Lancaster."

During his temporary leave from the opera house, Yecker became a United States citizen. He was fifty-five years old and had waited more than forty years to "abjure all allegiance and fidelity to any Foreign Prince, Potentate, State or Sovereignty whatsoever, and particularly to the Emperor of Germany"—this last phrase being written by hand into his naturalization papers. For the first time in his life, Yecker could call himself an American.

Built into the desire for home, it seems, is the impulse to leave, to hit the road or the airways and *see scenery*, as an Amish friend of mine once put it. Coming as we do from such disparate geographic and cultural homes, Americans may be peculiarly wired for this activity. Perhaps some portion of our wanderlust has to do with the wish to recover the lost (or imagined) dwellings of our past. In his later years, Blasius Yecker went back to Europe multiple times. He enjoyed the ocean crossings, "which seemed to be very beneficial to his health," the press observed. "He never lost his love for the Fatherland." We keep circling back, he and I.

Here in the middle of Water Street, row houses to my right, opera house to my left, I am pulled in both directions. I want to stay, burrow down, nest; I want to flee. I've done my share of traveling, have circled the country twice as an actor doing church plays, sleeping in strangers' beds and eating their salty bread (or more accurately their Jell-O salads). Each time I leave Lancaster I wonder if it's for the last time. And then, like the performers who stoked the American dream with their peregrinations, I return.

After his single appearance at the Fulton in 1886, Edwin Booth toured the country for another few years before retiring from the stage in 1891, at the age of fifty-seven. In the last years of his life he opened a club for actors, The Players, on New York's Gramercy Park. He wanted to create a refuge for performers, a place where they would be treated with respect. "I do not want my club to be a gathering place of freaks who come to look upon another sort of freak," he said.

Booth himself moved into a suite of rooms on an upper floor of The Players, and it was here that shortly after one o'clock in the morning on June 7, 1893, with his daughter beside him, he died. Moments earlier a thunderstorm struck—as at birth, a celestial omen—and the lights went out. "Don't let father die in the dark!" Edwina screamed, but when the lights came back he was gone. The mass of reporters who'd camped outside on the sidewalk, waiting for news of the actor's condition, filed their sad stories. Not long before, Booth had told friends he was tired of traveling, that he was waiting for his "cue to quit." All along he seemed to understand—better than most—that he was just passing through.

Booth and Blasius Yecker were both, in their way, outsiders whose real allegiance was to the theater, which they loved and chafed at and could not leave. Born just three months apart, these two men of the nineteenth-century stage remind us that to live is to wander, to etch a spot in the world and then move on. "Life is itself exile," William Gass suggests, "and its inevitability does not lessen our grief or alter the fact."

Some years after I stopped working at the Fulton, the rail lines that ran down the center of Water Street were removed. In my mind, however, they are still there, and whenever I visit the theater I half expect to see a train bearing down the street toward the opera house. Maybe it will happen. Maybe a locomotive will whistle, and somewhere in the sky the pages of an imaginary calendar will peel away, as if in a movie, and I'll look up to see Yecker's stagehands standing above me in the old doors to the scene dock. "Up here!" they'll shout to the workmen on the train. "Whoa, boys! Hand her over!" A little further down Water Street, at the end of the block, I'll glimpse a figure making his way toward the Stevens House Hotel. It is the great Booth, on the road once more, still playing.

16

WOMEN'S WORK: 1870–1931

The binding has faded, but the title of the volume, which I picked up a few years ago at a used bookshop in Michigan, is plain: *Manners, Culture and Dress of the Best American Society*. The year is 1894, and, as the book's author notes in his preface, the lack of knowledge about etiquette is now so widespread that a guide like this is needed, so that "*any one*" can "acquire the perfect ease of a gentleman, or the gentler manners of a well-bred lady."

"A gentleman," I read a few pages later, "is distinguished as much by his composure as by any other quality. Throughout life he avoids what the French call *scenes*—occasions of exhibition, in which the vulgar delight. He of course has feelings, but he never exhibits any to the world."

Women, on the other hand, are known for their histrionics. Absent training in etiquette, we gossip, criticize, interrupt; we obsess about trifles. In conversation we talk too fast, or worse, lisp, "which at once betrays childishness and downright nonsense." At the piano we shrug, sigh, pant, roll our eyes, grimace. To the dismay of our families we wander about the house in "disordered and soiled clothes."

"Beauty may be woman's weapon," the author of *Manners, Culture and Dress* instructs, but it "must be feathered by the Graces, pointed by the eye of Discretion, and shot by the hand of Virtue!" Only then can woman play her role in the "vast drama" that is society, "in which every person has the part allotted to him most appropriate to his abilities." The parts available to woman, we're told, are: dutiful daughter, affectionate sister, tender wife, judicious mother, faithful friend, and amiable acquaintance.

I turn the pages of the guide and hear my grandmothers, one born in 1897, the second in 1898: *Stand up straight, Leslie. Tuck in your tummy. Don't make a scene.* What future did these women raised in an age of stockings and stays envision for their tantrum-prone granddaughter? If I didn't get my way, I threw things. I traced swear words onto the tablecloth with the blunt end of my knife. I wore mismatched plaids.

On page 26 of *Manners, Culture and Dress* I read that "a woman strong and womanly in all ways, in whom the heart of a husband can safely trust—this is the perfect lady." Neither of my grandmothers went to college; both married, brought up children, made careers of running a home. I don't mean to judge; it's what was available to them.

They evolved with the century. Rummaging through their attics and photo albums, I would find bathing suits and flapper gowns tucked among the gloves and handkerchiefs. When I told them I wanted to work in the theater, one grandmother gave me a biography of Fanny Kemble, and the other paid for acting lessons and took me to my first Broadway show, Keir Dullea and Blythe Danner in *Butterflies Are Free.* The actors spent most of the second act of the play in their underwear.

"*Well*," my grandmother announced afterward as we left the theater. "I didn't expect *that*." She gripped my elbow as we started to cross the street. "You didn't mind, did you?"

I was thirteen and horrified at the thought of stripping onstage. "No," I lied.

"Good. Because the human body is nothing to be ashamed of, you know."

May Fisk, a female minstrel who brought her troupe of blondes to the Fulton in 1878 and again in 1879, would have liked my grandmother. Fisk drew a big house for her first Fulton appearance, despite the fact that it was August, and hot, and despite a program note reminding ticket holders that Fisk and her blondes had recently been denied permission to play a theater in small-town Iowa. No matter: the Lancaster crowd relished the company's salty jokes and burlesque finale. On a return visit to the Fulton the

next year, in a show called *Our Naughty Girls*, Fisk and her blondes caused
a stir when a fire alarm went off in the middle of their show, and one of
May's girls cried out from the stage that there was no need to evacuate the
theater because "the drinks will be brought in!"

The girls never came back. But the churchgoing Blasius Yecker, devoted
husband and father of seven, brought in May Howard's Burlesque Company, Billy Andrew's Lady Minstrels, the Ida Siddons Burlesque Company,
the Nellie Maskell European Burlesque Combination, Madame Girard
Gyer's English Novelty Company and Star Troupe of Roman and Heathen
Statuary, and more. He displayed women on trapezes, showgirls on swings
suspended from the flies, women in trousers masquerading as men, women
in blackface, female pugilists, dancers in short skirts and pink tights,
actresses in deshabille reclining on lounges. He offered productions of *The
Black Crook*, *Ixion*, *Mazeppa*, and the Kiralfy brothers' *A Tale of Enchantment*—spectacles fabled for their sensual display of the female form. So
great was the turnout for these productions that in 1880 the *New Era* concluded, "Legs are held in much higher estimation by the people of Lancaster city than brains."

In the parlors of well-bred Lancaster it was a different story, naturally.
Yecker's wife, Mary, and their three daughters, Annie, Lizzie, and Ida, trussed
themselves up like poultry with corsets and hoops, as did most of their
acquaintances. A turn-of-the-century image shows the Yecker girls wearing the same high collars, long sleeves, and wasp-waisted skirts my great-
grandmothers favored—attire that led anthropologist Havelock Ellis to
ask, in his 1894 examination of the sexes, *Man and Woman*, whether woman's quicker pulse rate and inferior respiratory capacity might not be due
to the constrictive nature of her undergarments.

If Yecker's daughters went to any of their father's leg shows, they left
no record of it, but a Margaret Rawn who attended a musical at the Fulton in the early 1890s complained in her diary that "the chorus girls were
ugly." Beauty was prized. With little effort, pretty girls who longed to
escape the tedium of home could find employment in the theater. (Dreiser's Carrie Meeber is an example.) Burlesque—which after 1870 came to
be linked almost exclusively with the display of women's bodies—was
cheap to produce, especially when you were hiring for looks instead of
talent. The pay might be low, but the job was easier and more lucrative
than domestic or factory work, and it offered freedoms most women
could only dream of.

That's not to say families, especially those in the middle class, didn't shudder at the prospect of their daughters going onstage. What distinguished an actress from a whore, after all? In a society that liked its women to stay home, actresses and prostitutes moved about freely and unchaperoned; they slept in hotels and on trains, ate in restaurants, peddled their images on postcards, hung out in theaters.

Years before I expressed any interest in going onstage, my mother told me that while I could of course do whatever I wanted with my life, she hoped I wouldn't become an undertaker or an actress. I've always wondered why she paired the two. It was more than just a matter of trying to protect me from an unsavory business, I think—it had to do with the flesh, with the way it literally decays on the mortician's slab and with the moral and physical decadence long associated with theater people. "Alas! No," cried the actress and women's rights advocate Olive Logan in an 1869 speech decrying the leg show or "nude drama," as she called it. "I cannot advise any woman to go upon the stage with the demoralizing influences which seem to prevail more every day when its greatest rewards are won by brazen-faced, stained, yellow-haired, padded-limbed creatures—while actresses of the old school, well-trained, well-qualified, decent, cannot earn a living."

It wasn't acting per se Logan hated—in fact she praised the theater as "a channel for gifted and intelligent young women to gain a livelihood by honest exertion"—but the way some shows, notably burlesque, compromised women and "stained" their flesh. To lose a daughter to this kind of enterprise was to experience not only a drop in status (hers as well as yours) but a symbolic death. A prostitute, at least, worked in private, but the chorus girl strutted her made-up self for the world to see. What parent didn't mourn a child's descent into that underworld?

Theater has always been a flesh trade. The actor's use of his body as the medium of his art—as a language at least as important as the script—"creates a special response in his audience," writes Michael Goldman. Playwright Valère Novarina says that nothing "but the desire for the actor's body" propels him to write for the stage, for it is in the process of physically rewriting the text that the actor creates theater. "Seeing the actors' and actresses' bodies is what is beautiful: to show the true and mortal, sexed and tongued flesh to the castrated public."

Jerzy Grotowski argued that theater exists foremost in the memory of the body, in the most primal parts of the actor's physical and psychological being, and he defined the actor as "a man who works in public with his body, offering it publicly." When the person making that gesture is a woman—a woman in a decorous era, no less—the exchange is that much more provocative. The Fulton Opera House was one of the few places Lancastrians could go, collectively and in public, to gaze at women. Torso, skin, hands, eyes, feet, breasts, buttocks, crotch, neck, shoulders, elbows, hair, ears, waist, fingertips, knees, hips, eyebrows, lips: Yecker's theater freed audiences to stare.

The object of their scrutiny was a hybrid, of course, as actors must be, and as women often are. Simone de Beauvoir saw that "the least sophisticated of women, once she is 'dressed,' does not present *herself* to observation. She is, like the picture or the statue, or the actor on the stage, an agent through whom is suggested someone not there—that is, the character she represents, but is not." Without artifice, Beauvoir hints, we do not exist. (Or as the rhyme I learned in childhood put it, "Powder and paint make a girl what she ain't.") Beauty—our weapon—renders us visible.

Women who refuse to play the game court scorn, as Olive Logan herself did when she spoke at the Fulton in 1870. "Her appearance did not make a very favorable impression," a reviewer tut-tutted the next day. "She is not at all good-looking." The critic allowed that Logan, then thirty-one, had a clear and pleasantly musical voice and enough wit to keep her substantial crowd amused, but he dismissed her talk, on the topic of "Girls," as "an out-and-out 'women's rights' effort" whose sincerity he questioned. "We doubt whether the fair Olive herself believes in all she says about female suffrage, but merely wishes to indulge herself in the luxury of a little spicy talk."

Logan blurred the boundaries between the sexes, and that made men (and more than a few women) uncomfortable. She had her own career and called on other women to do the same ("Now girls, be men!"). She refused to be pretty or even to admit that prettiness had its advantages. In her Fulton talk, she disparaged "the insipid, brainless girl of fashion, whose whole soul, such as it is, is absorbed in dress," and warned that women who trust to their "beauty *alone*" face a dismal end, for they will first be courted, then "flattered, adored, betrayed, deserted and damned." It's little wonder reporters who covered her queried Logan's integrity—to agree with her would have been to challenge the social status quo.

Much less threatening were troupes like Madame Rentz's Female Minstrels, who brought their short skirts and saucy skits to the Fulton a few days before Logan gave her lecture. The Boston-based burlesque company, one of the country's first, was just two months old and already a hit up and down the Northeast. "A crowded house may be looked for," ads in the Lancaster papers advised. "Go early." And people did—as they would continue to do, week-in, week-out, whenever a leg show came to town, well into the twentieth century.

Rentz's girls and their many imitators served up a lucrative combination of minstrel buffoonery and sexual titillation that reinforced contemporary thinking about female physiology, temperament, and intellect. In his 1871 *The Descent of Man, and Selection in Relation to Sex*, Darwin theorized that since males so obviously excelled in the arts, history, literature, science, and philosophy, "the average of mental power in man must be above that of women." He was not alone in believing anatomy was destiny. The female sex, wrote anthropologist James Hunt, is "in some respects as inferior to man as Negroes are to Europeans" ("On the Negro's Place in Nature," 1863–69). Women's brains are smaller than men's (*Popular Science Monthly*, 1878). Women and children belong, with blacks, to the "lower human races" (Cesare Lombroso, 1878). Menstruation induces a monthly "languor and depression which disqualify [women] for thought or action" (James McGrigor Allan, "On the Real Differences in the Minds of Men and Women," 1869).

Proof strutted nightly across the stages of America's theaters. Sitting in the dark, watching the steady parade of gaslit girls, Yecker's audiences could be forgiven for thinking women had nothing to offer but looks and sex. Even as it pried them from the constraints of domestic life, the Fulton's gilt-edged proscenium kept women in their place—kept everyone in their places.

A few voices cried otherwise, seldom to much effect. Four years after Logan brought her feminist pitch to the Fulton, thirty-six-year-old Victoria Woodhull strode onto the same stage in an elegant black dress with white cuffs and collar and called for men and women to be treated as equals; for the union of the two sexes to be grounded in free love, not marital obligation; for children to be taught the basics of their "sexual organization" so as not to inadvertently "abuse it"; and for the "wicked libertines who destroyed female innocence"—many of them men of the cloth—to be castigated. The *Intelligencer* pounced:

> In truth we do not clearly see what manly privileges Mrs. Woodhull wants that she does not enjoy. . . . She is—woman-like—exceedingly

impatient that public opinion does not coincide with her private opinion. . . . It was strange indeed to see a woman of so fair a presence utter, as this one unflinchingly did, language which could not fail to avert from her the sympathy of decent people. . . . It is a pity that talents such as she certainly has, should be prostituted in the evil cause in which she is engaged.

Unsettling, too, were her looks. Woodhull had recently taken a pair of shears to her long brown hair, and the result gave her "a masculine appearance."

The year was 1874. A quarter century had passed since the Declaration of Rights and Sentiments at Seneca Falls demanding women's civil, social, religious, economic, and electoral equality. To the small crowd in Yecker's hall—just over a hundred men and only twelve women—Woodhull must have seemed the human embodiment of that document. A divorced mother of two (one of them a severely disabled boy whose tottering walk and vacant cries Woodhull imitated onstage that evening), this tall, strangely graceful creature was known to have engaged in all sorts of marginal activities: spiritualism, prostitution, acting, feminism, politics. With her sister, Tennessee Claflin, who came with her to Lancaster, Woodhull had opened the first Wall Street brokerage firm for women and launched a weekly newspaper that lavished attention on taboo topics, most notoriously the Reverend Henry Ward Beecher's adulterous affair with one of his parishioners. In 1872, Anthony Comstock had arrested and briefly jailed the sisters for sending obscene material through the mail. That same year, Woodhull ran for president of the United States as the nominee of the Equal Rights Party; she received no recorded votes.

The *Intelligencer* reminded readers of Woodhull's involvement in the Beecher scandal—then front-page news—and of her prison term, but said nothing about her stock firm or her historic presidential candidacy. The paper acknowledged her acting skills and intellectual powers, and even conceded the truth of some of her arguments, but claimed Woodhull had discredited herself with "the promulgation of so much that is false and vile. . . . She pretends to be astonished that the ladies of the towns she visits do not come to her lectures, a fact which is very creditable to their good sense."

One is left to imagine how Lancastrians felt having this libertine in their midst. Woodhull had toured the country promoting free love and blasting the institution of marriage, which she equated with prostitution.

Accounts of her villainy filled the press; cartoonist Thomas Nast demonized her as "Mrs. Satan." Who in Lancaster came out to see her, and why? The *Intelligencer* reports that after her lecture Victoria and Tennessee did a "brisk trade" selling packets of Woodhull's speeches for a dollar apiece. I envision a throng of men packed tight around the handsome sisters, the rush for autographs, murmurs of thanks, a hand extended and, thrillingly, taken, the tingle of being so close to infamy. If there were women in the crowd, their numbers were small, and they must have felt the same faint shiver of disapproval I experienced a century later watching Dullea and Danner strip.

As she did wherever she went, Woodhull gave a ladies-only talk the next afternoon. Two dozen women attended, but the *Intelligencer* refused to cover the session, claiming it was "no business of ours nor of anybody else." I suppose the paper's editor didn't want to devote further space to her profligate views, or maybe Woodhull herself banned the press from attending. I wish I knew more about the Lancaster women who braved the censure of their neighbors to hear her. Perhaps, like their speaker, they chafed at the bonds of marriage and at laws that viewed them as mere extensions of their husbands. Perhaps they too were seeking a better world for their daughters.

Or maybe they were just voyeurs. (Why do I always assume my hometown is incapable of radical thought?)

Woodhull advertised a third lecture that evening, but so few people showed up she canceled the talk and refunded everyone's money. Lancaster, it seemed, had heard enough; Yecker never brought her back.

All through high school I played Broadway musicals on my record player while I was getting dressed for school in the morning. I had a white-and-gold-checked turntable that looked like a small suitcase when it was shut and an assortment of LPs I had borrowed from my dad's collection downstairs. Day in, day out, as I was pulling on my pantyhose and struggling to make my hair as straight as Peggy Lipton's, I'd listen to Richard Harris wonder how to manage Guinevere, and Rex Harrison curse himself for having let Eliza Doolittle into his life, and Rodgers and Hammerstein's nuns prattle on about the problem of Maria. We were midway between *The Feminine Mystique* and *The Women's Room*, and these matters were on our minds. How do you handle a woman? The answer, I sensed, was more complicated than "simply love her." Besides, it was the wrong question. How do you handle *being* a woman? That's what I wanted to know.

In my own family, women either married and raised children or had careers, but not both—unless it was the sort of thing, like portrait painting, that my mother's cousin did at home with her kids underfoot. My dad went off "to work" every day and my mom, who "didn't work," stayed home and picked up after us, washed our clothes, packed our lunches, baked after-school snacks, cooked dinner, did the dishes, changed the beds, and car-pooled us to and from our lessons and rehearsals and jobs. She helped my disabled sister dress and bathe and do her homework. Once a week she volunteered for Planned Parenthood, but if she did so from any feminist impulse, I never knew it. (She later told me her involvement, like that of my dad, who served briefly on the board, sprang from their personal experience of family planning—three kids in three years.)

Very occasionally my mother would take out a paintbrush and indulge in the vocation for which she'd trained in college and spent a year at the Art Students' League in New York, but a whiff of guilt always seemed to cloud her sojourns at the easel, and before long she'd go back to house-work—not that any of us did much to stop her.

It was a liminal period. On the pages of *Newsweek* women were burn-ing their bras, while up and down my parents' street they were trying to be June Cleaver. Betty Friedan never made it into our house, but I can recall the odd copy of *Ms.* sneaking home with the groceries, and with it an inkling of a wider world. A century after Victoria Woodhull held her private talk with the women of Lancaster, Gloria Steinem was reviving the conversation.

Of course we'd made progress—we could vote, my mother could help women get birth control, I could attend a previously all-male college—but the fundamental questions hadn't changed much. Marriage, motherhood, work: What was woman's role? How far could I dream?

Not very, it sometimes seemed. At the ribbon cutting for a new park-ing garage on Prince Street, a block north of the Fulton, city officials had the mayor's wife drive down the seven-story exit ramp to prove that any-one, even a woman, could navigate its spiraling descent. Lancaster didn't elect its first (and to date only) female mayor until 1990. My teachers at Franklin and Marshall were mostly men, as were the lawyers in my dad's office and the ministers at my parents' church and the directors I worked with at the Fulton and in college. But the director who asked me to join the Fulton children's theater company in 1980 was a woman, and so, by then, were the managing director of the opera house and the development director who hired me later that year to be her assistant, and these last two women were also mothers.

Somewhere in the molecules of air that spun through the building where I soon sat drafting fundraising letters and tallying annual gifts were the atomic vestiges of the struggles our ancestors had waged. If I had cared to listen, I might have heard Woodhull urging me to marry for love, not financial security, or Logan assuring me, as she had assured her Fulton audience more than a hundred years earlier, that "a woman could not be unsexed by any avocation she was engaged in, but would be a woman always as long as true womanly sentiments filled her breast." Had I lingered beside the actresses whose posters hung in the hallways outside the dressing rooms (and now hang in a glossy two-story lobby and bar adjoining Christopher Hager's original hall), I might have seen how their journeys fed into mine. We had all stood on the same stage and looked out into the gauzy shadows of an expectant house; we had all laced our shoes, patted our hair, left our fingerprints in this echo chamber called a theater, whose future they had helped to create and I was now working to preserve.

Cushman, Marlowe, Janauschek, Modjeska, Barrymore, Russell, Minnie Maddern Fiske: here were the women on whose fortunes whole troupes of players depended, leading ladies who ran their own companies, commanded men's wages, got top billing in the newspapers. This was the flip side to the chorus girl story—legitimate actresses praised for their "mental, moral and artistic superiority" (as critic William Winter said of Charlotte Cushman). If Yecker paid his bills with the likes of May Fisk and Madame Rentz, he bought his reputation with what Olive Logan called the "rarest birds in the theatrical land": female stars whose talents and labors had vaulted them to the top of their profession.

Along with every other manager of an American theater in the mid- to late nineteenth century, Yecker understood that if he wanted to stay afloat, his opera house had to look respectable, and for that to happen his audiences must include middle-class white women. Hence the rules posted prominently inside the Fulton and on the pages of its programs ("Spitting on the floor is unlawful and is positively forbidden"). Hence the emphasis on propriety in publicity notices and ads—even for leg shows. Hence the money Yecker lavished on Victorian décor, plaster goddesses and gods, velvet curtains. He wanted the ladies of Lancaster to feel comfortable inside his theater, to bring their children to see shows, to come, unchaperoned, to matinees where they could weep and giggle free from the admonishing gazes of husbands and fathers and fiancés.

Yecker needed actresses with impeccable credentials (or as a local reporter phrased it, "first-class representatives of dramatic art"). Of Fanny Janauschek's 1874 debut at the Fulton, in Schiller's *Marie Stuart*, the *Intelligencer* rhapsodized, "The entertainment was of a character seldom, if ever before, witnessed in this city," and the audience "fashionable, intelligent and appreciative." A day later, when the Czech-born tragedienne failed to attract an equally impressive crowd for the melodrama *Adrienne Lecouvreur*, the paper wagged its finger like a disappointed parent. "We manifestly have no need for an opera house here. The dingy old Fulton Hall was good enough for the minstrel shows which furnish the highest art that the city is willing to patronize. For the sake of our fair name and the gratification of those who enjoy really artistic performances, we regret that the cultivation of the majority of our citizens is not such as to hereafter warrant the appearance among us of first-class representatives of dramatic art."

Yecker persisted. Over the next two decades he brought Janauschek back to Lancaster no fewer than six times. He brought in the Polish-born star Helena Modjeska, famed for the naturalness of her acting and her ability to perform in multiple languages. Modjeska traveled in a private rail car, smoked cigarettes, and (as the *Intelligencer* stressed) was a mother. At her 1882 Fulton premiere—in *Adrienne Lecouvreur*, no less—an "uncommonly brilliant assemblage" representing "the wealth, fashion and highest culture of the community" filled the seats of Yecker's theater. He invited Modjeska back four more times. The energetic manager also introduced Lancastrians to Fanny Davenport, Charlotte Cushman, Kate Claxton, Lotta Crabtree, Annie Pixley, Julia Marlowe, Lily Langtry, Lillian Russell, Mrs. John Drew, and Mrs. Drew's granddaughter Ethel Barrymore.

On September 25, 1895, Yecker staked a small claim to theatrical history when he presented the popular American actress Minnie Maddern in her first professional appearance as "Mrs. Fiske." The thirty-year-old New Orleans native had retired from the stage five years earlier after marrying Harrison Grey Fiske, editor of the *Dramatic Mirror*, but she'd hated housekeeping and didn't want children, and so she'd come back to the theater. Whatever misgivings her husband may have had—the record is discreet— he had written the play she was to give that evening, *The Queen of Liars*, a reworking of a French melodrama. Yecker hyped the event ("she has not been seen on the stage except for charity in five years"), and although the audience was sparse and the play a disappointment, its blue-eyed, red-headed star dazzled. Minnie Maddern Fiske, a critic exulted, is "a better, subtler, more mature actress" than her unmarried predecessor had ever been. To a reporter who asked what she had done during her years away from the stage, the former ingenue laughed. "I got older." But marriage had tempered her. The tiny crowd at the Fulton clapped so feverishly she had to make several curtain calls.

The elusive Mrs. Fiske: I walked by her poster so many times I came to regard it as part of the Fulton architecture. Square face, ivory skin, bovine eyes, a nimbus of dark hair. I'd seen the look in my grandmothers' photo albums: dreamy, self-conscious, eyes fixed on a limitless future. "I am not so sure there is no immortality for the actor," Mrs. Fiske remarked to a biographer. Her idols were Eleonora Duse, Edwin Booth, Madames Modjeska and Janauschek, and Sarah Siddons—dead thirty years before Minnie Maddern was born. "Who shall say her work does not survive in still another way? . . . I like to think that the players Sarah Siddons inspired have handed on the inspiration from generation to generation."

She drew on her antecedents as I do mine, Mrs. Fiske, dead twenty-three years before my birth. I jot down the outlines of her life: the decades of touring (freezing theaters, firetrap hotels, a train that nearly plunged into a ravine); the marriage that blistered and then scabbed into companionship; the long and ultimately successful fight against a theatrical syndicate that sought to control every manager, playwright, and actor in America. (Mrs. Fiske was playing the Fulton, again, when word came in early 1910 that Syndicate leader Charles Frohman had been arraigned.) Little if any of this is visible in the pristine face that hangs on the Fulton wall, but yes, Mrs. Fiske, the life inspires.

She spoke of the need for a "current of new air" to blow through the theater. She said, "If as author, producer, director, or actor you become theatricalized, you are lost." She believed a director must wage war against an actor's vanity "from morning till night." In her sixty-year career as an actress she embraced realism and battled, in her words, "the hysterical emotionalism of a day gone by." Mrs. Fiske's "sobriety of method," wrote an admiring Edith Wharton, "her marvelous skill in producing effects with the smallest expenditure of voice and gesture . . . will do more than all the managers and all the dramatic critics to raise the theatrical ideals of the public and restore the dignity of the drama."

She created the kind of theater I wanted to see (the kind of theater the Fulton still, too rarely, attempts). The techniques I learned in acting class, the plays I studied in college and later graduate school, had their roots in her world. Smug me, thinking the hinges between us had snapped. She had grown up, as I had, loving the touch and sound and smell of the theater, "that odoriferous medley of gas, paint, and mold dear to the hearts of all true children of the stage," as she phrased it. But she had renounced the theater of her childhood—the tawdry melodramas with their preening stars—and worked instead to haul the American stage into the twentieth century.

During her first tour as Mrs. Fiske, in the fall of 1895, she offered two shows in repertory: her husband's *Queen of Liars* and Ibsen's *A Doll's House*. Yecker booked the first but not the second. It was a busy week at the Fulton—the old crowd-pleaser *Mazeppa*, with its skimpily dressed female star; the American Gaiety Girls Burlesque Company in *The Bloomer Club*; a production of *Othello*. Low and high. But even if he had had room for Mrs. Fiske's Nora, I'm not sure Yecker would have wanted her. The actress later admitted that her *Doll's House* was not profitable in its first year, "but, then, that was my own first season as Mrs. Fiske, and it was but one of a number of plays in a financially unsuccessful repertory." A decade earlier, Modjeska, too, had failed with the drama—even though she had changed its title to *Thora* and given it a happy ending. Nineteenth-century Americans had little patience with Ibsen. They appeared to share William Winter's view of him as a gloomy Scandinavian who had "altogether mistaken the province of the theater in choosing it as the fit medium for the expression of sociological views, views, moreover, which, once adopted, would disrupt society." Winter couldn't fathom why someone like Mrs. Fiske would choose Ibsen when she had "a good repertory of old plays."

Maybe you had to be female to get it. In my lifetime Betty Friedan would cite Nora as a symbol of "what feminism was all about. . . . Not very many women then, or even now, dared to leave the only security they knew—dared to turn their backs on their homes and husbands to begin Nora's search," Friedan wrote in 1963, the year I turned eight. "But a great many, then as now, must have found their existence as housewives so empty that they could no longer savor the love of husband and children."

When I first read the play in college it was a revelation. All through high school I had listened to Eliza Doolittle slip quietly home to Henry Higgins, bearing his slippers, but here was a woman who in the year 1879 had slammed the door on her husband. Why would Mrs. Fiske want to produce anyone *but* Ibsen, Winters might have asked. She had more than a little of Nora in her, this tough American actress who divorced her first husband, struck the vows of obedience from her second wedding ceremony, refused to keep house, and renounced children. In the same decade my grandmothers were born—the decade in which the author of *Manners, Culture and Dress of the Best American Society* reminded wives not to engage in activities outside the home "without previously consulting your husband and obtaining his full concurrence"—Minnie Maddern Fiske was traveling the United States in a play about a woman who walks out on her family.

"Rightly projected in the theater, Ibsen always has paid and always will," Mrs. Fiske declared. "And that is worth shouting from the housetops, because sensibly and rightly projected in the theater, the fine thing always does pay." She carved a place in the American theater for the Norwegian playwright. Even the Fulton eventually presented *A Doll's House*, although it was Yecker's son Charles who booked the first production, starring Eugenie Blair, in 1905. Mrs. Fiske herself brought Ibsen to the opera house in 1926, in a production of *Ghosts* in which she played Mrs. Alving, a woman some critics have described as Nora twenty years after *A Doll's House*—but a Nora who never left home.

To the gallery of ghosts who haunt the theater I am building on these pages, I add Mrs. Fiske. I feel an affinity with this woman who toured the country with a poodle named Fifi and at age fifty-six adopted a homeless baby boy; who cherished Ibsen and Shakespeare and the Bible and once said she would prefer life in a penitentiary to life in society, because in jail she could catch up on her reading. She brooked no fools. ("Dear! Dear! How seriously we take ourselves!" she liked to exclaim.) To ensure her anonymity she wore veils—at times two or three—when she went out in public.

I don't know that she solved the riddle of being a woman any more successfully than Woodhull or Logan or my grandmothers or my mother or I have. Work, marriage, children: that old trinity. Do any of us get it right? Money woes kept Mrs. Fiske onstage long after she had hoped to retire. She was still acting four months before her death, from cancer, in 1932. (Ravaged by pain, she played the Fulton a last time in 1931.) "I'm a thousand years old," she said toward the end of her life. "And I'm tired." She claimed she was the reincarnation "of a great many people," and that "long after this uncomfortable body of mine can't digest even the food I'm taking tonight," she would go on living.

As perhaps she has, inside this theater where the turntable of the past keeps spinning. Who shall say their work does not survive? she asked of her forebears.

Who, indeed?

17

CARTOGRAPHY

One night I got into my car and drove through Lancaster in the dark, past all the theaters where I'd once performed. The elementary school auditorium where I had played Lady Macbeth, the Methodist and Lutheran churches in whose rec halls and sanctuaries I had learned to act. I drove by Franklin and Marshall's Green Room, as empty as the campus around it, then over to West End Avenue and the red-brick kindergarten where I'd been a Pilgrim one Thanksgiving, then down Chestnut and Water Streets to the Fulton. I pulled into the parking lot and cut the engine and sat there in the massive black shadow of the building for which I was then performing the late twentieth-century art of development. I was twenty-five and headed to graduate school in Massachusetts in the fall, and I was starting to say goodbye to things.

After a few minutes I left the car and walked over to the theater and let myself in the front door and went up to my office on the third floor. It was nearly midnight. The neon sign on the Army-Navy store across the street had bathed the room in a pale yellow light, and the desks and file cabinets were drained of color. I was the only person in the building. The place smelled faintly of wood. I opened the window. Below me a truck was grinding its way south along Prince Street, but mostly the city was quiet on this warm evening a few days after the solstice. For a moment things seemed inverted: night was morning, walls the most permeable of openings, solitude companionship.

The long, slender room where I worked by day was cluttered with paper. Old playbills, letterhead and envelopes, donor solicitations, a box of the newsletters I had begun writing for the theater ("Meet Cliff Clayton, Fulton Technical Director"). There was the hot pot my boss had accidentally knocked out of the window one day (it landed on top of the marquee, at the toes of a disapproving Robert Fulton). Along the west wall of the room were three stained-glass windows that swiveled open over the upstairs lobby so that you could spy on patrons as they headed toward their balcony seats. No one knew when the windows had been installed or by whom, but we all relished the dimly illicit frisson we experienced whenever we opened them. On the opposite side of the office, along the wall that faced Prince Street, were the flaking plaster remains of a set of Indian portraits that had adorned the mid-nineteenth-century meeting place of the all-white Lancaster tribes of the Improved Order of Red Men. If you looked hard, you could make out a russet nose.

It was a room full of incongruities, more corridor than compartment. People were always passing through: board members, volunteers, staff. I might as well have worked in a train. You'd hear a thud on the stairs, then the wincing floorboards, and a passenger would arrive. Plumbers, electricians, contractors at work on the building next door, which the Fulton had acquired and was turning into new office space. All day long we heard the buzz of their tools through the walls. All day long the opera house creaked and groaned, an aching centenarian longing for a nap.

But tonight the building was quiet. To be here, alone, was to enter the sleeping heart of this place. The windows that swung in and out like valves, the thrumming passageways and dark chambers. *You are here*, the map I carried inside my brain announced.

I sat on the floor and tried to memorize the space around me, my *terra cognita*. I was leaving home, possibly for good, and it mattered. I traced the light from the Army-Navy store as it splashed across the old two-sided desk I shared with a colleague and onto the typewriter where I had secretly begun writing poetry in the mornings when no one was around. I charted the shadows on the ceiling. I pictured the auditorium beyond the walls to my right, the rows of empty seats breathing in the dark, the unguarded stage. Inch by quiet inch, I took possession of this building that so possessed me.

Earlier in the year I had traveled to Greece with my parents and for the first time seen the Theater of Dionysus on the south slope of the Acropolis. I had walked the remains of its stage, the stone circle around which the people of Athens had gathered for the sacred dance known as the dithyramb, from which the drama eventually sprang. Some vestige of that ritual arena lurked inside the Fulton's rectilinear frame. Perhaps it was the way the city bled through the windows of the room where I sat. I had seen how the theaters of ancient Greece merged with the landscape, each seeming to absorb the other, so that nature and art, stage and polis were one, and to experience the first was to know the second.

The desire, and thus the effort, to locate ourselves: to plot our coordinates in time and space. The Pilgrims who settled New England in the seventeenth century and forged tenuous ties with the Wampanoag discovered circular pits along native trails in the wilderness, which the Indians had dug to indicate the places where important events occurred. Each time the Wampanoag passed one of these memory holes, they told the tale of what had happened there. The Pilgrims understood that they were treading on mythic land.

No less resonant was the story pit into which I had crawled on this placid June night. The windows to my left looked out on streets I had known since I was a kid. The floorboards under my feet smelled like the attic in my grandmother's house outside Philadelphia. The corridors and lobbies and auditorium beyond the wall to my right, the stage itself, with its spectral light, spoke of the enterprise that had gripped my imagination for two decades and to which I intended to devote my life—I was starting an MFA program in dramaturgy in the fall—an enterprise whose outlines, it seemed, had been scored into the earth wherever people lived.

Is it a coincidence that the first modern atlas, produced in 1570 by the Flemish scholar and geographer Abraham Ortelius, was called a "theater" (the word "atlas" not coming into use until 1585)? Among the seventy maps Ortelius included in his *Theatrum Orbis Terrarum*, or *Theater of the World*, is an early rendering of the Americas, North and South, parts of which—Canada, Hispaniola, Cuba, Peru—hint at the shape of the hemisphere to come. The origins of my own known world—my *theater*—lie somewhere in a pale green wilderness called Nova Francia, which extends from the northernmost edge of Ortelius's map all the way down to La Florida. Small copper-colored emblems dot the region, marking the spots where Europeans, I presume, had settled the land. Looking closely I see that each is a cluster of buildings, the means by which human beings domesticate space and signal "our mortal sojourn on earth," in Robert Pogue Harrison's elegant phrasing.

The counterpart of our primitive human desire for domestication—for grounding—is our impulse to roam. In the waters to the east of Ortelius's *Americae*, in the *Mare Atlanticum*, a majestic galleon points its bow toward the New World. With what sense of fear and expectation, I wonder, did its crew leave home to chart the future? What instinct compelled them to exchange the familiar for the unknown?

I had flown across the same ocean myself earlier that year to see the Old World, the ancient source of Western culture. Late one evening in Athens, as I sat at the desk of my hotel room, writing in my journal, I heard a strange sound in the distance, as if a subway car were rumbling toward me in the night. The noise grew louder and more rhythmic, a metric ticking, and then suddenly the room swung violently back and forth, back and forth, back and forth. The lights went out. I threw myself under the bed and waited in the dark for the convulsions to stop.

I was lucky; our building held. I crawled out from under the bed and found my way to my parents' room next door, and together we stumbled down nine flights of unlit stairs to the hotel lobby and out into the street, which was packed with people. A couple from Argentina stood near us, intoning the word *terremoto*. Someone was pointing to the sky, as if it held answers. We stayed on the sidewalk in front of our hotel for maybe an hour, until the crowd began to scatter and the hotel staff started shepherding us back to our rooms. Hours later, at four A.M., an aftershock awoke me, and I heard sirens outside. The sound was comforting: I wasn't the only one awake and frightened in this city whose foundations were suddenly fragile. The next day at breakfast we learned we had experienced a 6.7-magnitude earthquake. At its epicenter sixty miles away, near Corinth, more than a dozen people had died. Their pictures were on the front pages of the papers in the kiosks, face after lifeless face.

That morning my parents and I traveled to Delphi, to the ruins of the Temple of Apollo, home of the Delphic Oracle, whom the ancients consulted before all major undertakings. The temple itself had been destroyed by an earthquake in the fourth century B.C., rebuilt, then destroyed by human plunder.

The aftershocks kept coming. I remember thinking we were nuts to be driving in a bus on twisting mountain roads the day after an earthquake, but there we were, slaves to our itinerary. It could happen like this, then: a shrug of the earth's surface, a rumble in the night. The structures we build to last may collapse, probably will. No wonder we cling to them in our minds. "In the fusion of place and soul," Harrison writes, "the soul is as much of a container of place as place is a container of soul." One breathes life into the other.

In Delphi there was also a theater, another spectacular half circle etched into the side of a hill, opening onto a mist-laden valley once thought to be inhabited by gods. (But doesn't every theater play to the spirits?)

Back in Lancaster, on that quiet June night on the third floor of the Fulton Theatre, I pressed my face against a square of window and looked out at the city. Here was the neat line that circumscribed my first quarter century. The market and hardware store. The tea shop where I went every morning for a cup of Assam. The bookstore whose clerk knew what I was reading that week. My dad's law firm. The courthouse where I'd worked part-time my first year of college. As I stood there at the window, inhaling the view, I realized I didn't need to say goodbye just yet. I was taking my theater with me.

18

IMAGES, MOVING AND STILL: 1896–1930

Mary Yecker, née Mary Schreck, born in Germany and a resident of the United States for the past half century, was dying. She had grown so frail she could no longer sit up by herself. On the day that her husband and five surviving children gathered at her bedside to have a last family portrait made, in the first months of 1902, her daughter Annie had to squeeze into bed behind her mother and prop the ailing woman against her lap so that Mary's small, pain-stricken face could be seen.

Her sons Victor and Charles and daughters Lizzie and Ida arranged themselves in front of their mother, and her husband of nearly fifty years sat behind her and with his left arm helped to angle his invalid wife toward the camera. For the occasion Blasius Yecker wore a dark jacket and vest and a white shirt with a winged collar and a crisp bow tie. He was nearly seventy, and tired, the depth of his exhaustion visible in the deep circles beneath his eyes, but he remained a handsome man whose silver goatee and aquiline features bore a passing resemblance to those of the iconic cowboy who had so often appeared in Yecker's theater, William F. Cody.

They had all lived long enough to see the century turn, Cody and Yecker and Yecker's wife and the five Yecker children, one of whom, Charles, now managed the day-to-day operations of his father's opera house. In Lancaster the arrival of the new century had been festive: crowds on the streets; gun-shots and pennywhistles and bells. A number of churches had held vigils, an annual rite, but in that auspicious year one freighted with an extra measure of wariness and hope. So much had changed. More and more of Lancaster's streets were macadamized; there were gas and gasoline lamps, electric arc lights, telephone wires, automobiles and street cars—so many that the city had been compelled to pass an ordinance requiring wheel guards and front fenders on street cars powered by anything other than a horse.

There had been another war, its heroes and their exploits fodder for the front pages of the tabloid press and the moving-picture shows that were becoming regular fare at Yecker's theater. News traveled quickly. Trains and cars and telegrams and phonographs, Edison's kinetoscope and the Lumière brothers' cinématographe, had all conspired, it seemed, to make space and time contract. Not twenty years earlier, Andrew Carnegie had boasted that while "the old nations of the earth creep on at a snail's pace," the United States "thunders past with the rush of the express," and he had been right, as had Whitman, who had called the locomotive the "pulse of the continent."

Commerce and industry had rendered the old institutions quaint shadows of themselves. Department stores and vaudeville houses now drew more congregants than churches and theaters; workers toiled in factories where the rhythms of night and day had given way to shifts. In another year the Wright brothers would annex the sky. Yecker had played his part in it all. His advertising firm had bought up every billboard in Lancaster and helped turn the midcentury market town to which he had emigrated into a *fin de siècle* emporium of manufactured goods and entertainment. He had even tried to build a fence "for advertising purposes" in front of the Lancaster post office, but the federal government had turned him down. He had published circulars crammed with publicity for his theater and peddled the ad space inside his playbills. ("The mind, resting from the excitement of the play, and lulled by sweet music, finds natural refreshment in the reading matter and advertisements of the programme.")

For the past decade, as a member and then president of the select city council, Yecker had voted in favor of letting downtown establishments put up overhead and swinging signs and against a ban on burning coal inside the city limits. He had worked to expand the water supply system and had helped found the Lancaster Home Building and Loan Association. There had been talk of his running for mayor.

He had made several trips back to Europe to visit family and friends. When he'd first sailed to America in 1848 the journey had taken forty-two uncomfortable days, but now he could make the crossing in under two weeks, in circumstances so pleasant he deemed them a boon to his health. Here also technology had whittled time to a sliver of itself.

Or so it may have felt to Yecker as he sat beside his grown children and their dying mother on that somber day in Lancaster, waiting to be photographed. With the exception of Annie, who was struggling so to support her mother that she could not keep her own head from moving, they all sat still, hands firm, eyes unblinking, while the photographer clocked his exposure. It was a miracle, really, the way it worked: a click of the shutter and the living were preserved, even Mary, who would soon leave them, for in the act of registering the family's existence, the camera captured the light that emanated from their hair, skin, fingers, lips, and clothes, and thus something of their material selves found its way into the image whose Xeroxed likeness—made for me by Blasius and Mary Yecker's great-grandson Paul—sits beside my laptop more than a century later.

That same day, Yecker and his children gathered in a room hung with framed works of art and photography, and they had their picture taken again, this time without Mary and her sickbed, as though in anticipation of their lives to come. If the earlier image allowed them to possess the past, this one gave them a vision of the future. To look at either was, and is, to see the transience of the now.

Yecker and his wife belonged to the first generation of human beings to grow up having their pictures made at different stages of their lives. He and Mary had both been children in 1839 when the Parisian set designer and scene painter Louis Daguerre announced the invention of a means of making photographic images. ("I have seized the light," he rejoiced. "I have arrested its flight.") Not long afterward William Henry Fox Talbot announced that he too had mastered the medium, and from then on the world could be reproduced, it seemed, with an authenticity no painting could achieve. Talbot called the camera "the pencil of nature." Distant loved ones, fabled lands, celebrated actors and presidents, absent children and the cherished dead were suddenly accessible. Maybe time could be trapped after all. (An ad in the Lancaster *Evening Express*, April 20, 1861, from the W. L. Gill City Gallery on King Street: "In view of the great uncertainty of life, particularly during the coming struggle, we invite all men of our city, leaving a wife or children for the maintenance of our glorious and good flag, and the happy and free institutions of our country, and who are so situated as to be unable to pay for a picture, to call at our Gallery, with an order from their Captain, for a gratuitous photograph for their families.")

I have images of Blasius and Mary Yecker as newlyweds, a studio portrait of Blasius in thriving middle age, and this ghostly pair of photographs from the end of Mary's life. How did she feel, I wonder, having her picture "taken" just then? Did she believe, as Balzac did, that the process of being photographed robbed her of a layer of her being? It scarcely mattered, of course. The age of the image had arrived. The newspapers and magazines and books were full of them. Inside her husband's opera house a few blocks away, the images moved.

Mary Yecker died on June 13, 1902, and was buried three days later in the cemetery of Saint Mary's Catholic Church. President Yecker excused himself from his select city council meeting that evening but returned the following month to attend to the town's business. There were new amusement licenses to grant and telephone wires to be laid, parks and factories to open. Grief was no match for progress.

At a given point, one's memories of a city become a part of the city. You walk along the street and see not what is in front of you but what used to be there: the optical shop where you got your first pair of glasses (powder blue, with tiny comets in the corners), the music store where you studied guitar. You don't remember when it happened, the shift from then to now. Maybe it took place in the dark, while you were sleeping, or during one of your many trips abroad, and no one thought to tell you.

If you are Blasius Yecker you remember muddy streets and soldiers trooping off to the rail depot, the funerals of Buchanan and Stevens, and the day that Barnum's Circus filed through town in a procession so long one end ran into the other in the middle of Center Square, and the elephants and zebras got mixed up with the Bedouins on their camels, and the crowd squealed with excitement, and for a moment your life felt as infinite as Barnum's parade.

These images, too, you preserve.

At times it must have seemed to him that the town he had known in his teens had vanished altogether. Gone were the King Street saddlery where he had learned to make bridles and reins and the harness shop he had opened a few years later under his own name. Gone were the peddlers with their mules, the itinerant jugglers, the night watchmen. Some days, I imagine, he could scarcely recognize his own opera house. Where, in the red-and-gold theater that had lately become a venue for vaudeville and cinema, was the run-down hall he had purchased seven months after Appomattox?

Now it was up to son Charles to keep the enterprise going, no small matter at a time when every year, it seemed, a new music hall or vaudeville house or roof garden opened somewhere in downtown Lancaster, and the Fulton had to keep up. They had dropped the price of tickets and booked acts like the London Sports Burlesque and Athletic Club, and Hatton's Vaudevilles, and the Grand Graeco-Roman Wrestling Tournament, but audiences were free to go where they wished, and did. When Charles brought the celebrated Four Cohans to the opera house in 1901 in *The Governor's Son*, the first full-length musical by the troupe's twenty-three-year-old star, George, only a smattering of Lancastrians showed up to see it. "Unfortunately the company failed to tack the extra half-dollar to the admission fee, and the wise folk whose judgment is regulated by the prices charged allowed the show to pass unnoticed," the *New Era* observed.

Soon the city would get its first moving-picture house, the Theatatorium, with more to follow, buildings whose names spoke of glamour and ease: Dreamland, Gem, Electric Vaudeville, Bijou, Hippodrome. Americans had never had more money or time to spend on pleasure. Vaudeville acts played through the afternoon and evening; films ran from morning to midnight. Amusement parks, dance halls, restaurants, arcades, and fairs all fed the public lust for novelty. And shopping itself, that most sublime of spectacles: here too was consumption as theater. Behold the tableaux vivants of the vitrines at Hager's Department Store one block east of the Fulton and the bright displays of merchandise lining the aisles of Frank Woolworth's Five and Dime on Queen Street, the first store of its kind in the nation.

From his quiet perch in the center of the Yecker family portrait, Blasius Yecker looks out at me with grave but not unfriendly eyes, as if to say, *This is how it was for us, you see*. Charles, square-jawed and neatly groomed, with a mustache like President Roosevelt's, sits cross-legged on the floor at his father's left knee, ever the child. What counsel did he seek from the older man? His father, after all, had seen just about everything in his day: the whims of public taste, the grind of commerce, the tyranny of new technologies. Blasius Yecker had put up with unscrupulous managers and unsavory audience members, with stars who had switched shows on him at the last minute and companies that bailed long before reaching Lancaster because they had run out of money somewhere on the road. And oh, the scandals! Could anyone forget the actress who got into a fight with her manager late one night and lay sobbing on the ground outside the theater until the police came? Or the spiritualist troupe whose members were nearly arrested for charging admission on a Sunday? All of it recounted in the newspapers, of course, fodder for the town gossips.

Charles had been two years old when Blasius Yecker bought Fulton Hall in 1865, twenty-seven when his father made him a partner in the business, and thirty-five when he took over its management in 1898. The country was at war with Spain. (Ads for the five-act "semi-military" drama *Gettysburg*, which played the opera house that fall, read, "We have heard how our boys fought at Santiago. See how they fought at *Gettysburg*.") The old rep and stock systems were dying, stagehands and designers had begun to unionize, and a syndicate of theatrical producers had seized control of most of the country's major theaters and strong-armed countless performers into playing exclusively on its circuit.

Writing in 1916, the theater historian Arthur Hornblow would lament the "marked and steady decline" of the American theater at the turn of the twentieth century. "The stage," he said, "was engulfed in a wave of commercialism that gradually destroyed the art of acting, elevated mediocrities to the dignity of stars, turned playwrights into hacks, misled and vitiated public taste, and the drama, from an art, became a business."

I have never fully understood what led someone like Blasius Yecker to latch his fortunes to such a fickle trade in the first place. If he was stage-struck, he kept mum about it. Perhaps at heart he was a gambler, or a visionary who sensed the potential of this messy art to transform his century, as it had. Over the decades he had exercised prudence and thrift, and the business had rewarded him—enough to provide for a family of nine—although I've never had the impression it made him rich.

And the children who grew up in his opera house, who would in time bequeath it to their own children? (For Charles Yecker's son Raymond would take over the business in 1920.) I see them playing hide-and-seek in its shadows, trading ghost stories, catching the odd glimpse of some star in his flannels and clutching their guts in laughter. Who doesn't dream of a childhood in the theater? Toby Tyler and *Babes in Arms*, the showboat under the Christmas tree. (One year my grandmother gave me an even more beautiful little stage, a cream-colored theater made of wood, with pale blue taffeta curtains, which she had ordered up from some Germanic country; it came with complete sets of *Hansel and Gretel* and *Little Red Riding Hood*, and I have it in my basement still, boxed and waiting. Another image.)

Ask George Cohan what it was like—trundling about the country with his violin at the age of ten, going onstage four, five, six times a day with his family—and the picture dims. "A stands for Albany, good for one night," begins the ditty Cohan wrote about life on the vaudeville circuit. "B stands for Boston, for two weeks all right. C for Chicago, big money, no yaps." Critic John Lahr speaks of the "striving, anguish, and glory of the percentage play called vaudeville," the quintessentially American brand of variety that for a period of nearly thirty years was the country's most popular form of entertainment. The direct descendant of minstrelsy, with its gags and acrobatics, songs and skits, vaudeville "set the stage for the Darwinian struggle of American capitalism: the high drama of competition and adaptation to market forces where the fittest survived," Lahr writes.

Cohan spent the first years of his life on the circuit, sleeping in the top tray of his mother's trunk while his parents shuttled from one shabby gig to the next. His earliest ambition, he said, was to "be a black-faced comedian in a comedy musical act"—like his dad, a former end man. The boy did it all: took tickets at the box office, hawked autographs, distributed handbills to factory workers on their lunch hour. To promote his parents' appearance in a show about Daniel Boone he dressed up in a cowboy suit and rode around on a donkey. ("We were walking advertisements wherever we went.") He made his stage debut at age nine: "Master Georgie. Violin tricks and tinkling tunes." The images pile up: Cohan in blackface, Cohan dancing buck-and-wing, Cohan in striped pants and a boater, wagging his finger as he tells Irish jokes. He came to the Fulton four times in *The Governor's Son* and at least twice more on his own, after he had quit vaudeville and made his name as a composer, playwright, actor, director, manager, and producer. Thumb through the lavish playbill for Cohan's 1905 *Running for Office*, which rests inside an acid-free folder in the Fulton archive, and you glimpse the ego that prompted comedian Gus Williams to tell a teenaged George Michael Cohan, "If you've half as much talent as you have confidence, you'll be a great actor someday." The Fulton playbill promises "twelve big brilliant all satisfying musical numbers, each and every one a jingling, tingling, melodious gem. All composed and written by Uncle Sam's own song-writer Ge. M. Cohan."

The musicals were brash, vulgar, sappy; they have not aged well. Cohan lives instead in a few songs, in the statue erected in his honor on Broadway, and in places like the Fulton, where the trill of his tapping toes reverberates whenever a hoofer crosses the stage. At the end of his life, it was this era Cohan missed most. "In his endless reminiscence with the few friends to whom he was devoted his talk was never of the theater of the moment or even that of his years of greatest success, 1910 to 1915," biographer Ward Morehouse relates, "but nearly always of his knockabout vaudeville days, of the road adventures of the late Eighties, the Nineties and the early 1900s."

Childhood: the remembered paradise to which we so doggedly cling, its lines sharpening even as it recedes. Rerun the film and here they are again, the Four Cohans, parents and sister alive, family intact, the future beckoning. Here is Charles Yecker, watching them from the back of the house. And here in the auditorium, beside his laughing wife, is Blasius Yecker, in thrall to the ruddy-faced young man with the nasal brogue who has commandeered his theater on this February night. Another discovery; another page for the album he keeps in his mind.

The cancer revealed itself in the fall of 1902, a few months after Mary's death. Surgeons operated, and by November Blasius was well enough to attend a meeting of the select city council but too ill to fulfill his duties as president. He missed the next meeting entirely but returned in early December, still too weak to preside but able to vote on several motions. In February of 1903 he turned sixty-nine and underwent a second surgery. In April he resigned from the select city council, and in May he took to his bed. His oldest son, Victor, came home from England, where he worked as a candy manufacturer, to be with his father. As they had a year earlier for Mary, the family circled.

Outside, the days were long and gardens fragrant. Women exchanged their capes for parasols; men shed their vests and overcoats. Charles Yecker's three small children played outdoors in the sun. The youngest, Janet Olive, was nearly seven and as buoyant as her initials, "JOY," suggested. In another decade she would go to work in the box office of her father's theater, as Charles had in his day. The office now stayed open from eight thirty in the morning until nine P.M., seven days a week. Patrons could reserve seats up to six days in advance of a show by mail, telegraph, or telephone.

All through the winter and spring of his father's illness, Charles kept the opera house going, occasionally with week-long runs by stock companies but mostly with one-night stands: Walker and Williams, comedian Eddie Foy, the Indian actress Go-Won-Go-Mohawk, James O'Neill, Joseph Jefferson Jr., Stetson's *Uncle Tom's Cabin*, the Philadelphia Orchestra. In March the Four Cohans brought *The Governor's Son* to the Fulton for the third time in as many years. In April Lyman H. Howe's "America's Greatest Moving Pictures" company made its second Fulton appearance with a filmed journey from Cairo to Khartoum—"a Cook tour, at home, and with but little expense," the *New Era* wrote. Audiences were transported through the Suez Canal and up the Nile, past the Sphinx, south to the great dam at Aswan. They witnessed a wedding procession, toured a vegetable market, watched buffalo operate an ancient water wheel, climbed the pyramids. Some would remember the experience for the rest of their lives. It was as if they had been there in person, breathing the desert air, feeling the spray of the river on their skin. "No need to visit Egypt hereafter," ads promised, and people agreed.

What seemed to be movement, however, was a mirage: Howe's Egypt was nothing more than a sequence of celluloid stills projected so rapidly onto a screen they gave the impression of motion. This was the great trick that had deceived audiences for the past half century or so, the idea that you could trap action (which is to say time) and replay it at will. "Our era prefers the image to the thing, the copy to the original, the representation to the reality, appearance to being," the German philosopher Ludwig Andreas Feuerbach had written as early as 1834, two years after the debut of the phenakistoscope, a slotted disk stamped with images that seemed to move when you spun it before a mirror. Set the thing in motion and couples magically waltzed, horses leapt, a man performed sixteen successive dance steps. Instantaneous photography and magic-lantern shows, stereoscopy and a device called the photobioscope, reinforced the perception that human ingenuity had at last found a way to arrest the transient world. Trees now bent and rebent in the wind, leaves flickered and glistened, glistened and flickered, as they caught the sun's rays. A new faith, in the sanctity of illusion—illusion that gestured and grimaced and spooned food into babies' mouths—took hold.

The first moving-picture apparatus to play Yecker's Fulton Opera House was the animatagraph, part of the fare offered by Waite's Comedy Company during a two-week engagement in Lancaster in December 1896—one year after the Lumière brothers had screened the world's first motion picture at the Grand Café in Paris. Crowds eager to see the "wonderful French machine" (it was more likely English) lined up outside the Fulton long before the show. Inside the auditorium, between intervals of live melodrama and orchestral music, spectral scenes of contemporary American life fluttered across a canvas screen, and the audience, giddy with pleasure, erupted in applause. The opera house hadn't generated such excitement in years, a reporter observed. It was like old times: "The house was filled and the gallery was packed so full that it was impossible to get anywhere into it." As spectators watched in artless wonder, darkness blossomed into light, and the three-dimensional world evaporated. What need of sets and props and actors' flesh, the cumbersome trappings of the stage, when air alone could produce such marvels? Why travel, when you could stay put in downtown Lancaster and see firemen rescue children from a burning building in New York City, or a battalion of mounted police gallop out of Central Park and ride right up to the footlights? The waking dream of moving pictures required only that viewers sit passively in the dark and allow the pretense of reality to wash over them. It was a solitary business. "Alone, hidden in a dark room," critic André Bazin would write, "we watch through half-open blinds a spectacle that is unaware of our existence."

Lancastrians turned out again two months later to see Thomas Edison's "Great Vitascope," which played the Fulton in early 1897 as part of a "first-class" vaudeville act. Edison's machine unspooled images of Niagara Falls and Herald Square, a cannon artillery and yet another regiment of charging policemen. The giant pictures were "so real and the motions are so natural," a witness said, "that it is hard to realize that they are not actually alive." But they were not, of course: film had far less to do with the living than theater, and yet to the crowds in the opera house—to the crowds ever since who have been mesmerized by images drifting across screens—it seemed otherwise.

Later that year Lancaster audiences saw their first filmed sports event: a championship fight between heavyweight boxers James Corbett and Robert Fitzsimmons, projected blow-by-blow onto a screen that occupied the whole of the Fulton stage. Churches and other groups had opposed the program, but there was no stopping it. Fans took sides and applauded the "specially severe punches."

By the time Lyman Howe first came to the Fulton in 1899 with a moving-picture machine he called the war-graph, the novelty of the medium had worn off, and a smaller audience showed up to see the night's main offering: scenes from the battlefields of the Spanish-American

War, including a victorious American charge "with men falling on all sides, shells tearing up the ground and the Red Cross men rushing fearlessly in to care for the wounded." Unlike Edison's vitascope, which featured twenty-second loops of film spliced end-to-end and threaded onto a bank of rollers, Howe's projector used reels, which meant he could combine short films into longer and more complex sequences—a hint of cinematic delights to come. The war-graph was the first full-length program of moving pictures to play the Fulton, unaccompanied by a vaudeville or other live act. For Charles Yecker, the deal was handsome. Howe charged relatively little for his pictures, and although the ticket prices were low—between ten and fifty cents—the percentage was high, and Howe split the profits fifty-fifty with the opera house. Small wonder that Yecker brought the company back repeatedly during the next two decades. Live theater couldn't compete.

From the end of the century until 1916, Lyman H. Howe's "High-Class Moving Pictures" was the foremost traveling picture exhibition in the United States. Howe himself stopped touring with the company after 1899 but continued to oversee his business. A lanky Pennsylvanian with the bland good looks of a salesman, which he was, he called himself "the Barnum of them all." He had built his operation from scratch—designed his own projector, purchased raw footage from companies like Edison and Lumière, selected individual shots and organized them in sequences he thought audiences would enjoy. Onstage, he had run the projector and provided commentary, the standard format for early exhibitions of moving pictures. Howe's particular innovation was to add sound—initially from a phonograph and then from live performers who hid behind the screen and manufactured special effects. "We are able to reproduce pictures that speak," ads pledged. War-graph audiences heard the din of cannons and muskets as Howe's projector unloosed image after image of the American navy bombarding the Cuban fleet. There were even curls of smoke. Small though it was, the crowd at the Fulton went "wild." The Lancaster papers praised the "forcible naturalness" of Howe's pictures, their "true to life" details, the absence of so much as a "quiver or flicker" in the war-graph's remarkable views of history in action.

What was past could suddenly exist in the present—not only exist, as in a photograph, but walk and breathe. The cinema opened a fissure in the tenebrous wall between yesterday and today, there and here, the dead and the quick. It replicated the mind's habit of replaying old scenes, and thus to the men and women who settled into the padded seats of Charles Yecker's opera house, it felt real in a way that theater, with its fictions and pretense, did not. The sheer banality of the very first moving images—a watermelon-eating contest, a woman feeding a flock of doves, a runaway horse—deepened the illusion. The cinema rendered the world "a smaller and more ordinary place," writes film historian Eric Rhode. It harnessed the dynamism of everyday life.

And yet for years it was not clear what purpose film served. Archival? Sentimental? Pedagogical? Was it simply a more bracing way of delivering the day's news or baseball scores? Lyman Howe composed elaborate travelogues using footage he had bought on trips to Europe, and these had their following. For a time the Fulton presented one or two of his travel programs yearly, often to sellout crowds. People liked the way Howe made it seem as if you were sitting at the front of a moving train, watching the world's scenery unfold. The proscenium disappeared and the auditorium flattened, and for two hours you rolled right along with the pictures. With plays you always knew where you were—the light from the stage splashed onto the seats and walls, the actors paced themselves according to your laughter—but film plunged you into shadow and then carried you off to some exotic locale, to Paris or London or Shanghai or Delhi or Cairo. There you were, gazing up at the Sphinx.

It's how I first knew the Fulton: sitting in the dark as an eleven-year-old, looking up at an unfamiliar city, the space around me, my own city, of no consequence, released from the humdrum events of my life and thrust into someone else's story. Here was the secret: film as narrative, a vaporous, larger-than-life drama you could enter at will and revisit any time you wanted for the price of a ticket.

That moving pictures could be a powerful mechanism for the telling of stories became apparent at roughly the same time Blasius Yecker lay dying in his home on West Orange Street, just around the corner from the opera house whose survival had been his preoccupation for almost forty years. The canvas screen that men like Howe ferried under their arms would become a permanent fixture of Charles Yecker's theater. Was it possible that something so inconsequential—a rectangle of fabric bobbing in the flies—could threaten the whole enterprise? When the exhilaration of film "has been blended in the right proportions with the psychic ingredient it commands," Antonin Artaud was to predict, "it will leave the theater far behind and we will relegate the latter to the attic of our memories." Artaud envisioned a different kind of cinema from the "venial hybrid art" of commercial movies that came to dominate twentieth-century entertainment, but he was right to foresee film as theater's rival, at least in the beginning.

Over the next decade Charles Yecker would seek to counter the seductions of moving pictures with the extravagance of the real. He would gut the interior of his opera house, add a second balcony with wooden benches and a separate entrance, install a new ceiling with elaborate plaster molding and four "handsomely decorated" box seats on either side of the proscenium. He would expand the Fulton's stage and orchestra pit, create new dressing rooms and fire escapes, enlarge and tile the front lobby, and build a magnificent new staircase and foyer with marble walls and carpeted floors.

Twice he would bring in Klaw and Erlanger's colossal production of *Ben-Hur*, which featured a live camel, hundreds of actors and stagehands, thousands of square feet of scenery, and eight horses galloping full-speed toward the audience on treadmills. Charles would present Stetson's Big, Double Spectacular *Uncle Tom's Cabin*, with Southern cakewalkers, two brass bands, donkeys, bloodhounds, and wagons drawn by Shetland ponies. He would book showgirls from Ziegfeld's Follies, vaudeville stars like Eva Tanguay and Lillian Russell and May Irwin, and the temperance crusader Carrie Nation, whose diatribe so enraged the college boys in Yecker's audience that he had to call the police. He would introduce Sarah Bernhardt to Lancastrians in a production of *La Dame aux Camelias* that few could understand but everyone wanted to see. (The sixty-seven-year-old legend arrived on a train with seven Pullman sleeping cars, including her own, which she insisted be parked miles from the opera house to protect her from "curious people.") To boost sales for a stock company, Charles would persuade one of its members to get married onstage at the end of a show. Hundreds of spectators paid to watch the real-life ceremony.

Charles Yecker signed contracts with the Shubert brothers, Klaw and Erlanger, Nixon and Zimmerman. In 1911, he announced a full season of vaudeville and moving pictures. Bulldogs and comedians, travelogues and newsreels took the place of legitimate theater. In 1916, in what papers called a "coup," he obtained the rights to present the Lancaster premiere of D. W. Griffith's *Birth of a Nation*, accompanied by a twenty-piece orchestra and a cast of live actors. "Business at the Fulton Opera House seems to be on the mend," the *Intelligencer* volunteered hopefully. But a group of locals deemed the film, as they had its theatrical predecessor, *The Clansman*, which Charles had also tried to present, an insult to the memory of Thaddeus Stevens, and the mayor banned the picture one day before it was due to open. *Birth of a Nation*—with its cartoonlike depiction of Stevens—moved ten miles west of Lancaster to the opera house in Columbia, Pennsylvania, and the "almost unprecedented" crowds who had bought tickets to see the three-hour epic at the Fulton took trolley cars out to the little town, a two-hour journey each way. Yecker was furious. He had spent huge sums advertising the premiere—money he couldn't recoup, he told reporters. "Why did not the mayor act when the show was first advertised and not wait until the week of the performance?" Griffith's revisionist take on Reconstruction America fueled outrage in Columbia as well, where members of the Negro Waiters Association protested its screening. The town's chief burgess intervened. "The members of your race would be benefited by attending it," he lectured the group. "It would make better men of them."

In Lancaster, where the press had begun referring to "this depression in the amusement business," Charles soldiered on. Increasingly, high art (Mrs. Patrick Campbell in Shaw's *Pygmalion*, Walter Damrosch and the New York Philharmonic) surrendered to low: minstrel shows, second-rate musical revues, cheap burlesque, more and more moving pictures. Is it any surprise that one day, in the spring of 1920, as he was walking home from the opera house, Charles Yecker suffered a sudden stroke and died? He was fifty-six and heartsick, I want to believe, at what had become of his father's theater. For a few months Charles's son Raymond took over the business and served up more of the same tawdry fare. When a group calling itself the Law and Order Society demanded he cease, Raymond refused, and the society had him arrested for "exhibiting immoral shows." Raymond promptly sold the opera house to a pair of businessmen who refurbished the inside of the Fulton, added a bright marquee to the front entrance, and brought back real plays.

For a time hope sputtered. Then came the talkies, the stock market crash, the Depression, and the cinema sealed its grip on American life. By 1933 half of New York City's theaters had closed, and seventy million Americans were attending movies weekly in the country's fourteen thousand "houses" devoted exclusively to moving pictures. Lancastrians could choose from the Colonial, with its green leather seats and electric fans; the Hamilton, with its pipe organ and lobby sofas; and the Capitol, with its marble drinking fountains. Or they could go to the Fulton, for in 1930 the building's newest manager announced that with few exceptions the "Fulton Theatre" would from this point forward present only motion pictures. A fireproof projection booth was installed on the second balcony, and columns that had obstructed people's view of the screen were removed. Stars who in recent years had graced the Fulton Opera House in person—Douglas Fairbanks, Ethel Barrymore, Otis Skinner, Billie Burke, Helen Hayes, Theda Bara, W. C. Fields—returned to the building as celluloid apparitions of themselves.

I write these paragraphs exactly one hundred and six years to the day after Blasius Yecker died in his home on West Orange Street. The papers give the time of his death—which came as a shock, despite his illness, and was thus accompanied "with more than the usual poignancy of grief"—as 10 A.M., Friday, May 15, 1903. As I write, my words take shape on a small screen on which I have lately been watching early footage by the Lumière brothers and the Edison company and Googling contextual information on Louis Daguerre and Lyman Howe. The screen on my desk also reports the day's news, allows me to book flights to Pennsylvania, lets me purchase tickets to the Fulton (and see video previews of what's onstage), puts me in touch with colleagues, and delivers whole books for me to peruse. (Perhaps you too are reading this on a screen.) What Blasius Yecker would think of this I cannot say, but it's a safe bet his great-great-great grandchildren, of whom there are more than forty, find these technologies as handy as I do.

All along I have been drawn to the immigrant showman who crossed the Atlantic in 1848 in search of a future that Europe, with its monarchs and empires, blights and rebellions, could not provide. The obituaries praise Blasius Yecker as "an upright and honorable man" who "never faltered in doing what he thought was right"—an image somewhat at odds with the entrepreneur who gave Lancastrians their first coon songs and leg shows. He may have passed for a bourgeois with his pinstriped suits and watch fobs and city-council appointment, but Blasius Yecker was a working man who knew what it meant to pool your pennies for a bit of gaiety on Saturday night. The bleak northern skies and harsh pieties of his birthplace, the widow's penury that was his mother's fate even before his birth—these stripped him of any bourgeois complacency and fueled his great striving, the will that propelled a fourteen-year-old boy to leave home by himself and sail to a country he had never seen. Of course he would wind up in the theater: his very life was a thing of fantasy.

In America he learned to make saddles and set type and run a box office, anything to secure himself in the wilderness of a new world. He married, had children, joined a church, went into business. He became a citizen and bought property—a pair of homes, a harness shop, an ad agency, and a cavernous hall perched on top of a stone jail whose doors had once opened onto a stream that led to a timbered Eden. Yecker turned this unlikely construction into a limelit haven where the people of his adopted city could engage in the rituals of theater, that ancient art of appearances by which we transcend the boundaries of self and place and time.

In his last will and testament, Yecker bequeathed $500 for the upkeep of his grave—a slab of Pennsylvania limestone inscribed with his name and the names of his wife and children. He instructed his heirs to do as they wished with the rest of his property, "to sell all my Real Estate by public sale or private contract," which they did, his grandson Raymond disposing of the Fulton in 1921, after the building had nearly ruined him.

But Raymond's sister Janet, whose initials spelled JOY, went on working in the box office of her grandfather's opera house even after the Fulton became a movie theater. "She had a heart for it, a feel," remembers Sister Rosemary Mulac, the nun who took care of Janet at the end of her life. Blasius Yecker's granddaughter lived to be 103 years old. She never married. In 1995, in her one hundredth year, the Fulton underwent another major renovation and expansion—the fourth complete overhaul of the building since its construction in 1852. Sister Rosemary suggested to Janet that they visit the new theater, but Janet said no, "I'm afraid I'm going to be hurt." Eventually she relented, and the two women set off in Sister Rosemary's car. When they pulled up in front of the theater, however, Janet refused to get out. She was afraid, Sister Rosemary saw, "of losing what she loved." Brother, father, uncles, aunts, grandfather: they were all there, behind Samuel Sloan's freshly restored ivory façade, the assembled dead, her one family, and it seems the old woman did not want to break the spell.

19

GHOST DANCE: 1896–1997

Among the first moving pictures to play the Fulton was a short sequence showing one of William F. Cody's cowboys riding a bucking pony. The primitive Western delighted viewers. Savage nature, stoic man: the essential components of the genre were there. The real West, as everyone knew, had vanished—tribal lands domesticated, once-measureless prairies cut and stitched by rail lines and barbed-wire fences. "Only Buffalo Bill remains," a reporter for the *Kansas City World* ventured in 1896, the same year Cody's cowboy lurched onto the Fulton's canvas screen. "Standing as the connecting link between the past and the present, he draws back the curtain of retrospection and reveals the picturesque figures who played dramatic parts in the border life of American history."

The great man himself continued to bring his Wild West Show to Lancaster's fairgrounds every few years. Cody's last appearance, in 1913, coincided with the release of his own cinematic homage to the West, *Indian Wars Pictures*, a reenactment of the Plains Indians wars of the 1870s, shot on location with veterans of the battles—the lost frontier revived as imagery. The year 1913 also saw the debut of the Indian-head nickel, stamped with the austere but genial features of the Sioux warrior Iron Tail, who became an instant star. His face turns up in a photograph of Cody's Wild

West troupe as the company parades through Lancaster during a visit to the city. Cody, gray-haired and regal, leads the entourage in a horse-drawn carriage, the mythic Buffalo Bill trailed by his retinue of friendly Indians, one of whom is the guy whose likeness you can now exchange for candy. Meanwhile, out in the real West, Edward Curtis was busy photographing native chiefs before their race went extinct, as was widely expected. Some predicted that by 1935 the process that had begun, in part, with the annihilation of the Conestogas in Lancaster's workhouse would be complete.

Memory, it turns out, is both a physical and a psychological phenomenon. In the process of recalling an event, our brains reactivate the neurons that fired during the original experience, so that it is possible, with the use of electrode implants, for scientists to now pinpoint the location of specific memories in the human mind. Buildings likewise retain and reanimate the past. "The heights of rooms, the amount of window openings, the rhythm of open spaces and closed spaces, of wall surfaces and windows, the relation of roof and façade—all these things reflect social habit and spiritual need, as well as structural necessity and climatic conditions," writes Lewis Mumford. "That is why architecture tells history, for it shows how, and why, and to what end, people have lived."

When that end is violence—the extermination of a race of human beings, for example—a building not only tells history but becomes what Victor Hugo termed its "terrible and inseparable witness." A mute witness, mostly, except on those occasions when the walls are moved to speak. A cowboy floats across a screen on a bucking horse; a column of Indians files through town. The past wakes, and with it the phantoms in the stones.

The first recorded sighting occurred in the mid-1920s, not long before the Fulton became a movie house. A man working backstage claimed he had seen a wraith in white skulking in the wings. Subsequent sightings put the same spectral being in the narrow stairway between the stage and the dressing rooms. Over the years actors and stagehands would report white vapors in the auditorium, sudden applause from empty seats, doors bursting open, a piano playing in a vacant room, spirits on the pin rail and balconies, gusts of icy *something* in the basement, a shadowy presence seventy feet above the stage that seemed to drift, like Prometheus, in perpetuity up and down a ladder, eternally bound, with all the others, to this building.

"If a house," writes Robert Pogue Harrison, "a building, or a city is not palpably haunted in its architectural features—if the earth's historicity and containment of the dead do not pervade its articulated forms and constitutive matter—then that house, building, or city is dead to the world. Dead to the world means cut off from the earth and closed off from its underworlds. For that is one of the ironies of our life worlds: they receive their animation from the ones that underlie them."

In February 1959, when the Fulton reopened as a theater for the first time since 1930, the production of choice was *Our Town*—Thornton Wilder's classic work about small-town America, in which the dead take their place onstage next to the living. The production's real-life stage manager, John Binkley, told a reporter that backstage between performances, he often had "the uncanny feeling" that spirits were present. "Crazy feeling, I know, but we all noticed it, every so often. Wasn't scary as you might think, either. Whoever—or whatever—it was didn't seem to pay any attention to us."

The Fulton in those days was a relic of itself, a theater turned movie house turned theater. Actors got dressed in a plywood cubicle in the unheated scene dock. The auditorium was so filthy they had to wash down the seats before performances. The ropes in the fly system, long unused, were frayed, and some had rotted, and between rehearsals the play's director took it on himself to replace them. Small wonder the talk in Lancaster was of tearing the Fulton down, putting up a parking garage in its place, modernizing. But the plays continued. One month after *Our Town*, Luther Adler brought *A View from the Bridge* to the city, the Fulton's first road show in years. A summer stock season was soon announced.

Writing in 1968—four years after a group of citizens calling themselves the Fulton Opera House Foundation purchased the theater for $75,000 and began restoring it, and one year before the U.S. Department of the Interior designated the Fulton a Registered National Historic Landmark—director Peter Brook suggested, in his seminal meditation on the stage, *The Empty Space*, that the "only vital question" to be asked, the question that "measures the whole structure," is "why theater at all? What for? Is it an anachronism, a superannuated oddity, surviving like an old monument or a quaint custom? Why do we applaud, and what? Has the stage a real place in our lives? What function can it have? What could it serve? What could it explore? What are its special properties?"

Many would argue that its special property is life itself, "the closeness of the living organism," in Jerzy Grotowski's phrasing, the one element "of which film and television cannot rob the theater." But isn't death equally its business? The peculiar charge we feel inside theaters—the tingle I invariably sense when a show is over, and the ushers are making their way through the empty auditorium, picking up playbills—is this not because I've just witnessed a ceremonial death? Something visibly alive has ended (even bad theater can have this effect). Not just ended, vanished: the actors who slip out of the stage door, shorn of costumes and makeup, are not the same people we've been watching onstage. Those people have died, and their absence elicits a blend of awe and gratitude and sadness not unlike the sensations we experience at a funeral. Even the tiny, subversive thrill I felt as a child bringing my cardboard Heidi to life in my showboat, drawing words from her immobile mouth, was a kind of resurrection. "The actor is death speaking, is the deceased speaking to me!" exults the playwright Valère Novarina.

"The simultaneous attraction to and fear of the dead, the need continually to rehearse and renegotiate the relationship with memory and the past, is nowhere more specifically expressed in human culture than in theatrical performance," writes Marvin Carlson in his evocative book about theater and memory, *The Haunted Stage*. To watch a play is to see a thing born, grow, and die. For this living organism, this performance, is one and only.

In Western culture we recognize three basic forms of divine space: wilderness, tomb, and those instances of human architecture that connect their occupants to the mysteries of the cosmos. Churches, tabernacles, temples, theaters. If the Fulton Theatre has survived into the twenty-first century, it is because it puts us in touch with what we know to be holy.

Jesse Nighthawk learned about the massacre of the Conestogas at "some pow-wow or something at Lancaster's Jewish Community Center, of all places," he tells me by phone from Arizona. I am in Michigan. It is the first decade of the twenty-first century, and we are both preoccupied with what happened to the Indians in Lancaster County in the winter of 1763. Jesse's voice rasps and drawls; to my surprise he seems willing to talk as long as I'm willing to listen. I am the impatient one, in a hurry to get the story, as if another hundred years might speed by and I'd miss my chance.

Neither of us is exactly sure why we're obsessed. Nighthawk—born Roy L. Rogers in Oklahoma, a full-blooded Cherokee who served in Vietnam in the 173rd Airborne and admits he's "in and out of a mental institution from time to time," who tells me, "All my life I've always been in trouble with the authorities"—says, "I'm drawn to all the people, for whatever reason. I do feel kinship to all Native people."

I can't bring myself to tell him I feel a similar kinship with a building. Instead I ask if he finds it odd that a theater should have been constructed on the site of the workhouse killings. "Not necessarily," he considers. "They weren't really into city planning back then."

He and his then-wife and two daughters were living in Lancaster in the mid-1990s when the Fulton board raised $9.5 million to renovate the opera house and add a four-story annex to its north side. The theater had become a firetrap and either had to be rebuilt from top to bottom or abandoned. Work on the project began in 1994 and continued for eighteen months. At the last performance in the old Fulton, a pianist played Liszt's "Mephisto Waltz." As she struck the final note of the piece, a white key suddenly burst from the instrument, soared into the air, and exploded. The effect was not part of her act, and no one who saw it could explain it.

During the renovation itself, construction workers reported an upsurge of otherworldly activity inside the gutted opera house. The local press, avidly tracking news of the renovation, hinted that the spirits who famously haunted the Fulton were unhappy at being disturbed. One construction worker became so unhinged by an encounter he had in the shadows with some unnamed presence that he ran screaming from the theater and had to be taken to the psychiatric wing of the local hospital. He never went back.

At about this time, Nighthawk's wife, Pamela, had a dream. She was in a longhouse, surrounded by older people who were smiling at her and nodding their heads, saying, "Everything's OK, everything is all right." She told Jesse about the dream, and he thought about it for a while and realized she'd had a vision. By then he had become an activist for Native American issues in the region, and he was upset about recent plans to dig up an Indian burial plot near the Susquehanna River. ("They're always doing shit like that," he told Pamela. "They throw up a smoke screen, and the next thing you know there's a subdivision.") He had also been reading about the "noises and stuff" at the Fulton. Somehow Pamela's dream brought all of this together in his mind, and Nighthawk decided he needed to honor the Conestogas, to console their wandering spirits and restore peace to the place where the last of their people had died.

Thinking not about the distant past but about the Vietnam War and its memorial on the Washington, D.C., Mall, writer Barry Spector observes, "The need to make meaningful narrative out of trauma leads to the search for authentic community and for art." Spector evokes Toni Morrison's phrase *disremembered past*—"that which is neither remembered nor forgotten, but haunts the living as a ghost"—to suggest that the only way for the human soul to achieve what we call "closure" is by remembering and grieving rather than forgetting. "Only then can the 'corpses' of a life—all one's losses and disappointments—receive proper burial," Spector continues. "In other, older cultures, authentic grief rituals align the ego's wish for closure with the deeper intentions of the soul to know itself."

The Eastern Woodlands Indians who inhabited what is now Pennsylvania saw ritual as a sacred gift, one so powerful its bestowal could lead a recipient into other dimensions of the universe. To convey both reciprocity and respect toward the natural world and to gain access to sacred powers, the Indians developed a vast repertoire of rites: hunting and planting ceremonies, rituals of supplication and appeasement, healing and mourning. They devised new rites as the occasion demanded, especially in the late eighteenth century, as they sought to resist colonial expansion. Dreams often provided the rationale for new ceremonies, and natives relied on clairvoyants able to divine dreams and prescribe appropriate rites for alleviating particular ailments.

In the late spring of 1997, a little more than a year after a drastically refurbished and much bigger Fulton Theatre had opened to clamorous reviews, and nearly two hundred and fifty years after the Paxton "boys" had attacked the Lancaster workhouse and butchered its inhabitants, Nighthawk and a group of friends and activists designed a ceremony to cleanse the murder site and ritually bury the souls of the slain. The performance took place on Sunday, June 15, in front of the old jail wall on Water Street, near the entrance to the Fulton greenroom. Two plaques were unveiled, honoring the Indians who had died in the village of Conestoga and in the Lancaster workhouse. Nighthawk and others sang songs, a man named Wayne Cave pounded a ceremonial drum, and four bowls placed in the four directions of the compass, each containing stalks of burning cedar and sweetgrass—cleansing plants traditionally used to help usher the dead from this world to the next—sent fragrant wafts of smoke into the air. A hundred spectators looked on. The afternoon heat was searing, but several people in the crowd, including Nighthawk, felt a chill wind suddenly gust through the street in the midst of the ceremony. At that point, Nighthawk would remember, "I think there *was* a presence, there most definitely was a presence. Maybe that breeze means some relief for those that had gone on." As quickly as it had come, the wind left.

After the ritual, Nighthawk and his friends went off to a park by the Conestoga River to eat fry bread and smoke a peace pipe. Barry Kornhauser, the Fulton's playwright-in-residence and director of children's programs, went back to his office on the third floor of the theater. He had been given a braid of sweetgrass from the ceremony to store in the Fulton archives, and he tossed it onto his desk, locked the door, and went home. When he came to work the next morning and opened the door to his office, he saw that his desk—perennially heaped with scripts and papers and gadgets and books—had been swept bare, its clutter strewn across the floor, "as if a wind had blown through the office," Barry would tell people again and again. "Only the sweetgrass braid was on the desk, lying by itself in the middle."

I don't believe in ghosts. Neither does Barry, whom I've known since 1981, when he and I worked together at the Fulton for a few months, sitting on opposite sides of the same desk that two decades later would be scoured clean by an inexplicable force. It was the end of my last stint at the Fulton, the start of his first. We've stayed in touch all these years, linked in part by our mutual compulsion to *get* the story of this building we both love, this sublime and elusive sphinx that stands in the middle of a city that's lately been named one of the best places in America to live, a red-brick city that was once the largest inland settlement in the British colonies.

We're not alone. While I was working on this book, Lancaster journalist Jack Brubaker was writing a history of the workhouse massacre, and he concluded, with strong evidence, that the magistrates of Lancaster were complicit in the killings that took place two days after Christmas in 1763, on a snowy afternoon while many of the town's leading citizens were in church, celebrating the birth of Christ. The Conestogas were a problem, and in the vigilantes from Paxton, Brubaker believes, the magistrates saw a solution. Warned of a possible assault on the jail, they turned a blind eye and let it happen.

Rites and memorials, histories too, can only go so far. They seem to help us feel better about things we can't change, events that belong to us by default. Maybe that cool breeze really did bring relief to the lost souls of the dead Conestogas. Maybe the grounding we crave, and that rituals seem to provide, really does happen, and in the performance of symbolic actions we apprehend the sacred. Whatever. We keep on doing them.

In all of this story, the Conestogas surface and plunge like deep-sea divers. Kyunqueagoah, known as Captain Jack, and his wife, Betty, or Koweenasee. Tenseedaagua and his wife, Kanianguas. Saquies-hat-tah, and his wife, Chee-na-wan, and their son, Quaachow. The little boys Shae-e-kah, Ex-undas, Tong-quas, and Hy-ye-naes. The girls Ko-qoa-e-un-quas, Karen-do-uah, and Canu-kie-sung. Destroyed two days after Christmas by the forebears of Buffalo Bill and all the cowboys, real and imagined, who would return to this spot as if on a pilgrimage, the Indians' mutilated corpses hauled off to a common grave and later exhumed, reinterred, dug up again, their bones lost, the very idea of them scattered into the clouds like the ashes of the village they once inhabited in William Penn's endless woods. That a theater—a house of spirits, living and dead—should occupy the ground where they died is perhaps, in the end, not so strange after all.

I drove away from Lancaster in August 1981 in my late aunt's Pontiac, the same car I had wrecked the previous year on a two-lane highway not far from a former boyfriend's house. I had been brooding about him, my head in a vengeful fog, and sped right through a stop sign and into a moving car. Another brush with Thanatos. No one was hurt, but the Pontiac had taken months to repair. Now it was crammed with theater books, dictionaries, my dog-eared thesaurus, clothes, cookware, and a black IBM Selectric the Fulton had let me buy for twenty-five dollars, the theater having earlier that year entered the digital age.

As I drove north, from the cornfields of south-central Pennsylvania into the granite hills of Massachusetts, where the trees were already beginning to rust, the poets I had been reading compulsively all summer—Sexton, Plath, Kumin, Sarton—rode with me. Theirs was the world I meant to inhabit. I half expected to run into Plath and Ted Hughes in Amherst, where I'd be renting a room in a white clapboard house on Pleasant Street, a few blocks from Emily Dickinson's manse and the stone library that held Robert Frost's papers. My rebuilt Pontiac lumbered north around Reading, through the Delaware Water Gap and the Poconos, along the Hudson River, past Sing Sing, into Connecticut. I was climbing. Somewhere outside Waterbury I pulled off the highway and opened the letter my mother had tucked into my purse that morning. She knew, even if I didn't, that I was leaving home for good this time. For weeks I had been practicing saying goodbye. Bike rides through the countryside around my parents' house, lunches with friends, a party at the Fulton a few days after my last official week on the job. My desk inside the theater was emptied and my successor trained. Funny how dispensable I had turned out to be.

In Amherst I would study theater history and criticism, costume and lighting design, acting theory, directing, Greek drama, the Irish Renaissance, Spanish theater. I would work on plays by Shakespeare and Jonson and Mamet and O'Neill. I would meet the unexpectedly plump, Pepsi-guzzling guru of the ascetic stage, Jerzy Grotowski. I would spend the better part of two years reading scripts for the Hartford Stage Company and another six months running the theater's summer program for kids. I would begin work on a biography of Lorca that would take me to Spain and my first husband and eventually to Michigan, where I would finally and somewhat reluctantly *settle*, whatever that means.

Aren't we supposed to leave home? Wasn't that my fundamental task, the one I'd been preparing for ever since my mother and father had carried me out of the Lancaster General Hospital a quarter of a century earlier and back to their second-story apartment on Frederick Street?

No false starts this time, no last-minute retreat down the interstate. I was doing it, bidding farewell, *moving*.

New England. The storied beginnings of the country. The Pilgrims and Plymouth Rock. Concord. Bunker Hill. Dickinson herself. And in my own century, O'Neill, whose ghosted Monte Cristo Cottage stood beside the ocean a few hours south of Amherst. O'Neill understood American wanderlust: he'd spent a lifetime leaving home and looking for one.

When I was still an infant my parents had built a new house on the east side of Lancaster, on a piece of farmland overlooking a creek that fed into the Conestoga River. As soon as I could, I'd built my own dwelling on that same property—a "fort," consisting mainly of a fallen tree, in the woods outside my bedroom window. The tree's damp, buggy interior was just big enough to let me curl up inside and spy on my parents' home from a distance of maybe twenty yards. Mother, father, brother, sister: they were all there, behind the walls, actors ready to perform, if only I would reveal myself, their one audience. But I preferred to stay inside my makeshift fort, the one I've been constructing for myself ever since.

"All really inhabited space bears the essence of the notion of home," Bachelard writes. Perhaps this is why I cling to the Fulton thirty years after I cleared out my desk and surrendered my keys to the building and drove off in my dead aunt's car. "If I were asked to name the chief benefit of the house," Bachelard continues, "I should say: the house shelters daydreaming, the house protects the dreamer, the house allows one to dream in peace." Echoes of one's "first, oneirically definitive house" reverberate in subsequent structures, and these in turn nourish our imaginative wanderings, so that "the places in which we have *experienced daydreaming* reconstitute themselves in a new daydream."

I would exchange the pinwork fields and gentle hills of Lancaster for rocky New England and treeless Spain and forested Michigan, but I would keep the dwelling places of my past with me, among them my old theater, this iconic *house*, cradle of reverie. The Fulton is more than a history of the American stage or the odyssey of a young nation—it is a reflection of my being. In its tug of war between stone and glass, cellar and façade, prison and box office, I see the material incarnation of my own struggle to reconcile body and spirit, to build up and away from the chaos of instinct. Here is bedlam chiseled into order, darkness framed by light, desire and heartbreak, laughter and violence redrawn as play. And in the midst of it all, waiting to be claimed, a vast and uncanny silence. Empty space. Temple of the soul. The old Greek *theatron*—a place for seeing, which is to say knowing. The stage around whose incandescent glow I continue to orbit.

At about the same time that Samuel Sloan was sketching his plans for Fulton Hall, another Philadelphia architect was giving a series of lectures on their art, one of the first attempts by an American to lay out a formal theory of architecture. Thomas U. Walter, who was to design the dome and wing extensions of the U.S. Capitol in the 1850s and early '60s, believed that, properly conceived, buildings could "excite in us the purest sentiments of infinity," could lead the soul on an "upward flight . . . from the visible to the invisible," all the way to God. (A few decades later James Joyce would suggest that "any object, intensely regarded, may be a gate of access to the incorruptible eon of the gods.") Walter compared buildings to books, inasmuch as both rely on an established language to communicate ideas. He believed the act of design was as intellectual a pursuit as that of writing a book.

My own book of the Fulton keeps writing itself. While I was at work on its last chapters, Randy Harris, a Lancaster-based consultant for historic preservation and community development, unearthed evidence demonstrating that the theater is "a site of significance" to the Underground Railroad. Harris found two separate sources indicating that in 1835, a jailer known as "Dare Devil Dave" Miller deliberately allowed two fugitive slave women to slip out of the Lancaster prison—site of the future Fulton Theatre—on his watch. One of the women was later recaptured, and Miller, a member of the Anti-Mason Party and a staunch foe of capital punishment, was subpoenaed to testify at her trial. He claimed to know nothing about how the women had escaped. But to a questioner who subsequently asked him in private "how it happened that he allowed two negro women to slip through his fingers," Miller "winked and laughed," according to an account in R. C. Smedley's 1883 *History of the Underground Railroad in Chester and the Neighboring Counties of Pennsylvania*. "It was afterward discovered," Smedley reports, that Miller had simply "opened the door and let them walk out." Harris submitted his findings to the National Park Service in 2008, and that same year the service designated the Fulton an official part of its nationwide Underground Railroad Network to Freedom.

When I first learned of the designation, I thought I had found a romantic ending to my story. But history is inconvenient. Miller, it seems, was the exception. Inside the archives of LancasterHistory.org, a small cache of legal documents—jail lists, depositions, affidavits, writs of habeas corpus—attests to the fate more typically experienced by those desperate African Americans who fled north into Lancaster County, only to be found and incarcerated in the town prison whose walls form the foundation of my theater. In their banality, the documents in the archives still the heart:

> To any Constable, and to the Keeper of the Prison of Lancaster County, Greeting:
> These are to authorize and require you, the said Constable, forthwith to convey and deliver into the custody of the Keeper of the said Prison, the body of Richard Jackson Col'd Man brought before me, Daniel Moore, Esquire, an Alderman of the said city, by Henry Chalfant charged with having run away from his Master Patrick Begley, and on examination he confessed the fact.
> And you, the said Keeper, are hereby required to receive the said Richard Jackson into your custody in the said prison, and him there safely to keep until he shall thence be delivered by due course of law. And for so doing this shall be your sufficient warrant.
> Given under my hand and seal, this 23rd day of August 1825. Daniel Moore

Jackson was luckier than many. A writ of habeas corpus attesting that he had committed no "criminal or supposed criminal matter" was filed on his behalf—presumably by a Lancaster County abolitionist (Jackson himself signed the document with an "X")—and although he spent several months in prison, Jackson ultimately appears to have been freed. But countless others were remanded to their enslavers. Thus does the

Fulton remain a haunted house. Any vision of God it might afford is a troubling one.

A last episode. Diagnosed with terminal cancer in the winter of 2008, Michael Mitchell, artistic director of the Fulton during the preceding decade, told the theater's board of directors he was at peace. When people asked him how that was possible, he said to the board members, his answer was simple: "Living my life in places like this. Grand spiritual enterprises. Not all theaters are like this. In fact, very few. But those of us who are lucky enough to *listen* recognize the voices you can hear here. And if you listen, the sounds are always here. How to sustain yourself, how to enrich every moment of your life, how to be enveloped, how to find peace, are in this space, even when there's no one in this space but me and this space."

Mitchell died a few months later, and his funeral, which he scripted himself, was a grand public event, a mix of Protestant ritual and street theater and musical-comedy schmaltz. The ceremony began with the rites of burial and communion in Saint James Episcopal Church—the site where Edward Shippen and the magistrates of Lancaster attended Christmas services on the day the Paxton gang attacked. The presiding minister, acknowledging the huge number of unfamiliar faces in the congregation, most of them friends of Mitchell's from the Fulton, welcomed the crowd "to our house just as you have so often welcomed us into your beloved house." The church's organist and music director, Ron Barnet, also the Fulton's music director, played both hymns and show tunes. A soprano sang "Climb Every Mountain." Afterward a bagpiper, retracing the route Shippen and his fellow congregants took on the day of the Paxton killings, led us out of the church, down Orange Street, onto Prince Street, and into the Fulton, where we settled into the auditorium for a theatrical homage to Mitchell.

It was a radiant October afternoon, the kind of day that recalls summer and forecasts autumn—leaves falling with soft scrapes onto the sidewalk, heat compelling us to shed jackets and put on sunglasses. I walked down Orange Street beside the mayor and his wife, and we talked about the city: the new hotel and convention center, the burgeoning gallery district, a half dozen good new restaurants. My mother, who had spent years volunteering in the Fulton box office after I left home in 1981, walked with us. She and my father had at last sold their old home, my childhood fortress, and now lived in a retirement community on the west side of town. Everything had changed, and everything was somehow the same. Even the dead were with us. Through the small miracle of the Fulton's sound system, Michael Mitchell was able to speak to us as we sat in his theater that afternoon, another voice from the other side. Onstage, actors and musicians belted their eulogies. It was its own communion, this boisterous service.

The performance ended, and the auditorium faded to black. In the darkness an actor walked onto the stage carrying a single lightbulb mounted on a metal stand—a ghost light, that old bit of theatrical hocus-pocus meant to ward off unwelcome spirits. But this afternoon it seemed to embrace them, Michael and all the voices that had kept him going in his time and have kept me going in mine, the wandering dead, our constant companions.

NOTES

PROLOGUE: 1961

The national touring production of *The Sound of Music*, starring Barbara Meister and John Myhers, came to Philadelphia in 1961.

CHAPTER 1: HAUNTED

Thaddeus Stevens called for "Abolition!" during the Republican Party's county convention at Fulton Hall in September 1862 (quoted in the *Lancaster Intelligencer*, July 7, 1863). My information on Sarah Bernhardt's insistence on entering through the front door of the Fulton comes from a September 2000 conversation with June Yecker, who remembers her great aunt Janet Yecker recounting the anecdote. On Lincoln's inaugural stop in Lancaster and the passage of his funeral train through the same rail depot, see Martin; *Lancaster Evening Express*, April 20 and 21, 1865; Hoch; and Eshleman, "Lincoln's Train." On the funeral train in general, see Reynolds, *Walt Whitman's America*, 445; Smith, *American Gothic*, 192; and Herndon and Weik, 459–60. On the atmosphere of early Lancaster, including its taverns, see Mombert, Ellis and Evans, Rupp, Wood, and Loose, *Heritage*. For the story of Robert Fulton sketching British prisoners, see Wood, 82. I saw Julie Christie and Alan Bates in both *The Go-Between* (1970) and *Far from the Madding Crowd* (1967). The American Heritage Festival ran from July 2 to September 2, 1974; the program note on Michael Lewis is taken from my copy of the festival playbill. Lewis died on March 6, 1975 ("Michael Lewis, the Actor, Sinclair's Son, Dies at 44," *New York Times*, March 7, 1975). Costume designer Ruth Tighe discovered a man's body in a dumpster outside the Mack building in 1976 ("Dead Man Found in Water Street Dumpster," *Lancaster New Era*, July 12, 1976). On theater as a memory machine, see Carlson, *Haunted Stage*, 142–43; Yates; and Malkin. My thanks to director Mark Lamos for reminding me that I am not alone in my fascination with American theaters and their ghosts.

CHAPTER 2: MR. YECKER OPENS A THEATER: 1866

Background on post–Civil War culture and society in Lancaster and the United States in general is derived from Delbanco, 269; *Lancaster Examiner and Herald*, April 26, 1865; Loose, *Heritage*, 115; Reichmann; and Mombert, 486–87. I am grateful to Paul E. Yecker Sr. and June Yecker for supplying me with biographical information on Blasius Yecker, including his birth certificate, birth records for his children, and photographs;

Yecker's May 15, 1903, obituary in the *Lancaster New Era* is a further source. Yecker traveled to America with his childhood friend Michael Haberbush, whose career is the subject of the richly detailed article "Born in Hertzfelden: "Michael Haberbush, the Well-Known and Successful Saddler," *Lancaster Weekly Intelligencer*, August 14, 1886; information on Blasius Yecker also appears in "Old-Time Play Houses: Some Reminiscences of the Ancient Lancaster Theatres," *Lancaster Weekly Intelligencer*, February 27, 1886. An industrious Paul E. Yecker Sr. located both articles while recuperating from a heart attack. I was able to verify Blasius Yecker's 1848 emigration route in Glazier. Information on Lancaster's mid-nineteenth-century German community is found in Ellis and Evans, 464; and Hosch. According to "Born in Hertzfelden," Yecker's fellow saddler Michael Haberbush profited from the war ("The Patriot Daughters who did so much for the volunteers overwhelmed Mr. Haberbush with orders for skeleton knapsacks and other fixings, that he was obliged to work his men almost day and night, Sundays included, to meet the demand. Later on as the war progressed, he took sub-contracts from Philadelphia manufacturers to furnish harness for cavalry regiments. His local trade also increased day by day, so that he found it necessary to secure increased room"). I infer that Yecker did the same, even though my efforts to secure concrete evidence of such from both the Pennsylvania State Civil War Archive in Harrisburg and the National Archives proved fruitless. Yecker and Hilaire Zaepfel purchased Fulton Hall on November 23, 1865 (Lancaster County Courthouse Deed Book I, vol. 9, 493–94); Yecker bought out Zaepfel's share in the hall in 1869 ("Old-Time Playhouses"). On Yecker's early competition, see Reichmann; on the fire company fair and Chang and Eng, see the *Daily Evening Express* (November 28, 1865; December 15, 1865). Accounts of the *Miltonian Tableaux* appear in Reichmann, 69; and the *Evening Examiner* (December 29, 1865; January 2, 1866). My understanding of the issues that gripped post–Civil War America is drawn primarily from Delbanco, Lemann, Brodie, and Reynolds's *Walt Whitman's America*. In the years immediately after the Civil War, Thaddeus Stevens became the architect of what Fergus Bordewich calls "the most radical plan of congressional reconstruction of the South" (*Bound for Canaan*, 327). Stevens also drafted the Fourteenth and Fifteenth Amendments. Sherman's statement is quoted in Solnit, 63. Papers documenting Yecker's avoidance of the draft can be found in the Sener/Sehner Collection, 1805–1911, Folder 2, LancasterHistory.org; J. P. McCaskey, whose name still graces Lancaster's high school, is among those who contributed money to avoid the draft. On the 1866 renovation of Fulton Hall, see Reichmann, Greiner, and "Old-Time Playhouses," as well as coverage in the *Evening Express* and the *Intelligencer* (February 2–21, 1866). Tickets to see the George W. Harrison Company at Fulton Hall in 1866 ranged from 35 to 75 cents a head. On Harrison's presentation of *Our American Cousin,* see the *Evening Express,* February 22, 1866, and the *Intelligencer,* February 23, 1866. On Lincoln's assassination and the antitheatrical mania it spawned, including its impact on Edwin Booth, see Smith, *American Gothic*; Winik; Brodie; Copeland; Clarke; Reynolds, *Walt Whitman's America*; Lockridge; Wilmeth and Bigsby, *Cambridge History*, vol. 1, 6, and vol. 2, 174; and Olszewski. For response to the assassination in Lancaster, see the *Evening Express*, April 17 and 20–22, 1865; Edwin Booth's statement appeared in the April 18, 1865, edition of the same paper. An ad for Henry Struble's "first-class saloon" appears in the *Lancaster Intelligencer*, February 23, 1866. On the Fulton's waning attendance in the spring of 1867, see Greiner; Marty Crisp, "Old and New Wrinkles," *Lancaster Sunday News* (October 6, 2002); and the *Daily Evening Express* (June 17, 21, and 22, 1867). In June 1867, the McKean Buchanan Dramatic Company canceled a week-long run at Fulton Hall after just one performance because the house was half empty. Buchanan complained that Lancaster did not appreciate good theater (*Intelligencer*, June 19, 1867, quoted in Greiner, vol. 1, 89). *The Great Lincoln Memorial Tableaux* played Fulton Hall on November 8, 1866 (*Lancaster Examiner and Herald*, November 7, 1866; *Daily Evening Express*, November 10, 1866). On the odds of a theater manager's succeeding, see Henderson, 12–13. Barnum's advice appears on page 4 of his *Autobiography*. Ruskin's comment is from his *Lectures*. For his help in explaining Lancaster County geology to me—and in verifying that the stone foundations of the Fulton are, indeed, limestone—I am grateful to Rob Sternberg of Franklin and Marshall College's Department of Earth and Environment.

CHAPTER 3: THE KILLING OF THE CONESTOGAS: 1763

Paul Nevin of Wrightsville is the de facto curator of the Susquehanna petroglyphs and has written extensively about them on his website, Susquehannariver.net, and in Nevin, "Rock-Art Sites" and "10,000 Years." Susquehanna boulders with petroglyphs can also be seen at the Pennsylvania State Museum in Harrisburg. Lancaster County's first jail was built at Wright's Ferry (now Columbia) in 1730–32. Construction of the Lancaster city jail and workhouse seems to have taken place in three stages: a log prison was built in 1739–40, followed by a limestone expansion of the prison in 1745–46 and the erection of a workhouse in February 1763, for sheltering "idle and strolling vagrants" who are guilty of "drunkenness and profane swearing, breach of the Sabbath, tumults, and many vices" (Pa. Archives Series 8, vol. 6, 5397–98; Brubaker; "Old-Time Playhouses"; Douglas Harper, "Huddled in Jail, the 14 Indians Had No Chance," *Lancaster Intelligencer Journal*, June 21, 1997; Mombert, 427; Ellis and Evans, 207–8; Fulton Theatre plaque). Again, my thanks to Franklin and Marshall's Rob Sternberg for his geological expertise. On Lancaster's colonial period, see Wood; Rupp, *History*; Loose, *Heritage*. Background on John Smith and the Susquehannocks comes from Kent; Richter; Jennings; Swanton; Loose, "Along the Susquehanna"; Eshleman, *Lancaster County Indians*; and John Smith's *Generall Historie*, which I consulted at the University of Michigan Clements Library. The sad history of the Conestogas is told in numerous documents, including such early sources as Heckewelder, Parkman, Mombert, Rupp, Ellis and Evans, and Eshleman, *Lancaster County Indians*. More reliable contemporary sources are Kent; Merrell; Dowd, *A Spirited Resistance* and *War Under Heaven*; Richter; Pencak and Richter; Silver; Wood; and Brubaker. The Conestogas were so fond of some of their Pennsylvania neighbors they named their children after them. My thanks to Jim Heistand of Conestoga for putting me in touch with Betty Witmer, and to Jim, Betty, and Mark Hershey for guiding me through the Witmer farm and helping me to visualize the Conestoga settlements that once occupied the property. On Pontiac's rebellion, its impact on Pennsylvania, the Paxton rangers, John Elder, and the killings of the Conestogas at Conestoga and in the Lancaster jail, see Dowd, *War Under Heaven*; Richter; Stroh; Shannon; Wood; Merrell; Dunbar; Silver; and Olson. In his indispensable book about the Paxton killings, *Massacre of the Conestogas*, Jack Brubaker argues powerfully that the Lancaster magistrates were complicit in the workhouse slaughter, and he traces the subsequent historiography surrounding the killings, deftly separating fiction (of which there is much) from fact. Edward Shippen's letters have been widely reprinted (see, for example, Mombert, Dunbar, and Brubaker); the originals are found in the American Philosophical Society in Philadelphia. As a slaveholder, Shippen was far from alone: as Ira Berlin notes in *Many Thousands Gone*, between 1759 and 1780, the slave population in Lancaster County underwent an eightfold increase. Rhoda Barber's "Journal of Settlement at Wright's Ferry," which includes a poignant account of her family's response to the killing of the Indians at Conestoga, belongs to the collection of the Historical Society of Pennsylvania, in Philadelphia. Although it is generally agreed that the Paxton vigilantes killed the last of the Conestogas, two members of the group, a man named John and a woman named Mary, had in fact left Conestoga Town prior to 1763 and found shelter on a farm in northern Lancaster County; they left no known descendants. For a detailed guide to early American masonry, see McKee; Botton, 176–77, also writes eloquently about stone masonry. Ellis and Evans, 208–9, report that on March 23, 1745, the commissioners of Lancaster entered into a "memorandum of agreement with James Webb to do ye Mason work and find his material for ye same for doing ye Stone work of ye New Prison." I am indebted to Jack Brubaker for clarifying the layout of the Lancaster jail; Brubaker notes that the murders took place in the workhouse, a later addition to the prison and current site of the Fulton Theatre. Copies of the Paxton pamphlets and dialogues are reprinted in Dunbar; on their significance, see also Silver; Olson; Jensen; and Wilmeth and Bigsby, *Cambridge History*, vol. 1, 4. I consulted an original copy of Franklin's *Narrative* at the University of Michigan Clements Library; on Franklin himself, see Isaacson. In the 1750s, Benjamin Franklin paid several visits to Susannah Wright and her family, Quaker residents of Wright's Ferry, in western Lancaster County, some fifteen miles from Conestoga (Schaefer, 150–53). I am grateful to Steve Warfel, Janet Johnson, and their colleagues in the Archaeology Section at the State Museum of Pennsylvania for allowing me to see firsthand some of the hundreds of artifacts from Barry Kent's 1972 excavation of Conestoga Indian Town. My thanks to Barry Kent, as well, for his insights. On Charles Mason, see Mason, Clerc, Danson, and Pynchon. In 2010, during a ceremony at Lancaster's First Presbyterian Church, members of the Presbytery of Donegal formally acknowledged the role John Elder and the Paxton Presbyterian Church played in the massacre of the Conestogas.

CHAPTER 4: SACRED SPACE

As a member of Lancaster-based Maranatha Productions, I performed a concert of gospel music at the Fulton in 1971 and played Anne Frank on the same stage in 1973. Rick Fisher, president of the Paranormal Society of Pennsylvania, has conducted several ghost-hunting sessions at the Fulton, and with his colleague Scott Ditmer was gracious enough to demonstrate the process to me in 2003.

CHAPTER 5: MR. HAGER BUILDS A HALL: 1852

The Victor Hugo quotation, from his "Preface à Cromwell," appears in Carlson, *Places*, 27–28. My account of Stoffel Heger is drawn from multiple sources: the Hager family archive; the records of Trinity Lutheran Church (which I consulted with the expert aid of church archivist Joan Kahler); Wood, 8–9; Strassburger; Rupp, 359; *Biographical Annals*, 178; and documents in the Lancaster County Courthouse. Among the latter, Stoffel Heger's will, dated September 15, 1815, and signed with a wobbly "X," is a priceless record of one family's status in early nineteenth-century Lancaster. The document bequeaths to Hager's (Heger's) third wife, Catharine, all his household belongings, including two beds, three quilts, one coverlet, six bedsheets, two window curtains, one dining table, one breakfast table, six Windsor chairs, one spinning wheel, two washtubs, one bucket, two iron pots, a teakettle, six knives and forks, six pewter plates, one coffee mill, six China teacups and saucers, one large German Bible, a hymnal, and a prayer book. For background on Christopher Hager (1800–1868), see Trinity Lutheran Church, Birth Records; *Memorial Volume*; William Hager; Klein, *Lancaster's Golden Century*; Dowd; *Biographical Annals*; Ellis and Evans. A clipping from the *Lancaster Daily Intelligencer* dated May 1, 1937, in the Hager family archive documents Christopher Hager's buying trips to Philadelphia. On Hager's involvement in the Lancaster Colonization Society, see Mark C. Ebersole, "German Religious Groups," 182. The renowned Pennsylvania artist Jacob Eichholtz (1776–1842) painted both Christopher and Catherine Sener Hager in ca. 1825 and ca. 1830 (Beal, 98.) On life in the city of Lancaster in the first half of the nineteenth century, see Mombert; Bordewich, "Digging into a Historic Rivalry"; Loose, *Heritage*; Reichmann; "Report of the Centennial Observance"; Klein, *Lancaster's Golden Century*; Dowd; Rupp; Ellis and Evans; Winpenny. John Durang's "War and Scalp Dance" is described in Loose, *Heritage*, 45; and Kieffer, 34. In 1838, a "bachelor of eighty" recalled the "bustle and confusion" of Lancaster's streets (quoted in Everts and Stewart, xiii–xiv). Hager's purchase of the Lancaster jail is documented in "Old-Time Play Houses"; Lancaster County Commissioners Minutes (March 15, 22, and April 12, 1852), LancasterHistory.org; Ellis and Evans, 211; "Transformation"; Riddle; *Lancaster Examiner and Herald*, April 7, 1852. A public sale of "The Old Prison" took place in Lewis Sprecher's tavern on April 5, 1852 (*Saturday Examiner*, April 3, 1852; *Lancaster Intelligencer*, April 13, 1852). Hager actually purchased the jail with a partner, Peter G. Eberman, who almost immediately sold off his interest, leaving Hager the "sole owner" ("Old-Time Play Houses"; Lancaster County Deed Book X, vol. 7, 549–52). Background on the prolific Samuel Sloan comes from *Samuel Sloan*; Coolidge; and Philadelphia Architects and Buildings, http://www.philadelphiabuildings.org/pab/index.cfm (accessed April 24, 2007). Sloan's thoughts on architecture appear in his two-volume *The Model Architect*. Shortly after he hired Sloan to design Fulton Hall, Hager was instrumental in securing the same architect's services to design a pulpit at Trinity Lutheran Church; that elegant work, which includes a charming "backstage" space for robing, is visible in the church today. My thanks to Lancaster architect Richard Levengood for spending the better part of an afternoon guiding me through the Fulton's architectural past. Thanks also to architect Edward Francis of William

Kessler and Associates, Detroit, Michigan, for helping me to understand the Fulton's unique qualities and for allowing me to consult the invaluable "Fulton Opera House Master Plan" (revised version, September 9, 1992). On the 1852 construction of Fulton Hall, see Walter Hager; "Transformation"; Lestz; as well as coverage throughout the spring and summer of 1852 in the *Intelligencer*, the *Saturday Express*, and the *Examiner and Herald*. Reports of a worker felled by sunstroke appear in both the *Intelligencer* (June 22, 1852) and the *Saturday Express* (June 19, 1852). The building was first used on September 2, 1852, by the Odd Fellows (*Intelligencer*, September 7, 1852). I consulted numerous texts on the growth of the American theater in the mid-nineteenth century, chief among them Henderson; Reynolds, *Walt Whitman's America*; and Wilmeth and Bigsby's indispensable three-volume *Cambridge History*. The history of theatrical entertainment in Lancaster is recounted in Reichmann; "Old-Time Play Houses"; and Henke, "From Public House to Opera House" and "Three Nineteenth-Century Lancaster Theatres." On the lifting of the ordinance requiring a tax on entertainment, see the *Lancaster Intelligencer*, October 19, 1852, and Greiner, vol. 1, 71–72. Accounts of the grand opening of Fulton Hall appear in the Lancaster press, October 12–20, 1852. Judge Alexander Hayes's remarks were reprinted in the *Lancaster Examiner and Herald*, October 20, 1852. Samuel Sloan elaborates on the necessity of and requirements for lightning rods in *The Model Architect*, vol. 2, 85–86. Although the woman in the crinoline is my invention, her thoughts on her first photograph are lifted verbatim from Douglas.

CHAPTER 6: "WHAT HAS THE NORTH TO DO WITH SLAVERY?": 1852–1861

On architecture in general, I am indebted to Alain de Botton's *The Architecture of Happiness* (the source, on p. 47, of the Ruskin quotation) and to Lewis Mumford's several books on the topic. An ad for Kendall and Dixon's Ethiopians at Fulton Hall appears in the October 13, 1852, *Examiner and Herald*; the *Lancaster Intelligencer* reports on October 26, 1852, that the troupe played the city's Mechanics Hall. I have been unable to find a review of the company's Fulton appearance, if in fact there was one. On the impact of the Fugitive Slave Law, see Delbanco, 153, who quotes Emerson's "Address to the Citizens of Concord on the Fugitive Slave Law," May 3, 1851. For details on Lancaster's burgeoning mid-nineteenth-century cotton industry, see Winpenny. When I asked Winpenny why Thaddeus Stevens would have supported the mills, knowing their link to slavery, Winpenny told me, "From the perspective of Lancaster, the mills meant jobs for 1,300 young women and economic prosperity for a town trying to make the transition from artisan dominance to the early factory system. For the Red Rose City textile mills meant boom, boom, boom. This is what Thaddeus Stevens saw, I suspect" (Thomas Winpenny, e-mail to author, November 30, 2005). Hayes's remarks on the mills appear in the *Lancaster Examiner and Herald*, October 20, 1852. On the early days of Fulton Hall and attendant business establishments, see Greiner; Walter Hager; Lestz; Joseph Wilson Lahr. See also local press coverage of events in the hall from October through December, 1852. Ross I. Morrison (34–36) notes that for a period of three months in 1858, Fulton Hall served as the site of crowded evangelistic meetings—part of the Evangelical Awakening. Colonel

Reigart's engraving of Fulton Hall is reported in the May 18, 1853, *Intelligencer*. The October 20, 1852, edition of the *Examiner and Herald* said of Fulton Hall, "A great desideratum has been supplied, and through the agency of an enterprising and public spirited gentleman who we hope will reap a plentiful harvest from the investment." On October 26, 1852, the *Intelligencer* listed the range of amusements then available in Lancaster, among them infant drummers, a boa constrictor, a panorama of Mexico, and Ole Bull, the famed "Norwegian Paganini," who gave the first professional performance at Fulton Hall on October 21, 1852; he was accompanied by nine-year-old soprano Adelina Patti (Walter Hager). Trustee James Buchanan spoke during Franklin and Marshall College's first-ever commencement, held in Fulton Hall on June 7, 1853 ("Formal Opening of Franklin and Marshall College, in the City of Lancaster, June 7, 1853," *Intelligencer* [June 14, 1853]; also Franklin and Marshall College Board of Trustees Minutes, 1853, in Archives and Special Collections Department, Franklin and Marshall College). An ad for shawls appeared in the October 30, 1852, edition of the *Saturday Express*. On Robert Fulton's statue, see Walter Hager; Eleanore J. Fulton; Duing; *Saturday Express*, March 25, 1854; and *Examiner and Herald*, March 22, 1954. The original (and recently restored) statue now stands inside the Fulton Theatre, and a replica occupies the outdoor niche above the marquee. Rose Merrifield's *Uncle Tom's Cabin* opened in Fulton Hall on March 21, 1854, and ran through April 5, 1854 (*Examiner and Herald*, March 22, 1854, and April 5, 1854; *Intelligencer*, March 21, 1854). The play itself is the subject of Harry Birdoff's *The World's Greatest Hit*; see also Wilmeth and Bigsby; Henderson; Sundquist; Reynolds, *Mightier than the Sword* and *Walt Whitman's America*; Lott; and Gossett. The Pillsbury quote appears in Reynolds, *Mightier than the Sword*, 145. Information on Rose Merrifield comes from C. R. Foreman, "'Uncle Tom' on His Travels," *Clipper* (February 19, 1877) and "'Uncle Tom's Cabin': Its Early Days, and the People Who Played in It," *Clipper* (February 10, 1877), both of which I found on Stephen Railton's excellent website Uncle Tom's Cabin and American Culture: A Multi-Media Archive, http://utc.iath.virginia.edu/ (accessed June 1, 2007). Railton confirms that Rose Merrifield was white and used blackface, and that she and her company used George Aiken's script of *Uncle Tom's Cabin* (e-mail to author, June 5, 2007). The Lancaster newspapers from 1850 through 1861 are filled with accounts of political events at Fulton Hall, and are a reminder that in some ways we live in tamer times today. The reference to Thaddeus Stevens's club foot ("Thump, lump") appears in the *Intelligencer*, October 7, 1856. The incident with Buchanan and the student orator took place on July 24, 1856; Buchanan had become the Democratic nominee for U.S. president during the first week of June 1856, and, as was the custom at the time, gave no speeches during his candidacy, hence the heightened interest in this encounter on the stage of Fulton Hall. For coverage of the incident, see Franklin and Marshall College Board of Trustees Minutes, 1856, and "College Commencements. Commencement at Franklin and Marshall College. Buchanan on Brooks. Lancaster, July 24, 1856," undated *New York Tribune* clipping, in Archives and Special Collections Department, Franklin and Marshall College; Philip S. Klein, 79–80; *Lancaster Intelligencer*, July 29, 1856; Dubbs. I am grateful to F&M College historian Sally Griffith for steering me toward this incident. David Wilmot appeared at Fulton Hall on October 3, 1857 (Douglas, 56).

Herschel Johnson campaigned from the Fulton stage on September 17, 1860 (*Intelligencer*, September 25, 1860); Heiges. On his way to Washington on February 22, 1861, Lincoln spoke at the Lancaster railroad depot, some three blocks from Fulton Hall (Martin; also Lancaster press coverage, February 22–27, 1861). Buchanan's March 6, 1861, homecoming was widely reported in the Lancaster press; the *Examiner and Herald*'s derisive sketch appeared on March 27, 1861. My description of the Fencibles' departure is drawn from articles in the *Lancaster Evening Express*, the *Intelligencer*, and the *Examiner and Herald*, April 16–22, 1861. Edward Hager is listed among those members of the Fencibles who departed Fulton Hall on April 19, 1861 (*Examiner and Herald*, April 24, 1861).

CHAPTER 7: INTERLUDE

I owe the inspiration for this chapter to my former student Geoffrey George and his ingenious essay "Realized Images: A Study of Maps and Perception," in which George communes with the spirit of mapmaker Henry Francis Walling. The Marriott Hotel and Lancaster County Convention Center opened on Penn Square in the spring of 2009; the Thaddeus Stevens House and cistern are visible inside the center's Vine Street entrance. As of 2013, LancasterHistory.org was coordinating efforts to fund a museum dedicated to Stevens on the site of his former law office (Bernard Harris, "U.S. Aid Sought to Plan for Thaddeus Stevens Museum," *Intelligencer Journal / Lancaster New Era*, March 4, 2013). I am grateful to archaeologist James Delle for allowing me to visit the Stevens property during his excavation of the site. For information on Lancaster's Central Market, see http://www.centralmarketlancaster.com/. John Adams's observation appears in Bobrick, 62, who cites Bailyn. The greatest of Lancaster's eighteenth-century peace-treaty sessions took place in 1744 and lasted days (see Kent, 66; Mombert, appendix, 51–89; Eshleman, 340–47; Wood, 82, 208; Merrell, 258). The marquis de Lafayette visited Lancaster in July 1725, and the city decked itself out for the occasion (Everts and Stewart, xiv). Buchanan returned to Lancaster on March 6, 1861 (*Evening Express*, March 7, 1861; *Examiner and Herald*, March 13, 1861; Mombert, 392); the former president died on June 1, 1868, and some twenty thousand people attended his funeral in Lancaster (Philip S. Klein, 427; Mombert, 392–93). Debates over Buchanan's legacy persist to this day; see, for example, Fergus Bordewich's comparison of Buchanan and Stevens, "Digging into a Historic Rivalry," which sparked a small uproar in Lancaster when it came out in *Smithsonian Magazine* in 2004. *Buchanan Dying* opened at F&M's Green Room Theatre on April 29, 1976, and was amply covered in both the *Lancaster Intelligencer Journal* and *New Era*. The play itself is available from Stackpole Books in a 2000 edition with a foreword in which Updike mentions our production. On acting onstage and in life, see Goffman and Stanislavski. I appeared in Norman Corwin's *The Rivalry*, about the Lincoln-Douglas debates, in March 1976. Background on Robert Fulton, who was born in Lancaster County in 1765—one year after Stoffel Heger's arrival—comes primarily from Philip. Fulton died in 1815 and is buried in the graveyard at Trinity Church in lower Manhattan, the small sanctuary that improbably survived the collapse of the Trade Towers on September 11, 2001. The Santayana quote appears in Goffman, 56–57.

CHAPTER 8: THEATER OF WAR: 1861–1865

On the audience at Bull Run, see Oates, 254–55. On Grant's careful handling of Lee's surrender at Appomattox, see Winik, 181–91. Hundreds of troops poured into Lancaster in April 1861, among them two regiments of Ohio Volunteers, who were lodged inside local churches, the courthouse, and Fulton Hall (*Lancaster Evening Express*, April 22, 1861; *Examiner and Herald*, April 24, 1861, and May 6, 1861). The girl with the canary is my invention but was inspired by a scene in Antonio Blitz's *Life and Adventures of Signor Blitz*; Blitz played Fulton Hall on April 8, 1865. The Fencibles returned to their armory on July 27, 1861, after ninety days' active service; the exchange between the reporter and the Fencibles is drawn from accounts of their homecoming in the *Lancaster Examiner and Herald* (July 31, 1861); the *Intelligencer and Weekly* (July 30, 1861); and the *Evening Express* (July 29, 1861). Thaddeus Stevens spoke at Fulton Hall on September 3, 1862, during the Republican County Convention; his remarks are lifted verbatim from the *Examiner and Herald* (September 10, 1862). On his "reptilian" appearance and "sepulchral" voice, see Jolly. The Boy is my invention. My rendering of the Fencibles' reunion at Fulton Hall on June 4, 1863, stems from an article in the *Lancaster Inquirer* (June 5, 1863); the reporter's words, with their striking use of theatrical imagery, are authentic. "The Southern Refugee" played Fulton Hall on June 15, 1863 (*Lancaster Inquirer*, June 12, 1863); the actor's words and the contents of his cabinets—billed in the Lancaster press as a "Rebel Museum of Wonderful Curiosities"—are inspired by the *Inquirer's* description of the act. Lancaster County's great moment in the war came in late June 1863, as Lee's troops occupied neighboring York County and threatened to cross into Lancaster en route to Philadelphia. An agitated Christopher Hager spoke out during a mass meeting of citizens in the Lancaster courthouse on June 25, 1863, and the next day informed a colleague in Philadelphia that his city was "in danger of invasion and destruction" should the rebels cross the Susquehanna into Lancaster County (the letter is found in the Records of the Department of Military and Veterans' Affairs, Pennsylvania State Archives, Harrisburg). On June 28, 1863, county officials burned the Columbia-Wrightsville Bridge connecting York and Lancaster Counties, thus sending Lee's troops west toward Gettysburg. The original foundations of that bridge, encrusted with vegetation, still stand, an eerie reminder that not so much time has passed since those desperate days. Mayor Sanderson's remarks are my invention; Hager's comments are drawn verbatim from an account in the *Lancaster Inquirer*, June 26, 1863. Buchanan's letter to Harriet Lane is quoted in Curtis, vol. 2, 609. An apocryphal story (quoted in McDermott) has it that Fulton Hall was used to house the wounded from Gettysburg, but as the late John Loose reminded me, without the Columbia-Wrightsville Bridge, it would have been next to impossible to bring soldiers from Gettysburg to Lancaster. Volunteers and curious onlookers from Lancaster did, however, make their way to Gettysburg within days of the battle. Frederick Douglass was slated to speak at Fulton Hall on July 15, 1863, in conjunction with a recruitment drive for African American soldiers, but near-riots in front of both the Lancaster courthouse and Fulton Hall on July 14 prompted local authorities to cancel the event; to my knowledge, Douglass never spoke at Fulton Hall. The Lancaster press published ample reports of these events, which coincided with Lincoln's draft proclamation and draft riots in New York City; the cancellation notice that the Boy reads is from the *Evening Express* (July 15, 1863). Although some historians have claimed that Fulton Hall remained dark throughout the war, press accounts prove otherwise. On July 17, 1863, Dr. Harry Lee gave a demonstration of laughing gas inside the hall; my reconstruction of a portion of that evening is drawn from an ad in the *Evening Express* (July 15, 1863). On April 10, 1865, crowds who had gathered in front of the Lancaster courthouse to celebrate Robert E. Lee's surrender lit a bonfire that spelled out the word "Victory" (*Daily Evening Express*, April 11, 1865). Magician and ventriloquist Antonio Blitz was slated to play Fulton Hall on April 10 and 11, 1865, and there is no evidence to suggest he did not fulfill that obligation. In his 1872 memoir, Blitz recalls performing for hundreds of wounded Civil War soldiers in Philadelphia, including two young soldiers, both without legs, who laughed with glee at his antics; their faces, Blitz writes, were "remarkably beautiful, of a feminine character, with a great delicacy of feature and complexion, scarcely ever seen on any manly form. Apparently in the full enjoyment of mirth, they had forgotten their helpless condition. Their countenances beamed with pleasure, and almost inclined me to wish that even I was not less discontented or aggrieved by misfortunes incidental to life." The exchange between Blitz and the Girl is drawn almost verbatim from the same memoir. Although theaters throughout the United States closed after Lincoln's murder, Fulton Hall seems to have stayed open. The Davies and Co. Polyorama and Parlor Entertainment played Fulton Hall Thursday through Saturday, April 13–15, 1865; although I don't know the specific content of the Davies polyorama, I know that a popular 1864 polyorama (Antonio and Chambers, proprietors) included several war scenes, among them, in the words of an ad, the "Arrival of the Monitor; terrific engagement with the Merrimac; the most remarkable naval [*sic*] on record; the Merrimac driven back beyond Sewell's Point, and the little Monitor is triumphant, amid the booming of cannon and the conflagration of the Congress" ("Polyorama of the War at Laing's Hall!," *Leavenworth (Kansas) Daily Times*, May 15, 1864, http://www.uttyler.edu/vbetts/leavenworth_times_64.htm [accessed October 2, 2009]).

CHAPTER 9: MR. YECKER OPENS AN OPERA HOUSE: 1873

Blasius Yecker presented a panorama of the Confederate invasion of Pennsylvania in April 1868 (*Lancaster Intelligencer*, April 17, 1868; the same paper carries a notice for the "Ku-Klux Klan! When the Black Cat is sleeping, meet at the Den. First Year, Bloody Moon. Hush! And watch"). Tom Thumb and his diminutive family played Fulton Hall on December 9 and 10, 1867, and drew substantial crowds (*Intelligencer*, December 7–11, 1867). On the auction of James Buchanan's liquor collection, see the *Intelligencer*, October 14, 1868. Christopher Hager and James Buchanan are buried within several hundred yards of one another in Woodlawn Cemetery, on Lancaster's south side.

At his insistence, Thaddeus Stevens was buried in the African American section of Shreiner's Cemetery, which in its day, exceptionally, admitted both whites and blacks;

the graveyard is just a few blocks northwest of the Fulton Theatre. Blind Tom made his Fulton Hall debut on October 26, 1868; that same day both the *Lancaster Evening Express* and *Intelligencer* carried long articles detailing Tom's background and physical features, including the circumference of his head. Tom returned four times to the Fulton, in 1871, 1873, 1875, and 1876 (Greiner). Mark Twain spoke at Fulton Hall on January 19, 1872, as part of the theater's "Home Course" lecture series (Luck). Blasius Yecker traveled to Kansas to visit his son Victor in May 1886 (*Intelligencer Journal*, May 15, 1886); on his brief stay in Oregon, see the *New Era*, May 15, 1903. "Born in Hertzfelden" notes that Yecker, together with his fellow immigrants Michael Haberbush and Hilaire Zaepfel, attended night school during their first months in Lancaster, while also working twelve- and fourteen-hour days in the harness shop. Photographs of Blasius and Mary Yecker around the time of their wedding belong to Paul E. Yecker Sr., as do birth and baptismal records for all of Blasius and Mary Yecker's children; their first child, Victor Antonio, was born July 3, 1856. On Yecker's decision to develop the "amusement possibilities" of Lancaster, see "Old-Time Playhouses." The sobering tale of the vanishing American West is told in Heckewelder, Brown, and Solnit. Details on Charles Garnier and the aesthetics of the American theater in the Gilded Age can be found in Garnier; Henderson; and Wilmeth and Bigsby, *Cambridge History*, vol. 2. On Saint Mary's Church, see DeLaurentis and Hershey. Background on Edwin Forrest Durang and his family is found in Hare; Kieffer; Marty Crisp, "Pulling Strings to Rescue John Durang," *Lancaster Sunday News*, January 18, 2004; and John Durang. I am especially indebted to John Durang's biographer, Lynn Brooks, of the Franklin and Marshall College dance faculty, for generously sharing her wealth of Durang knowledge and for guiding me toward the delightful Edwina Hare. Playwright Christopher Durang kindly answered my e-mails and put me in touch with family members. In 2004, Rob Brock opened a John Durang Puppet Museum inside Brock's Hole in the Wall Puppet Theater on Water Street, two blocks from the Fulton Theatre; a plaque honoring Durang stands outside Brock's theater. On Edwin Forrest Durang's renovations, see "Fulton Hall—Its Reconstruction," *Lancaster Intelligencer Journal*, October 1, 1873, and "Transformation," *Lancaster Daily Express*, October 1, 1873. My thanks to architect Dick Levengood for helping me to understand the engineering behind Durang's renovations. On the grand reopening of the theater, see the *Lancaster Intelligencer Journal*, October 3, 1873; and Greiner, vol. 1, 142. Whitman's remark on America's future is from *Democratic Vistas* (1871) and is quoted in Wilmeth and Bigsby, *Cambridge History*, vol. 2, 109. On the "deed of horror" that took place beneath the Fulton stage, see "Transformation." Harris's remark appears in his *Biographical History*, 525n and 530n. The Young Ladies' Guild of the Moravian Church presented its tableau of the "Massacre of Indians at Lancaster, December 27th, 1763," during an evening of tableaux that also included the "Martyrdom of John Huss, July 6th, 1415"; "Zeisberger Preaching to the Indians at Geshgoshunk, October 1767"; and "Cleopatra's Toilet" (*New Era*, January 27, 1882; playbill, Fulton Theatre Archive). Thanks to Christopher Durang for his February 11, 2002, e-mail about his family's early support for his career; his reflections on playwriting appear in the introduction to Christopher Durang, x–xi.

CHAPTER 10: IN TRANSIT

The Acting Company brought *The Robber Bridegroom* to the Fulton Theatre in the spring of 1976. "Leslie Stainton Dreams of Being 'Really Fine Actress,'" by John Drybred, appeared in the *Lancaster Intelligencer Journal* in June 1976 (undated clipping in my scrapbook). On the human penchant for adopting masks, see Goffman, 17–20. David Mamet's thoughtful *True and False* is a welcome antidote to Stanislavski. When it comes to thinking about the significance of acting, I have long relied on Michael Goldman's insightful *The Actor's Freedom* and recommend it to anyone wishing to explore the actor's art and our obsession with it. Elizabeth Ashley's *Actress: Postcards from the Road* was published in 1978. Lorca's remarks on the ephemeral nature of the theater, which have deeply informed my own thinking on the art, come from "Encuentro con Federico García Lorca," a 1935 interview reprinted in García Lorca, 572.

CHAPTER 11: BUFFALO BILL AND THE AMERICAN WEST: 1873–1882

My portrait of William F. Cody is drawn primarily from Kasson; Ward; Hall; and Wickstrom. A visit to the Buffalo Bill Museum and Grave in Golden, Colorado, also yielded useful information. Cody's many appearances in Lancaster received substantial press coverage; key sources for this chapter are the *Intelligencer* (December 17–19, 1873; April 8, 1878 [in which the various kinds of shots Cody made inside Fulton Hall are listed]; April 25, 1881; December 28, 1881; December 30, 1882); the *Daily Examiner and Express* (February 16–18, 1880); and *The Footlight* (December 24, 1881), a copy of which can be found in the Fulton Theatre Archive. Thomas Nast appeared at the Fulton on November 21, 1873, and Charlotte (Lotta) Crabtree on October 22, 1873 (Greiner, vol. 2, 376–77). On the American love affair with dime novels, see Kasson, 27; Solnit, 74; Wilmeth and Bigsby, *Cambridge History*, vol. 2, 34; and Jill Lepore, "Westward Ho!," *New Yorker* (October 9, 2006), 76–80. It was during Cody's February 17, 1880, performance at the Fulton that Yecker's theater filled with "a mass of yelling and surging humanity" (*Daily Examiner and Express*, February 18, 1880). I have also cited these reviews: *New Era* (April 5–6, 1878); *Intelligencer* (December 28, 1881). Ads for Cody's presentation of *Knight of the Plains*, with a "Band of Genuine Indians" and a "Jew money lender," are found in the *Daily Examiner and Express* (February 16–17, 1880). I am indebted to Ty Greiner for his painstaking work compiling a master list of all the frontier (and other) dramas to play the Fulton in the nineteenth and early twentieth centuries. On Cody as an actor, Gordon Wickstrom's "Buffalo Bill the Actor" is indispensable; I am also grateful to Gordon for his generous assistance during the writing of this chapter, and for having introduced me as a college freshman to Arthur Kopit's *Indians*. The play says just about everything we need to know about Cody and the American West. On Yecker's visit to his sons, see the *Intelligencer Journal*, May 15, 1886. "What May Be Seen on the Plains," an extract from a Professor I. D. Rupp's journal of a trip from Philadelphia to the Rocky Mountains in 1866, appeared in the *Daily New Era*, April 5–6, 1878. Sheridan's statement is quoted in Brown, 265. Brown's *Bury My Heart at Wounded Knee* documents the continuing assault on the American Indian and demonstrates with chilling detail that the murder of the Conestogas was but the start of what can only be termed genocide; James Carleton's remark appears on p. 31 of the book. On the saga of the Conestogas' bones, see Kent, 67; Witthoft; "The Lancaster That Was: Our First Lockup," *Lancaster Sunday News* (October 28, 1984); Rupp, *History*, 360; Mombert, 189; Brubaker. On Buffalo Bill's Wild West exhibition as a "resurrection," see Kasson, 61, citing *Pomeroy's Democrat*, July 3, 1886. On Lancaster's role in the conquest of the West, see *Lancaster Intelligencer* (May 11, 1858).

CHAPTER 12: MEMORY MACHINE

The quotes from Rilke are from his "Ninth Elegy" (1922), translated by C. F. MacIntyre. Robert Pogue Harrison quotes Rilke on p. 44 of *The Dominion of the Dead*, a book whose discussion of human burial practices and their significance has informed parts of this chapter. Harrison cites Mumford, *City in History*, 7, on nomadic burial sites. On "eulogized space," see Bachelard, xxxi–xxxii. News of a body on the Fulton construction site appeared in the *Saturday Express*, October 30, 1852. Marvin Carlson first drew my attention to Camillo and his successor, Robert Fludd, in *Haunted Stage*, 143. For more on Camillo and Fludd, see Yates and Malkin.

CHAPTER 13: THE MINSTREL'S MASK: 1852–1927

The organization of this chapter reflects the traditional three-part structure of the nineteenth-century minstrel show: first, a group of songs and jokes presented by the full company; second, an olio section with stump speeches, specialty acts, and ensemble numbers; third, a full-blown burlesque skit usually set in the South. Many nineteenth-century guides to minstrelsy describe the process of corking up; see, for example, *The Original Christy's Minstrels: Complete Repertoire of Plantation Melodies, from which the Programme of Each Evening Is Selected* (1860); *Bones—His Gags and Stump Speeches; Nigger and Dutch Stories and Dialogues* (1879); *Morris Brothers, Pell and Trowbridge's Minstrels! Rules of the Hall* (185?); *Popular Ethiopian Melodies Including Many New and Favorite Songs, as Sung at Sanford's American Opera House* (1856); *Matt Peel's Banjo: Being a Selection of the Most Popular and Laughable Negro Melodies, as Sung by the Renowned Peel's Campbell's Minstrels* (1858); *Unsworth's Burnt Cork Lyrics*. I was able to consult the originals of these at the University of Michigan Clements Library and the University of Michigan Special Collections. Lyrics throughout this chapter are drawn from these sources and from Lott; Crawford; Bean, Hatch, and McNamara; and Hamm. On the general history of minstrelsy, see Taylor and Austen; Lott; Toni Morrison; Crawford; Bean, Hatch, and McNamara; Hamm; Wilmeth and Bigsby, *Cambridge History*, vols. 1 and 2; Henderson; Toll; Elam and Krasner. I also recommend Spike Lee's *Bamboozled* (2000) to anyone wishing to experience the unsettling power of minstrelsy. For background on Mark Twain's fondness for minstrelsy, see Kaplan; Ward, Ken Burns, and Duncan; Alexander Saxton, "Blackface Minstrelsy," in Bean, Hatch, and McNamara, 67. On Twain's single Fulton appearance, see Luck. Samuel Cartwright's statement is quoted in Crawford, 196. Ralph Ellison's description of minstrelsy appears in Mahar, 181. On the Georgia Minstrels, see Eileen Southern, "The Georgia Minstrels: The Early Years," in Bean, Hatch, and McNamara; Annemarie Bean, "Black Minstrelsy and Double Inversion, Circa 1890," in Elam and Krasner; and Reynolds, *Mightier than the Sword*, 180. On the troupe's many Fulton appearances, see Greiner; the description of them as "Nigger Minstrels" appears in the *Columbia Spy*, April 20, 1872. Taylor and Austen (50–51) note that with a few exceptions, nineteenth-century black minstrel troupes were distinguished from white by the designation "Georgia," "Colored," or "Slave" ("Negro" referred to whites in blackface). The quote on donning blackface "when we had something really *crazy* to say" appears in Taylor and Austen, 78; see pp. 77–79 of the same book for a discussion of minstrelsy's liberating impact on African Americans. Readers interested in the failure of Reconstruction should consult Nicholas Lemann's excellent *Redemption*. I am grateful to Alison Kibler and her Franklin and Marshall students for deepening my understanding of the complexities of race relations at the Fulton, and in particular for steering me toward the 1901 and 1904 performances by Walker and Williams in the theater. Their semester-long exploration of Williams and Walker at the Fulton led to the publication of Kibler, Richman, and Weinberg. On the 1863 demonstration in front of Fulton Hall and Douglass's canceled appearance, see Hopkins; the *Lancaster Evening Express* (July 14–15, 1863); and the *Lancaster Intelligencer* (July 21, 1863). Descriptions of local reactions to both minstrel shows and *Uncle Tom's Cabin* are drawn from the *Weekly Bean* (November 22, 1879), in the Fulton Theatre Archive; the *New Era* (January 27, 1882); the *Columbia Spy* (June 3, 1882); the *Intelligencer* (March 28, 1882); and Birdoff, 285. My thanks to Leroy Hopkins of Millersville University, both for his scholarship (see Hopkins) and for his prompt and wide-ranging responses to my queries. On Pennsylvania's 1887 antidiscrimination law, see Kibler, Richman, and Weinberg. On Darwinian concepts of racial inferiority, see Reynolds, 471–73; Crawford, 196; and Gross, 87. Whitman's comment on the "law of races" appears in Reynolds, 472. On Bert Williams, see Pierpont; Eric Ledell Smith; Charters; Taylor and Austen. On *In Dahomey*, see Riis; Kibler, Richman, and Weinberg; and Margo Jefferson, "Blackface Master Echoes in Hip-Hop," *New York Times*, October 13, 2004.

CHAPTER 14: EMPTY SPACE

It is possible my godmother saw the James Adams Floating Theatre, which toured this part of America starting in 1914 and was also seen by Edna Ferber. For parts of this chapter I've consulted my well-thumbed copy of Rosilyn Wilder's *A Space Where Anything Can Happen*. Johan Huizinga's essay "Nature and Significance of Play as a Cultural Phenomenon" appears in Schechner, 46–66. The chapter title, of course, is indebted to Peter Brook's indispensable volume by the same name.

CHAPTER 15: PLAYERS: 1886–1893

Photos of the Fulton under Blasius Yecker's management show today's rear doors at the front of "Yecker's Fulton Opera House"; architect Dick Levengood suspects the doors were removed to the rear of the building during Emlen Urban's 1904 renovation of the theater. Background on Blasius Yecker comes from photographs, birth records, and other documents in the possession of Paul Yecker, and from his obituary in the *New Era* (May 15, 1903). P. T. Barnum's advice appears in his *Autobiography*, 157. For local coverage of Edwin Booth's December 31, 1886, performance of *Hamlet* at the Fulton, see the *Intelligencer* (December 30, 1886–January 1, 1887) and the *New Era* (December 29, 1886). *Fun on the Bristol* played the Fulton on March 10, 1881 (*Intelligencer*, March 11, 1881, quoted in Greiner, vol. 1, 236); *Black Crook*, which played the Fulton on December 30, 1886, is widely considered the first American "leg show" (see Henderson, 123, and Dudden, 149). Background on Edwin Booth comes from Gene Smith; Clarke; Copeland; Alford; Lockridge; and Hutton. On the rigors of the road, see Wilmeth and Bigsby, *Cambridge History*, vol. 2, 150–51, 200–212. Kemble's remark is reprinted in Kemble, 182–83; Kemble played Lancaster in 1847. Eugene O'Neill's line about actors on the road comes from *Long Day's Journey into Night* (O'Neill, 61); on his deathbed in 1953, O'Neill famously said, "I knew it. Born in a hotel room— and God damn it—died in a hotel room." Thoreau's quote is from *Walden*; the passage from Dante's *Paradiso* (canto 17) is translated by Allen Mandelbaum; Whitman's complaint about touring actors is found in Wilmeth and Bigsby, *Cambridge History*, vol. 1, 9. On the proliferation of theaters in the United States between 1865 and 1900, see Henderson; Reynolds; and Wilmeth and Bigsby's *Cambridge History*. Of the nearly four thousand theaters that went up in these years, some three hundred survive. A visit to the largely untouched Tabor Opera House in Leadville, Colorado, allowed me to see the cramped and cold conditions under which most nineteenth-century actors labored. On Yecker's 1890 renovations to the Fulton, see the *Daily Intelligencer* (July 3 and August 25, 1890) and the *New Era* (August 8, 25, and 27, 1890). Blasius Yecker's granddaughter Janet Yecker later claimed that both her grandfather and her father, Charles, personally engaged the artists who performed at the Fulton and always screened performers to ensure that nothing inappropriate or inferior would be offered (unidentified newspaper clipping, Fulton Theatre Archive). Sometime in the mid-1870s, the City of Lancaster granted Yecker full control over the fare in his theater, a clear sign of its faith in his discretion; for that right, Yecker paid $75 annually, "the said sum to be in lieu of the special licenses provided by Existing Ordinances" (*Digest of the Ordinances of the City of Lancaster* [ca. 1875], 159, in Greiner, vol. 1, 138). On Yecker's method of playing "on shares," see the *Columbia Spy*, November 20, 1875. The *New Era*'s remarks on "sharps and tricksters" appeared in the paper's May 15, 1903, obituary for Blasius Yecker. Lancastrian Margaret B. Rahn would remember sitting in the lobby of Stevens House Hotel with her friends in the mid-1890s, hoping to see stars (Burns, 122). For a list of touring performers who played the Fulton between 1852 and 1930, see Greiner, vol. 2. The Fulton Theatre Archive has several theater diaries kept by local patrons. Milton Hershey liked to tell how one night, when he'd been roasting peanuts for peanut fudge at Royer's Ice Cream, he slipped away from the ice cream shop and went around the corner with a friend to see a show at the Fulton. As they were sitting in the gallery watching the show, Hershey suddenly smelled the stench of burning peanuts through an open window. He and his friend raced downstairs and out onto the street, where they saw, as Hershey put it, "a shower of peanut shells coming down." Hershey had forgotten to turn off the blower, and burned shells had been sucked up the flue and were drifting down to earth like leaves. Not long after working at Royer's, Milton Hershey founded his famous candy company (D'Antonio, 28–32). Information on Proctor and Soulier's short-lived Fulton adventure is found in Reichmann, 47; Greiner, vol. 1, 138; *Intelligencer Journal* (August 25, 1890); and *New Era* (August 27, 1890). My thanks to Paul E. Yecker Sr. for sharing a copy of Blasius Yecker's 1890 letter announcing his return to the Fulton. Blasius Yecker became a naturalized U.S. citizen on May 25, 1889 (Naturalization Records, LancasterHistory.org). The *Lancaster New Era* (May 15, 1903) mentions Yecker's "love for the Fatherland." I am grateful to curator Raymond Wemmlinger of The Players for showing me around Edwin Booth's club and allowing me to see the room where he died. The Gass quotation appears in Gass, 215.

CHAPTER 16: WOMEN'S WORK: 1870–1931

Quotes on manners are taken from Wells. May Fisk played the Fulton on August 8, 1878, and March 13, 1897 (*Intelligencer Journal*, August 7 and 9, 1878; Greiner, vol. 2, 411); a small note in the "Fulton Programme," vol. 1, no. 14 (November 1878) reads, "May Fisk's Blondes were refused permission to play at Keokuk, Ia., recently" (Fulton Theatre Archive). I am again indebted to Ty Greiner for the big-picture view of who played the Fulton and when; see Greiner, vol. 1, 118–19, for a discussion of burlesque at the Fulton. The following articles also detail some of the many burlesque shows to play Yecker's theater: *Intelligencer*, May 22, 1867 (on the "Lady Don Combination and Operatic Burlesque Troupe," one of the first companies of its kind to appear in Lancaster); *Intelligencer Journal*, December 31, 1886 (on Black Crook); *Evening Express*, May 18, 1868 (on the Walter A. Donaldson's Dramatic Co. production of *Mazeppa, or The Wild Horse of Tartary*); *Intelligencer Journal*, January 26, 1880, and *New Era*, January 23 and 29, 1880 (on the Kiralfy Company's *A Tale of Enchantment*). On Lancaster's affection for leg shows, see the *Columbia Spy*, January 31, 1880, which cites the *New Era*. Paul E. Yecker Sr. has generously provided me with copies of photographs in his family's archive. On nineteenth-century attitudes toward women, and on women of the nineteenth-century stage, see Kibler, *Rank Ladies*; Dudden; Auster; Wilmeth and Bigsby, *Cambridge History*, vol. 2; Russett; Brumberg; and Davis. Margaret Rawn's diary can be found in the Fulton Theatre Archive. Background on Olive Logan comes from Auster, 24–26, 144; and Logan. I've drawn my thoughts on the actor's body from a variety of sources, among them Goldman, *The Actor's Freedom*; Novarina and Weiss; Jerzy Grotowski, "The Theatre's New Testament," in Schechner and Schuman, 183; and Beauvoir, 533–34, quoted in Goffman, 57–58. Coverage of Olive Logan's November 10, 1870, lecture at the Fulton makes for lively reading; see the *Intelligencer Journal*, November 11, 1870. On Madame Rentz's visit to Lancaster, see the *Intelligencer Journal*, November 2–3, 1870; Rentz and her troupe returned to the Fulton on January 26, 1880, and drew large crowds (*Intelligencer Journal*, January 26–27, 1880). Darwin and his fellow nineteenth-century theorists are discussed in Russett, 40–47. For background on Victoria Woodhull, see Goldsmith's provocative *Other Powers*. Coverage of Woodhull's Fulton lectures appears in the *Intelligencer Journal* (October 22–26, 1874). To this day I am unable to exit Lancaster's Prince Street garage without thinking of the progress we've made in women's rights since the 1970s. Güner Gery managed the Fulton in 1980, and Johanna Brams was the theater's development director and my boss that same year; my thanks to both women for hiring me. William Winter's remarks on Charlotte Cushman are found in Auster, 16–17. Numerous playbills in the Fulton Theatre Archive include prohibitions against spitting. Fanny Janauschek made her Fulton debut on February 2, 1874 (*Weekly Intelligencer*, February 4, 1874; *Intelligencer Journal*, February 4, 1874); between 1883 and 1896 she returned to the Fulton at least six more times. Ty Greiner lists the many appearances by Janauschek, Modjeska, and other leading ladies; to anyone interested in the nature of these lives, I recommend Susan Sontag's fascinating novel *In America*. On Minnie Maddern Fiske, see Binns; Woollcott; Griffith; Cole and Chinoy, 584–87. Wilmeth and Bigsby, *Cambridge History*, vol. 2, 47, 215. On the American theater's timid embrace of Ibsen, see Auster, 77; Woollcott, 43–48; and Wilmeth and Bigsby, *Cambridge History*, vol. 2, 5, 38. Friedan's observations on Nora appear in Friedan, 140–41.

CHAPTER 17: CARTOGRAPHY

References to "Red Man" societies at the Fulton appear in Walter Hager and *Saturday Express*, May 8, 1852. In 1981 the Fulton expanded into the building immediately to its south. My understanding of the ancient Greek theater comes in part from Kitto; Hamilton; Taplin; and above all Professor Richard Trousdell's superb seminar on the topic at the University of Massachusetts in 1983. Information on the Wampanoag is from Russell Shorto, "Pilgrims and Indians," *New York Times Book Review*, June 4, 2006. On maps and mapmaking, see Turchi and Ehrenberg. The Harrison quotation is taken from his *Gardens*, 130. An earthquake with a Richter magnitude of 6.7 occurred near the eastern Gulf of Corinth at 10:57 P.M. local time on February 24, 1984 (Smithsonian/NASA Astrophysics Data System, http://adsabs.harvard.edu/abs/1982cger.rept.....C (accessed October 3, 2009).

CHAPTER 18: IMAGES, MOVING AND STILL: 1896–1930

My thanks again to Paul E. Yecker Sr. for copies of the Yecker family photographs described in this chapter. On Lancaster's 1900 New Year's celebration, see the *New Era*, January 1, 1900. Information on changes to Lancaster's infrastructure is largely drawn from the Journals of the Select and Common Councils of the City of Lancaster, which are available in the Gerald S. Lestz Reading Room of the Lancaster Public Library and at LancasterHistory.org; the journals are also the source of much of my knowledge of Blasius Yecker's comings and goings between 1893, when he first joined the Select City Council, and his death in 1903. For Andrew Carnegie's comment on American speed and Whitman's reflection on the locomotive, see Reynolds, 496, 512. An account of Yecker's failed attempt to advertise in front of the Lancaster post office appears in the C. Emlen Urban Collection, Book of Letters, Lancaster History.org. The playbills in the Fulton Theatre Archive are a treasure trove for anyone interested in turn-of-the-century advertising; the line quoted here ("the mind, resting from the excitement of the play") comes from a September 10, 1887, program.

On Yecker's trips to Europe, see the Journals of the Select and Common Councils of the City of Lancaster, June 7, 1899, through March 28, 1900; the *Intelligencer*, May 15, 1903; and the *New Era*, May 15, 1903. On the phenomenon of photography, see Sontag, *On Photography*; Dutton; and Solnit. An ad in the May 4, 1852, *Intelligencer* notes the opening of a "Daguerrian Gallery" in downtown Lancaster. Readers wishing to reflect on photography's role in the American Civil War should consult Faust's excellent *This Republic of Suffering*. Mary Yecker's death is mentioned in her husband's obituary in the *Intelligencer*, May 15, 1903; in family records belonging to Paul E. Yecker Sr.; and in the Record of Burials, Saint Joseph's Church, Lancaster. Yecker's absence from the Select City Council meeting on June 16, 1902, is noted in the Journals of the Select and Common Councils. A wonderful account of Barnum's parade through Lancaster appears in the *New Era*, April 23, 1881. For background on Yecker and the Lancaster saddlery trade, see "Born in Hertzfelden"; "Old-Time Playhouses"; *Intelligencer*, May 15, 1903; and *New Era*, May 15, 1903. Information on the booming early twentieth-century theater business in Lancaster comes from Henke, "From Public House to Opera House"; Henke, "Three Nineteenth-Century Lancaster Theatres"; Greiner, vol. 1, 182–83; Loose, *Heritage*, 110; Reichmann, 50; and Bryan. On changes in Lancaster itself, see the Journals of the Select and Common Councils of the City of Lancaster, 1897–1903; and Bryan, 110. For the Four Cohans' 1901 Fulton debut, see the *New Era*, February 20–21, 1901, and the *Intelligencer*, February 21, 1901; the family returned to the Fulton on April 11, 1902; March 24, 1903; and September 4, 1903. On his own, George M. Cohan played the Fulton numerous times between 1905 and 1920 (Greiner, vol. 2). I've drawn my portrait of George M. Cohan chiefly from Cohan; Wilmeth and Bigsby, *Cambridge History*, vol. 2, 52, 175; Greiner, vol. 1, 214; Cecil Smith, 147–52; Hamm, 312–13; and Morehouse. Frank W. Woolworth opened his first successful five-and-ten store in downtown Lancaster in June 1879 (Loose, *Heritage*, 132, 140); the city granted F. W. Woolworth an "amusement license" in 1901 (Journals of the Select and Common Councils of the City of Lancaster, July 10, 1901). Wilmeth and Bigsby note the theatricality of late nineteenth- and early twentieth-century American consumer culture (*Cambridge History*, vol. 2, 160). For the tale of the actress who fought with her manager outside the Fulton, see reports in both the *New Era* and the *Intelligencer*, September 4, 1890; on the spiritualist troupe that charged admission on the Sabbath, see the *New Era*, October 31, 1887. Ads for *Gettysburg* appear in the *Intelligencer* (October 30, 1898). The Syndicate has been much written about; see, for example, Auster, 34; Hall, 167; Wilmeth and Bigsby, *Cambridge History*, vol. 2, 6–7, 212–15; Greiner, vol. 1, 178–79; Henderson, 25–27, 168; Kibler, *Rank Ladies*, 96–97; Binns, 60–80, 157–89, 213–14; Griffith, 59–72; and Cole and Chinoy, 539. Arthur Hornblow is quoted in Wilmeth and Bigsby, *Cambridge History*, vol. 1, 9. John Lahr's informative review of *Gypsy* does much to illuminate the rigors of vaudeville. On Blasius Yecker's cancer, see the *Intelligencer*, May 15, 1903; the *New Era*, May 15, 1903; Journals of the Select and Common Councils of the City of Lancaster, November 11, 1902, through April 3, 1903. Information on Janet Yecker comes from her obituary in the *Intelligencer Journal* (February 24, 2000); and my conversation with Sister Rosemary Mulac of Saint Anne's Home on June 13, 2000. As ever, much of my knowledge of what played the Fulton is drawn from Ty Greiner's exhaustive thesis. Lyman Howe brought his Cairo-to-Khartoum travelogue to the Fulton in April 1903 (see the *Intelligencer*, April 21–23, 1903; *New Era*, April 23, 1903); Burns, 129, documents the effect Howe's travel shows had on Lancaster theatergoers. Feuerbach's statement appears in Sontag, *On Photography*, 153. On the evolution of moving pictures, see Mast and Cohen; Solnit; Gianetti; Abel, *The Red Rooster Scare*; Abel, *Silent Film*; Wilmeth and Bigsby, *Cambridge History*, vol. 2, 163; and Musser. Waite's Comedy Company brought its animatagraph to the Fulton for a two-week engagement beginning December 7, 1896 (Greiner, vol. 1, 297; *Intelligencer*, December 8, 1896; *New Era*, December 8, 1896); supplementary information on the animatagraph and other early cinema technologies comes from Tom Gunning, "'Now You See It, Now You Don't,'" in Abel, *Silent Film*, 75; Wilmeth and Bigsby, *Cambridge History*, vol. 2, 131; and Solnit, 24. André Bazin's remark appears in "From *What Is Cinema*," in Mast and Cohen, 280–82. "Edison's Vitascope and Refined Concert Co." played the Fulton on February 15–16, 1897 (*Intelligencer*, February 13–15, 1897; *New Era*, February 16, 1897; Greiner, vol. 1, 297). Twenty years earlier, on May 31, 1877, the Fulton had unsuccessfully presented "The Edison Telephone Concert," which consisted of a vocal duet performed by a singer onstage and a colleague a block away in the Stevens House Hotel; only six people bought tickets (Greiner, vol. 1, 268; "Fulton Opera House Highlights: 1852–1969," Fulton Theatre Archive). On the Corbett-Fitzsimmons fight, see Greiner, vol. 1, 297. Howe's war-graph is documented in Greiner, vol. 1, 298, and both the *New Era* and *Intelligencer* (April 11–17, 1899). See Abel, *Red Rooster*, for background on Howe and his work. I derive my understanding of Charles Yecker's payment system from Greiner, vol. 1, 298. Numerous writers have pondered the distinction between cinema and live theater, among them Siegfried Kracauer, "Basic Concepts," in Mast and Cohen, 7–21; Susan Sontag, "Film and Theater," in Mast and Cohen, 249–67; F. E. Sparshott, "Basic Film Aesthetics," in Mast and Cohen, 209–32; Erwin Panofsky, "Style and Medium in the Motion Pictures," in Mast and Cohen, 151–69; and Brook, 87, 99. Artaud's quote is found in Jamieson; see also Artaud, 12. Charles Yecker hired Lancaster architect C. Emlen Urban (who also designed the utopian town of Hershey, Pennsylvania) to renovate the Fulton in 1904; coverage of that process is found in the *Intelligencer*, April 25, 2904; the *New Era*, April 23 and 25, 1904; and Henke, "From Public House to Opera House," 77. Klaw and Erlanger's *Ben-Hur* is one of the glories of Charles Yecker's tenure at the Fulton; anyone wishing to know the details of the extravaganza, which played the theater in September 1907 and again in September 1910, should peruse both the *Intelligencer* and *New Era* (September 17–20, 1907); Burns; Mercer; and a 1910 playbill for the production in the Fulton Theatre Archive. Of the production, a reviewer for the *Intelligencer* wrote, "When the foaming horses . . . come into view, audiences forget to breathe." Sarah Bernhardt made her Fulton debut on February 20, 1911 (Greiner, vol. 1, 214; author conversation with June Yecker, September 12, 2000; unidentified newspaper clipping, Fulton Theatre Archive; Burns, 121; *Intelligencer*, February 18–21, 1911; *New Era*, February 21, 1911); Bernhardt returned to the Fulton in *La Dame aux Camelias* on April 10, 1912, by which time she had joined the vaudeville circuit (Greiner, vol. 2, 741; Kibler, *Rank Ladies*, 82). In a 1952 *Intelligencer Journal* article about the wedding, reporter Joseph T. Kingston issued the welcome news that the marriage lasted happily; see also the *Intelligencer*, April 21, 1913, and the *New Era*, April 22, 1913. Charles Yecker announced in May 1911 that the Fulton would offer vaudeville and moving pictures: "The vaudeville acts will be changed twice a week, and will be some of the biggest acts on the Nixon and Zimmerman circuit" (Kibler, Richman, and Weinberg; Greiner vol. 1, 239–40, citing the *New Era*, May 12, 1911, 2). The controversy over the Fulton's proposed showing of *Birth of a Nation* filled the local headlines for days (see the *Intelligencer* and the *New Era*, January 21–28, 1916). The Columbia burgess's remark appears in the *Intelligencer*, January 28, 1916. On Charles Yecker's vain effort to bring *The Clansman* to the Fulton, see the *Intelligencer*, November 12, 1906. On the direct links between *The Clansman*, *Birth of a Nation*, and *Uncle Tom's Cabin*, see Reynolds, *Mightier than the Sword*, 213–29. Charles Yecker died on May 4, 1920 (Yecker Family Archive; author interview with June Yecker, September 12, 2000). Raymond Yecker's brief run as Fulton manager lasted from his father's death in 1920 until the summer of 1921, when he sold the theater to Harry F. Butzer and John A. Guerrini, who in turn sold the theater to Ralph W. Coho in 1923; Coho and his family held onto the Fulton until 1963, when they sold the building to the Fulton Opera House Foundation (Greiner, vol. 1, 309–14). A projection booth was installed in 1930 (Gallagher and Weathersby). Blasius Yecker's death was front-page news in both the *New Era* and the *Intelligencer*; his will, dated March 18, 1883, with a codicil dated April 13, 1903, is found in the Lancaster County Courthouse, Will Book P, vol. 2, p. 230. Janet Yecker died on February 22, 2000 (*Intelligencer Journal*, February 24, 2000).

CHAPTER 19: GHOST DANCE: 1896–1997

Footage featuring a cowboy from Buffalo Bill's troupe played the Fulton during the Waite Comedy Company's two-week run in December 1896 (*Intelligencer*, December 8, 1896). Joy Kasson, 228–29, quotes from the *Kansas City World*, October 19, 1896; Kasson also chronicles Cody's Wild West shows and forays into film. I am indebted to Gordon Wickstrom for sharing a copy of his undated photo of Cody parading through Lancaster. On Curtis's photographic project, see Frazier. On the physiology of memory, see Benedict Carey, "For the Brain, Remembering Is Like Reliving," *New York Times*, September 5, 2008. Mumford's observation appears in *Architecture*, 25. Hugo writes of buildings and violence in the "Préface à Cromwell," which is reprinted in Carlson, *Places*, 27–28. On the Fulton Theatre's long and storied association with ghosts, see Adams; Jim Ruth, "The Haunting of the Fulton," *Lancaster Sunday News*, October 10, 1982; Elizabeth Thomas, "Is the Fulton Haunted? Local Ghost Hunter Find [*sic*] Answers!," *Fulton Opera House Bulletin* (n.d. [ca. 1998?]), Fulton Theatre Archive; Rochelle A. Shenk, "The Fulton's 'Ghosts,'" in "150 Years at the Fulton," special supplement to the *Lancaster Sunday News*, March 16, 2003; David Griffith, "In Search of the Eerie 'Woman in White,'" *Intelligencer Journal* (n.d. [1998?]), Fulton Theatre Archive; author interview with Rick Fisher, June 12, 2003. Harrison's reflections appear on p. 36 of *Dominion of the Dead*. For coverage of the Fulton's 1959 production of *Our Town*, including Binkley's "uncanny feeling," see Marty Crisp, "Open House, Open Hearts," *Lancaster Sunday News* (January 5, 2003), and Sam Taylor, "Sarah Bernhardt, the Barrymores, Lillian Russell," *Lancaster New Era* (April

16, 1973). Brook writes of the theater's purpose on p. 40 of *The Empty Space*. Grotow-
ski's "closeness of the living organism" is quoted in Wiles, 251; see also Novarina and
Weiss; and Carlson, *The Haunted Stage*, 167. On divine space in Western culture, see
Wiles, 24–25. I am immensely grateful to Jesse Nighthawk for his willingness to talk
to me at length in the summer of 2009 about the 1997 Fulton Theatre ceremony.
Details about the ceremony also come from P. J. Reilly, "Indians Hope Their Songs
Soothe Restless Spirits," *Intelligencer Journal*, June 21, 1997; Brubaker; and author
interview with Dennis Calabrese, April 6, 2007. A second reconciliation ceremony
took place in the fall of 2010 at Lancaster's First Presbyterian Church; during that
event, members of the Presbytery of Donegal, which represents Presbyterians in Lancaster, York, and Chester counties, acknowledged the role of the Paxton Presbyterian
Church in the killing of the Conestogas and criticized the church's then-pastor, John
Elder, for his implicit support of the massacre. Mayor Rick Gray of Lancaster cited
the "lack of justice" following the murders and said he regretted "the choices made by
our ancestors in Lancaster government that could've provided better protection for
the Conestoga native peoples." This was the first public admission that colonial
authorities in Lancaster allowed the massacre to happen (Jack Brubaker, "Community Leaders Had Role in Massacre," *Intelligencer Journal / New Era*, October 15, 2011).
The late Helen Hager, widow of Nat Hager and my dear friend, helped spearhead the
$9.5 million renovation to the Fulton in 1995. The key figures responsible for that
renovation—architect Edward Francis of William Kessler and Associates, Detroit,
Michigan, and theater designers Ann Sachs and Robert Morgan, of Sachs Morgan
Studio, New York, New York—generously shared their time and knowledge with me,
and I am grateful. Barry Kornhauser told me about the ghostlike piano key, the piece
of sweetgrass, and the construction worker who was spooked by an apparition; all
three incidents also found their way into the local press. Barry Spector's observations
are drawn from Spector, 87–88. On native ritual in the American Northeast, see Dowd,
Spirited Resistance, 3–9. I urge anyone interested in the Paxton killings to read Jack
Brubaker's *Massacre of the Conestogas*. The Conestogas are listed by name in Kent, 387.

EPILOGUE: 2008

Gaston Bachelard's *Poetics of Space* has been a crucial guide throughout this undertak-
ing; see p. 5 for his thoughts on home. Walter's architecture essays are collected in
Walter. The quotation from James Joyce's *Ulysses* appears in Lawlor, 12. My thanks to
Randy Harris for sharing his extensive research on the Fulton's Underground Rail-
road connections; details about his work can also be found in Susan E. Lindt, "The
Righteous Jailer," *Intelligencer Journal* (September 6, 2008), and Randolph Harris,
"Underground Railroad Clues Point Here," *Intelligencer Journal / New Era* (April 26,
2011). There is evidence to suggest that abolitionists may have used the Lancaster jail
as a weapon in their fight to liberate slaves. A September 19, 1817, deposition in the
LancasterHistory.org collection indicates that William Wright (1770–1846; a Quaker
and well-known abolitionist in the Lancaster County borough of Columbia) intervened in the case of a freedom-seeking slave named Jarret who had turned up in
Columbia. Although the local magistrate had been on the verge of returning Jarret to

his owner, "in consequence of the interference of William Wright the Magistrate ordered [Jarret] to be delivered over to Judge Franklin and he was sent to the gaol of Lancaster County." Wright, and perhaps other abolitionists, may have reasoned that it was better to incarcerate a fugitive and file a habeas corpus than simply return an enslaved person to bondage; Wright filed numerous writs of habeas corpus on behalf of freedom seekers. Despite his intervention in this case, however, Jarret was "remanded to his master by Judge Franklin" on September 20, 1817. I am grateful to Kevin Shue of LancasterHistory.org for alerting me to the relevant legal documents in the historical society's holdings, and to Harvey Miller, Todd Mealy, and Paul Finkelman for helping me to understand their significance. Barry Kornhauser graciously provided me with a recording of Michael Mitchell's remarks, as played at his memorial service on September 29, 2008.

BIBLIOGRAPHY

Journal of the Lancaster County Historical Society is abbreviated *JLCHS* throughout.

Abel, Richard. *The Red Rooster Scare: Making Cinema American, 1900–1910*. Berkeley: University of California Press, 1999.

———, ed. *Silent Film*. New Brunswick: Rutgers University Press, 1996.

Adams, Charles J., III. *Pennsylvania Dutch Country Ghosts, Legends, and Lore*. Reading, Pa.: Exeter House Books, 1994.

Alford, Terry. Introduction to Asia Booth Clarke, *John Wilkes Booth: A Sister's Memoir*. Jackson: University Press of Mississippi, 1999.

Artaud, Antonin. *The Theater and Its Double*. Translated by Mary Caroline Richards. New York: Grove, 1958.

Ashley, Elizabeth. *Actress: Postcards from the Road*. New York: M. Evans, 1978.

Auster, Albert. *Actresses and Suffragists: Women in the American Theater, 1880–1920*. New York: Praeger, 1984.

Bachelard, Gaston. *The Poetics of Space*. Translated by Maria Jolas. Boston: Beacon Press, 1969.

Bailyn, Bernard, ed. *Pamphlets of the American Revolution*. Vol. 1, *1750–1765*. Cambridge, Mass.: Belknap Press of Harvard University Press, 1965.

Barish, Jonas A. *The Antitheatrical Prejudice*. Berkeley: University of California Press, 1981.

Barnum, P. T. *The Autobiography of P. T. Barnum: Clerk, Merchant, Editor, and Showman*. London: Ward and Lock, 1855.

Bausman, Lottie M. "Massacre of Conestoga Indians, 1763: Incidents and Details." *Historical Papers and Addresses of the Lancaster County Historical Society* 18 (1914): 179–80.

Beal, Rebecca. *Jacob Eichholtz, 1776–1842: Portrait Painter of Pennsylvania*. Philadelphia: Historical Society of Pennsylvania, 1969.

Bean, Annemarie, James V. Hatch, and Brooks McNamara, eds. *Inside the Minstrel Mask: Readings in Nineteenth-Century Blackface Minstrelsy*. Hanover: Wesleyan University Press, 1996.

Beauvoir, Simone de. *The Second Sex*. Translated by H. M. Parshley. New York: Knopf, 1953.

Berlin, Ira. *Many Thousands Gone: The First Two Centuries of Slavery in North America*. Cambridge, Mass.: Belknap Press of Harvard University Press, 1998.

Binns, Archie. *Mrs. Fiske and the American Theater*. New York: Crown, 1955.

Biographical Annals of Lancaster County, Pa. Chicago: J. H. Beers, 1903.

Birdoff, Harry. *The World's Greatest Hit: Uncle Tom's Cabin.* New York: Vanni, 1947.

Blitz, Antonio. *Life and Adventures of Signor Blitz; Being an Account of the Author's Professional Life; His Wonderful Tricks and Feats; with Laughable Incidents, and Adventures as a Magician, Necromancer, and Ventriloquist. By Himself.* Hartford, Conn.: Belknap, 1872.

Bobrick, Benson. *Angel in the Whirlwind: The Triumph of the American Revolution.* New York: Penguin, 1998.

Bordewich, Fergus M. *Bound for Canaan: The Underground Railroad and the War for the Soul of America.* New York: Amistad, 2005.

―――. "Digging into a Historic Rivalry." *Smithsonian Magazine,* February 2004, 96–107.

Botton, Alain de. *The Architecture of Happiness.* New York: Pantheon, 2006.

Brady, Gerard. "Buchanan's Campaign in Lancaster County." *JLCHS* 53 (1949): 97–135.

Bridgens' Atlas of Lancaster County, Pennsylvania. Philadelphia: H. F. Bridgens, 1864.

Brodie, Fawn M. *Thaddeus Stevens: Scourge of the South.* New York: W. W. Norton, 1959.

Brook, Peter. *The Empty Space.* 1968. Reprint, New York: Touchstone, 1996.

Brooks, Lynn. "Staged Ethnicity: Early American Perspectives." *Dance Chronicle* 24, no. 2 (2001): 193–222.

Brown, Dee. *Bury My Heart at Wounded Knee.* New York: Henry Holt, 1970.

Brubaker, Jack. *Massacre of the Conestogas.* Charleston, S.C.: History Press, 2010.

Brumberg, Joan Jacobs. *The Body Project: An Intimate History of American Girls.* New York: Random House, 1997.

Bryan, Jodelle L. "From Vaudeville to the Silver Screen: Popular Entertainment in Lancaster, 1900–1930." *JLCHS* 95, no. 4 (1993): 108–28.

Burns, Doris. "Reminiscences of the Fulton Opera House." *JLCHS* 76, no. 3 (1972): 117–35.

Carlson, Marvin. *The Haunted Stage: The Theatre as Memory Machine.* Ann Arbor: University of Michigan Press, 2001.

―――. *Places of Performance: The Semiotics of Theater Architecture.* Ithaca: Cornell University Press, 1989.

Charters, Ann. *Nobody: The Story of Bert Williams.* London: Macmillan, 1970.

Clerc, Charles. *Mason & Dixon & Pynchon.* Lanham, Md.: University Press of America, 2000.

Clarke, Asia Booth. *The Elder and the Younger Booth.* Boston: James R. Osgood, 1882.

Clinton, Catherine. *Fanny Kemble's Civil Wars.* New York: Simon and Schuster, 2000.

Cohan, George M. *Twenty Years on Broadway (and the Years It Took to Get There): The True Story of a Trouper's Life from the Cradle to the "Closed Shop."* New York: Harper and Brothers, 1924.

Cole, Toby, and Helen Krich Chinoy. *Actors on Acting.* New York: Crown, 1970.

Cook, James W. *The Arts of Deception: Playing with Fraud in the Age of Barnum.* Cambridge, Mass.: Harvard University Press, 2001.

Coolidge, Harold N., Jr. *Samuel Sloan: Architect of Philadelphia, 1815–1884.* Philadelphia: University of Pennsylvania Press, 1884.

Cope, Thomas D. "Collecting Source Material on Charles Mason and Jeremiah Dixon." *Proceedings of the American Philosophical Society* 92 (1948): 111–14.

Copeland, Charles Townsend. *Edwin Booth.* Boston: Small, Maynard, 1901.

Crawford, Richard. *America's Musical Life: A History.* New York: W. W. Norton, 2001.

Curtis, George Ticknor. *Life of James Buchanan.* 2 vols. New York: Harper and Brothers, 1883.

Danson, Edwin. *Drawing the Line: How Mason and Dixon Surveyed the Most Famous Border in America.* New York: John Wiley, 2001.

D'Antonio, Michael. *Hershey: Milton S. Hershey's Extraordinary Life of Wealth, Empire, and Utopian Dreams.* New York: Simon and Schuster, 2006.

Davis, Tracy C. *Actresses as Working Women: Their Social Identity in Victorian Culture.* London: Routledge, 1991.

DeLaurentis, Ann, and Bernadine Hershey, eds. *Church of the Assumption of the Blessed Virgin Mary. Lancaster, PA: "Old St. Mary's," 1741–1991.* Lancaster, Pa.: St. Mary's of Lancaster, 1991.

Delbanco, Andrew. *Melville: His World and Work.* New York: Knopf, 2005.

Dickinson, H. W. "Robert Fulton's Birthplace as Historic Shrine." *Commonwealth of Pennsylvania Department of Internal Affairs Monthly Bulletin* 8, no. 8 (1940): 16–18.

A Digest of the Ordinances of the City of Lancaster, and of the Acts of Assembly Relating Thereto. Lancaster, n.d. [ca. 1875].

A Digest of the Ordinances of the Corporation of the City of Lancaster and of the Acts of Assembly Relating Thereto. Edited by William R. Wilson and James C. Carpenter. Lancaster, Pa.: W. B. Wiley, 1855.

Douglas, Henry Kyd. *The Douglas Diary: Student Days at Franklin and Marshall College, 1856–1858.* Edited by Frederic Shriver Klein and John Howard Carrill. Lancaster, Pa.: Franklin and Marshall College, 1973.

Dowd, Gregory Evans. *A Spirited Resistance: The North American Indian Struggle for Unity, 1745–1815.* Baltimore: Johns Hopkins University Press, 1992.

———. *War Under Heaven: Pontiac, the Indian Nations, and the British Empire.* Baltimore: Johns Hopkins University Press, 2002.

Dowd, M. Jane. "Landmarks in Commerce: Hager & Bro., Inc. Christopher Hager." *JLCHS* 65 (1961): 198–203.

Dreiser, Theodore. *Sister Carrie.* New York: Doubleday, 1997.

Dubbs, Joseph Henry. *History of Franklin and Marshall College.* Lancaster, Pa.: Franklin and Marshall College Alumni Association, 1903.

Dudden, Faye E. *Women in the American Theatre: Actresses and Audiences, 1790–1870.* New Haven: Yale University Press, 1994.

Duing, Parke. "A Study on the Life of Hugh Cannon, Nineteenth-Century Sculptor, and an Analysis of Works by the Artist." Ms., Franklin and Marshall College (May 1977).

Dumont, Frank. *The Witmark Amateur Minstrel Guide and Burnt Cork Encyclopedia.* New York: M. Witmark and Sons, 1899.

Dunbar, John, ed. *The Paxton Papers.* The Hague: Martinus Nijhoff, 1957.

Durang, Christopher. *Christopher Durang Explains It All for You: Six Plays by Christopher Durang.* New York: Avon Books, 1983.

Durang, John. *The Memoir of John Durang, American Actor, 1787–1816.* Edited by Alan S. Downer. Pittsburgh: University of Pittsburgh Press, 1966.

Dutton, Denis. *The Art Instinct.* New York: Bloomsbury, 2009.

Ebersole, Mark C. "Episcopalians and Slavery in Lancaster County from the Colonial Period to the Civil War." *JLCHS* 105, no. 2 (2003): 64–88.

———. "German Religious Groups and Slavery in Lancaster County Prior to the Civil War." *JLCHS* 107, no. 4 (2005–6): 158–87.

Ehrenberg, Ralph E., ed. *Mapping the World: An Illustrated History of Cartography.* Washington, D.C.: National Geographic Society, 2006.

Elam, Harry J., Jr., and David Krasner. *African American Performance and Theater History: A Critical Reader.* New York: Oxford University Press, 2001.

Ellis, Franklin, and Samuel Evans. *History of Lancaster County.* Philadelphia: Everts and Peck, 1883.

Eshleman, H. Frank. *Lancaster County Indians: Annals of the Susquehannocks and Other Indian Tribes of Pennsylvania, 1500–1763.* 1908. Reprint, Lewisburg, Pa.: Wennawoods, 2000.

———. "Lincoln's Visit to Lancaster in 1861; And the Passing of His Corpse in 1865." *JLCHS* 13 (1909): 55–81.

Evans, Harold, with Gail Buckland and David Lefer. *They Made America.* New York: Little, Brown, 2004.

Everts, L. H., and D. J. Stewart. *1875 Historical Atlas of Lancaster County, Pennsylvania.* Facsimile ed. Lancaster, Pa.: Lancaster County Historical Society, 1992.

Faust, Drew Gilpin. *This Republic of Suffering: Death and the American Civil War.* New York: Knopf, 2008.

Fenton, William N. *The Iroquois Eagle Dance: An Offshoot of the Calumet Dance.* Smithsonian Institution Bureau of American Ethnology Bulletin 156. Washington, D.C.: U.S. G.P.O., 1953.

Franklin, Benjamin. *A Narrative of the Late Massacres, in Lancaster County, of a Number of Indians, Friends of this Province, by Persons Unknown: With Some Observations on the Same.* Philadelphia, 1764. In Dunbar, 55–75.

Frazier, Ian. *On the Rez.* New York: Picador, 2001.

Friedan, Betty. *The Feminine Mystique.* New York: W. W. Norton, 2001.

Fulton, Eleanore J. "Robert Fulton as an Artist." *Papers of the Lancaster County Historical Society* 42, no. 3 (1938): 49–96.

Fulton Opera House. "The League of Historic American Theatres: Nomination for Outstanding Restoration Project; Fulton Opera House." Typescript, 2003.

The Fulton Opera House Restoration: Built in 1852; Saved for Restoration 1964. Pamphlet. Lancaster, 1964.

Gallagher, John, and William Weathersby Jr. "Fulton Opera House Returns to Grace in Lancaster, PA." *Theatre Crafts International* 30, no. 5 (1996): 23–24.

García Lorca, Federico. *Obras completas III: Prosa.* Edited by Miguel García-Posada. Barcelona: Galaxia Gutenberg / Círculo de Lectores, 1996.

Garnier, Charles. *Le théâtre.* Paris, 1871.

Gass, William H. *Finding a Form.* Ithaca: Cornell University Press, 1996.

Giannetti, Louis. *Understanding Movies.* 3rd ed. Englewood Cliffs, N.J.: Prentice-Hall, 1982.

Glazier, Ira A., ed. *Germans to America—Series II: Lists of Passengers Arriving at U.S. Ports in the 1840s.* 7 vols. Wilmington, Del.: Scholarly Resources, 2002.

Goffman, Erving. *The Presentation of Self in Everyday Life.* New York: Doubleday, 1959.

Goldman, Michael. *The Actor's Freedom: Toward a Theory of Drama.* New York: Viking, 1975.

———. *On Drama: Boundaries of Genre, Borders of Self.* Ann Arbor: University of Michigan Press, 2000.

Goldsmith, Barbara. *Other Powers: The Age of Suffrage, Spiritualism, and the Scandalous Victoria Woodhull.* New York: Knopf, 1998.

Gossett, T. F. *Uncle Tom's Cabin and American Culture.* Dallas: Southern Methodist University Press, 1985.

Greiner, Tyler L. "A History of Professional Entertainment at the Fulton Opera House in Lancaster, Pennsylvania: 1852–1930." 2 vols. M.A. thesis, Pennsylvania State University, May 1977.

Griffith, Frank Carlos. *Mrs. Fiske.* New York: Neale, 1912.

Gross, Ariela Julie. *Double Character: Slavery and Mastery in the Antebellum South.* Princeton: Princeton University Press, 2000.

Hager, Walter C. "Fulton Hall and Its Graven Image." *Papers Read Before the Lancaster County Historical Society* 22, no. 9 (1918): 141–48.

Hager, William H. "The Hager Family: 1741–1967." Unpublished ms., 1967.

Hall, Roger A. *Performing the American Frontier, 1870–1906.* New York: Cambridge University Press, 2001.

Hamilton, Edith. *The Greek Way.* New York: W. W. Norton, 1964.

Hamm, Charles. *Yesterdays: Popular Song in America.* New York: W. W. Norton, 1979.

Hare, Edwina. *The Durang Family.* Harleysville, Pa.: Alcom, 2000.

Harris, Alex. *A Biographical History of Lancaster County.* Lancaster, Pa.: Elias Barr, 1872.

Harrison, Robert Pogue. *The Dominion of the Dead.* Chicago: University of Chicago Press, 2003.

———. *Gardens: An Essay on the Human Condition.* Chicago: University of Chicago Press, 2008.

Heckewelder, John. *A Narrative of the Mission of the United Brethren Among the Delaware and Mohegan Indians, from Its Commencement, in the Year 1740, to the Close of the Year 1808 . . . .* Philadelphia, 1820.

Heiges, George L. "1860—The Year Before the War." *JLCHS* 65 (1961): 113–35.

Henderson, Mary C. *Theater in America: 250 Years of Plays, Players, and Productions.* New York: H. N. Abrams, 1996.

Henke, James Scott. "The Colonial Theatre of Lancaster: 1912–1965." *JLCHS* 92, no. 4 (1990): 121–24.

———. "From Public House to Opera House: A History of Theatrical Structures in Lancaster, Pennsylvania." Ph.D. diss., University of Michigan, 1987.

———. "The Jefferson Theatrical Family in Lancaster, Pennsylvania." *JLCHS* 92, no. 4 (1990): 118–20.

————. "Three Nineteenth-Century Lancaster Theatres." *JLCHS* 93, no. 2 (1991): 56–60.

Herndon, William Henry, and Jesse W. Weik. *Herndon's Life of Lincoln: The History and Personal Recollections of Abraham Lincoln.* New York: Da Capo Press, 1983.

Hoch, Bradley R. *The Lincoln Trail in Pennsylvania: A History and Guide.* University Park: Pennsylvania State University Press, 2001.

Hopkins, Leroy T., Jr. "No Balm in Gilead: Lancaster's African-American Population and the Civil War Era." *JLCHS* 95, no. 1 (1993): 20–30.

Hosch, Heinz L. "Three Hundred Years of German Immigration: 1683–1983." *JLCHS* 105, no. 2 (2003): 54–63.

Hutton, Laurence. *Edwin Booth.* New York: Harper and Brothers, 1893.

Isaacson, Walter. *Benjamin Franklin: An American Life.* New York: Simon and Schuster, 2003.

Jamieson, Lee. "The Lost Prophet of Cinema: The Film Theory of Antonin Artaud." http://archive.sensesofcinema.com/contents/07/44/film-theory-antonin -artaud.html. Accessed May 8, 2009.

Jennings, Francis. "Susquehannock." In *Handbook of North American Indians,* vol. 15, *Northeast,* edited by Bruce G. Trigger. Washington, D.C.: Smithsonian Institution, 1978.

Jensen, Merrill. *The Founding of a Nation: A History of the American Revolution, 1763–1776.* New York: Oxford University Press, 1968.

Jolly, James A. "The Historical Reputation of Thaddeus Stevens." *JLCHS* 74 (1970): 33–71.

Kaplan, Justin. *Mr. Clemens and Mark Twain.* New York: Touchstone, 1966.

Kasson, Joy. *Buffalo Bill's Wild West.* New York: Hill and Wang, 2000.

Kemble, Fanny. *Fanny Kemble's Journals.* Edited by Catherine Clinton. Cambridge, Mass.: Harvard University Press, 2000.

Kent, Barry C. *Susquehanna's Indians.* Anthropological Series 6. Harrisburg: Pennsylvania Historical and Museum Commission, 1984.

Kibler, M. Alison. *Rank Ladies: Gender and Cultural Hierarchy in American Vaudeville.* Chapel Hill: University of North Carolina Press, 1999.

Kibler, M. Alison, Lisa Richman, and Randi Weinberg. "The Fulton Opera House in Black and White: African-American Performers and Protest in Lancaster, Pennsylvania, 1890–1915." *JLCHS* 106, no. 2 (2004): 52–63.

Kieffer, Elizabeth Clarke. "John Durang: The First Native American Dancer." *Pennsylvania Folklore* 21 (1954): 26–38.

Kingston, Joseph T. "Couple Recalls Wedding on Stage of Fulton in 1913." *Intelligencer Journal.* [Undated clipping in Fulton Theatre Archive, 1952.]

————. "Current Move Revives Hopes of Fulton's Old Stage Manager." *Intelligencer Journal.* [Undated clipping in Fulton Theatre Archive, 1952.]

————. *History of Fulton Opera House.* Lancaster, Pa.: Lancaster County Historical Society, 1952. Also six-part series in *Intelligencer Journal,* March 27–April 5, 1952.

Kitto, H. D. F. *The Greeks.* New York: Penguin, 1973.

Klein, Frederic S. *Lancaster's Golden Century, 1821–1921: A Chronicle of Men and Women Who Planned and Toiled to Build a City Strong and Beautiful.* Lancaster, Pa.: Hager and Bro., 1921.

Klein, H. M. J., and William F. Diller. *The History of St. James' Church (Protestant Episcopal) 1744–1944.* Lancaster: Vestry of St. James Church, 1944.

Klein, Philip S. *President James Buchanan: A Biography.* University Park: Pennsylvania State University Press, 1962.

Kopit, Arthur. *Indians.* New York: Bantam, 1971.

Kurath, Gertrude Prokosch. *Dance and Song Rituals of Six Nations Reserve, Ontario.* Ottawa: National Museum of Canada, Bulletin 220, Folklore Series 4, 1968.

Lahr, John. "Mother Load." Review of *Gypsy. New Yorker*, April 7, 2008.

Lahr, Joseph Wilson. "Washington H. Keffer." *JLCHS* 109, no. 2 (2007): 88–116.

Landis, Bertha Cochran. "Ye Old Time Inns of South Queen Street." *JLCHS* 41 (1937): 130–32.

Lawlor, Anthony. *The Temple in the House: Finding the Sacred in Everyday Architecture.* New York: Putnam, 1994.

Lemann, Nicholas. *Redemption: The Last Battle of the Civil War.* New York: Farrar, Straus and Giroux, 2006.

Lestz, Gerald S. *143-Year-Old Love Story.* Lancaster, Pa.: Fulton Opera House, 1995.

Lockridge, Richard. *Darling of Misfortune: Edwin Booth.* New York: Century, 1932.

Logan, Olive. *Before the Footlights and Behind the Scenes: A Book About "The Show Business" in All Its Branches.* Philadelphia: Parmelee, 1870.

Loose, John Ward Wilson. "Along the Susquehanna." *JLCHS* 108, no. 3 (2006): 100–148.

———. *The Heritage of Lancaster.* Woodland Hills, Cal.: Windsor, 1978.

———. "A History of Sin and Vice: Lancaster—The Fallen Angel." *JLCHS* 94 (1992): 105–16.

Lott, Eric. *Love and Theft: Blackface Minstrelsy and the American Working Class.* New York: Oxford University Press, 1995.

Luck, William R. "'Roughing It' at the Fulton—Mark Twain Comes to Lancaster, January 19, 1872." *JLCHS* 97, no. 1 (1995): 13–18.

Mahar, William J. *Behind the Burnt Cork Mask: Early Blackface Minstrelsy and Antebellum American Popular Culture.* Champaign-Urbana: University of Illinois Press, 1999.

Malkin, Jeanette R. *Memory-Theater and Postmodern Drama.* Ann Arbor: University of Michigan Press, 1999.

Mamet, David. *True and False: Heresy and Common Sense for the Actor.* New York: Pantheon, 1997.

Martin, C. H. "Abraham Lincoln's Connections with Lancaster and Its Citizens." *JLCHS* 39 (1938): 13–32.

Mason, A. Hughlett, ed. *The Journal of Charles Mason and Jeremiah Dixon.* Philadelphia: American Philosophical Society, 1969.

Mast, Gerald, and Marshall Cohen, eds. *Film Theory and Criticism: Introductory Readings.* New York: Oxford University Press, 1974.

McDermott, John D. "Special Report: The Fulton Opera House, Lancaster, Pennsylvania. XX: Literature, Drama, and Music." United States Department of the Interior, National Park Service, the National Survey of Historic Sites and Buildings, December 17, 1968. Ms. in the Fulton Theatre Archive.

McKee, Harley J. *Introduction to Early American Masonry: Stone, Brick, Mortar and Plaster.* Washington, D.C.: National Trust for Historic Preservation in the United States, 1973.

Memorial Volume of the Evangelical Lutheran Church of the Holy Trinity, Lancaster, Pennsylvania. Discourses Delivered on the Occasion of the Centenary Jubilee, by Rev. C. F. Schaeffer, D.D., and Rev. Prof. F. A. Muhlenberg, A. M. From A.D. 1761–1861. Lancaster: John Baer's Sons, 1861.

Mercer, Tony. "Ben Hur—Live at the Fulton." *Susquehanna Magazine,* January 1986.

Merrell, James H. *Into the American Woods.* New York: W. W. Norton, 1999.

Mombert, J. I. *An Authentic History of Lancaster County: In the State of Pennsylvania.* Lancaster, Pa.: J. E. Barr, 1869.

Morehouse, Ward. *George M. Cohan: Prince of the American Theater.* Philadelphia: J. B. Lippincott, 1943.

Morrison, Ross I. "Manifestations of the Evangelical Awakening of 1857–1858 in the Lancaster Area." M.A. thesis, Millersville University, 1973.

Morrison, Toni. *Playing in the Dark: Whiteness and the Literary Imagination.* Cambridge, Mass.: Harvard University Press, 1992.

Mumford, Lewis. *Architecture.* Chicago: American Library Association, 1926.

———. *The City in History: Its Origins, Its Transformations, and Its Prospects.* New York: Harcourt, Brace, 1961.

———. *Sticks and Stones: A Study of American Architecture and Civilization.* 2nd ed. New York: Dover, 1955.

Musser, Charles. *High-Class Moving Pictures: Lyman H. Howe and the Forgotten Era of Traveling Exhibition, 1880–1920.* Princeton: Princeton University Press, 1991.

Nevin, Paul A. "Rock-Art Sites on the Susquehanna River." In *The Rock-Art of Eastern North America: Capturing Images and Insight,* edited by Carol Diaz-Granados and James R. Duncan, 239–57. Tuscaloosa: University of Alabama Press, 2004.

———. "10,000 Years of Native American Heritage in the Lancaster-York Heritage Region." Report prepared for the Lancaster-York Heritage Region Committee, January 15, 2001.

Novarina, Valère, and Allen S. Weiss. "Letter to the Actors." *TDR* 37, no. 2 (1993): 95–104.

Oates, Stephen B. *With Malice Toward None.* New York: HarperPerennial, 1994.

Olson, Alison. "The Pamphlet War over the Paxton Boys." *Pennsylvania Magazine of History and Biography* 123, nos. 1–2 (1999): 31–55.

Olszewski, George J., with Conrad L. Wirth, Randle B. Truett, and William M. Haussmann. *Historic Structures Report: Restoration of Ford's Theatre, Washington.* Washington, D.C.: United States Department of the Interior, 1963.

O'Neill, Eugene. *Long Day's Journey into Night.* New Haven: Yale University Press, 1955.

Parkman, Francis, Jr. *History of the Conspiracy of Pontiac and the War of the North American Indian Tribes Against the English Colonies After the Conquest of Canada.* Boston: Little, Brown, 1855.

Pencak, William A., and Daniel K. Richter, eds. *Friends and Enemies in Penn's Woods: Indians, Colonists, and the Racial Construction of Pennsylvania.* University Park: Pennsylvania State University Press, 2004.

Philip, Cynthia Owen. *Robert Fulton: A Biography.* New York: Franklin Watts, 1985.

Pierpont, Claudia Roth. "Behind the Mask." *New Yorker,* December 12, 2005, 102–8.

Prowell, George R. "The Invasion of Pennsylvania, by the Confederates, Under General Robert E. Lee, and Its Effect upon Lancaster and York Counties." *JLCHS* 29 (1925): 41–51.

Pynchon, Thomas. *Mason & Dixon.* New York: Henry Holt, 1997.

Reichmann, Felix. "Amusements in Lancaster, 1750–1940." *Historical Papers and Addresses of the Lancaster County Historical Society* 45 (1941): 25–56.

"Report of the Centennial Observance of Lancaster City." *JLCHS* 22 (1918): 57–70.

Reynolds, David S. *Walt Whitman's America: A Cultural Biography.* New York: Vintage, 1996.

Richter, Daniel. *Facing East from Indian Country: A Native History of Early America.* Cambridge, Mass.: Harvard University Press, 2001.

Riddle, William. *The Story of Lancaster, Old and New: Being a Narrative History of Lancaster, Pennsylvania, from 1730 to the Centennial Year, 1918.* Lancaster, Pa.: The author, 1917.

Riis, Thomas L. "*In Dahomey* in Text and Performance." In *The Music and Scripts of "In Dahomey,"* edited by Thomas L. Riis, xiii–xlvi. Madison, Wis.: A-R Editions, 1996.

Roach, Joseph. *Cities of the Dead: Circum-Atlantic Performance.* New York: Columbia University Press, 1996.

Roath, John R. "Me and Buffalo Bill." *JLCHS* 97, no. 2 (1995): 66–71.

Rupp, I. Daniel. *A Collection of Upwards of Thirty Thousand Names of German, Swiss, Dutch, French, and Other Immigrants in Pennsylvania from 1727 to 1776.* Baltimore: Genealogical Publishing Co., 1965.

———. *History of Lancaster County.* 1844.

Ruskin, John. *Lectures on Architecture and Poetry, Delivered at Edinburgh, 1863.* New York: John Wiley, 1864.

———. *The Seven Lamps of Architecture.* New York: 1849.

Russett, Cynthia Eagle. *Sexual Science: The Victorian Construction of Womanhood.* Cambridge, Mass.: Harvard University Press, 1989.

Samuel Sloan: Pennsylvania's Distinguished 19th Century Architect. Lewisburg, Pa.: Slifer House Museum, 2005.

Santayana, George. *Soliloquies in England and Later Soliloquies.* New York: Scribner's, 1922.

Schaefer, Elizabeth Meg. *Wright's Ferry Mansion: The House.* Columbia, Pa.: Von Hess Foundation, in association with Antique Collectors' Club, 2005.

Schechner, Richard. *Essays on Performance Theory, 1970–1976.* New York: Drama Book Specialists, 1977.

Schechner, Richard, and Mady Schuman, eds. *Ritual, Play, and Performance: Readings in the Social Sciences / Theatre*. New York: Seabury Press, 1976.

Shannon, Timothy J. "A Redesigned Pontiac for the Twenty-First Century." Review of *War Under Heaven*, by Gregory Evans Dowd. *Common-Place* 3, no. 3 (2003), http://www.common-place.org/vol-03/no-03/reviews/shannon.shtml.

Silver, Peter. *Our Savage Neighbors: How Indian War Transformed Early America*. New York: W. W. Norton, 2008.

Sloan, Samuel. *The Model Architect*. 2 vols. Philadelphia: E. S. Jones, 1852.

Smith, Cecil. *Musical Comedy in America*. New York: Theatre Arts Books, 1950.

Smith, Debra D., and Frederick S. Weiser, trans. and ed. *Trinity Lutheran Church Records, 1767–1796*. 2 vols. Apollo, Pa.: Closson Press, 1998.

Smith, Eric Ledell. *Bert Williams: A Biography of the Pioneer Black Comedian*. Jefferson, N.C.: McFarland, 1992.

Smith, Gene. *American Gothic: The Story of America's Legendary Theatrical Family— Junius, Edwin, and John Wilkes Booth*. New York: Simon and Schuster, 1992.

Smith, John. *The Generall Historie of Virginia New England and the Summer Isles . . . .* London: Michael Sparkes, 1624.

Solnit, Rebecca. *River of Shadows: Eadweard Muybridge and the Technological Wild West*. New York: Viking, 2003.

Sontag, Susan. *In America*. New York: Farrar, Straus and Giroux, 2000.

———. *On Photography*. New York: Farrar, Straus and Giroux, 1973.

Spector, Barry. "Memory, Myth, and the National Mall." *Jung Journal* 2, no. 3 (2008): 73–97.

Stanislavski, Constantin. *An Actor Prepares*. Translated by Elizabeth Reynolds Hapgood. New York: Theatre Arts Books, 1969.

Stoner, Fredric A. *A Musical Ghost Story*. Produced at Fulton Opera House, October 10, 1988.

Strassburger, Ralph Beaver. *Pennsylvania German Pioneers*. Vol. 1, *1727–1775*. Edited by William John Hinke. Camden, Maine: Picton Press, 1992.

Stroh, Oscar H. *The Paxton Rangers and Some Facts About Pontiac's Rebellion*. Harrisburg: The author, 1982.

Sundquist, Eric, ed. *New Essays on "Uncle Tom's Cabin."* Cambridge: Cambridge University Press, 1986.

Swanton, John R. *The Indian Tribes of North America*. Smithsonian Institution Bureau of American Ethnology 145. Washington: Smithsonian Institution Press, 1952.

Taplin, Oliver. *Greek Tragedy in Action*. Berkeley: University of California Press, 1979.

Taylor, Yuval, and Jake Austen. *Darkest America: Black Minstrelsy from Slavery to Hip-Hop*. New York: W. W. Norton, 2012.

Toll, Robert C. *Blacking Up: The Minstrel Show in Nineteenth-Century America*. New York: Oxford University Press, 1974.

Turchi, Peter. *Maps of the Imagination: The Writer as Cartographer*. San Antonio: Trinity University Press, 2004.

Unsworth's Burnt Cork Lyrics. New York: Robert M. De Witt, 1859. [University of Michigan Special Collections.]

Updike, John. *Buchanan Dying: A Play*. Mechanicsburg, Pa.: Stackpole Books, 2000.

Walter, Thomas U. *The Lectures on Architecture, 1841–1853.* Edited by Jhennifer A. Amundson. Philadelphia: Athenaeum, 2006.

Ward, Geoffrey C. "Showman of the Wild Frontier." Review of *Buffalo Bill's America,* by Louis S. Warren. *New York Times Book Review,* December 11, 2005, 26.

Ward, Geoffrey C., Ken Burns, and Dayton Duncan. *Mark Twain: An Illustrated Biography.* New York: Knopf, 2001.

Wells, Richard A. *Manners, Culture and Dress of the Best American Society, Including Social, Commercial and Legal Forms, Letter Writing, Invitations, etc., also Valuable Suggestions on Self Culture and Home Training.* Springfield, Mass.: King, Richardson, 1890.

Wickstrom, Gordon. "Buffalo Bill the Actor." *Journal of the West* 34, no. 1 (1995): 62–69.

Wilder, Rosilyn. *A Space Where Anything Can Happen: Creative Drama in a Middle School.* Rowayton, Conn.: New Plays Books, 1977.

Wiles, David. *A Short History of Western Performance Space.* New York: Cambridge University Press, 2003.

Wilmeth, Don B., and Christopher Bigsby, eds. *The Cambridge History of American Theatre.* 3 vols. Cambridge: Cambridge University Press, 1998–2000.

Wilmeth, Don B., and Tice L. Miller. *Cambridge Guide to American Theatre.* Cambridge: Cambridge University Press, 1996.

Winik, Jay. *April 1865: The Month That Saved America.* New York: HarperCollins, 2001.

Winpenny, Thomas R. "The Engineer as Promoter: Charles Tillinghast James and the Gospel of Steam Cotton Mills." *Pennsylvania Magazine of History and Biography* 105, no. 2 (1981): 166–81.

Winter, William. *Other Days: Being Chronicles and Memories of the Stage.* New York: Moffat, Yard, 1908.

Witthoft, John. "The Conestoga Towns." Ms. #4, 7b, on file. Division of Archaeology. William Penn Memorial Museum, Harrisburg, Pa.

Wood, Jerome H. *Conestoga Crossroads: Lancaster, Pennsylvania, 1730–1789.* Harrisburg, Pa.: Pennsylvania Historical and Museum Commission, 1979.

Woodruff, Paul. *The Necessity of Theater: The Art of Watching and Being Watched.* New York: Oxford University Press, 2008.

Woollcott, Alexander. *Mrs. Fiske: Her Views on Actors, Acting, and the Problems of Production.* New York: Century, 1917.

Yates, Frances A. *The Art of Memory.* New York: Penguin, 1966.